KU-079-975

Acknowledgments

In preparing this book we have been assisted by a number of people whom we wish to thank:

Members of the Institute of Personnel Management who responded to the questionnaire on industrial relations.

Staff of the Institute of Personnel Management who provided us with the names and addresses of members and with any other membership information which we asked for: Mr E. Tomkinson, Miss W. A. Kilgour, Miss E. M. Harris and Mrs V. Corinaldesi.

The Editor of the *Scotsman* for the pamphlet on 'Incomes' by John Graham; and Mr Hugh Parker of McKinsey & Co., for permission to reproduce the information appearing on page 194.

Miss M. M. Niven for commenting on the historical section; Mr M. B. Forman for the use of his notes on the development of personnel management, 1954–64; Miss M. Towy-Evans for stimulating some new ideas; Mr R. J. Lawson for suggestions about his findings in the South Wales study; Mr A. W. Wedderburn for his comments and suggestions.

We are also grateful to members of management and trade-union courses who reacted vigorously to some of the views we imposed on them and who are responsible for some of the additional amendments we made. It would be invidious to name them but they will, no doubt, identify the contributions for which they were responsible and will be assured of our thanks.

And last but not least, our helpers in Cardiff who assisted us with sending out, coding and sorting the survey data and in typing our manuscripts: Mrs D. Cameron, Miss S. Holmes, Miss H.

James, Mr M. Laugharne, Mr M. Page and staff at the Computer Centre of the Welsh Hospital Board, Mrs M. Spernas.

Our thanks should not be taken to implicate anyone other than ourselves in the mistakes and omissions we have made; for those the responsibility is entirely our own.

INDUSTRIAL RELATIONS
and the Personnel Specialists

Peter Anthony
Lecturer in Management

Anne Crichton
Senior Lecturer in Social Science
University College of South Wales and
Monmouthshire, Cardiff

B. T. BATSFORD LTD London

First published 1969
© Peter Anthony and Anne Crichton 1969

H55215

331.1

Made and printed in Great Britain by
William Clowes and Sons Ltd, London and Beccles
for the publishers B. T. Batsford Ltd
4 Fitzhardinge Street, London, W.1
7134 0951 7

Contents

Introduction

Public concern about industrial relations finds expression in newspapers, television, radio and in recommendations from various quarters for far-reaching changes. Britain's slow economic growth is blamed on work-people's lack of willingness to work and on time-wasting industrial conflicts between management and men. The institutions of industrial relations which were developed in the nineteenth century are now said to be, like the plant and machinery of the industrial revolution, as much a handicap as an advantage to the nation that pioneered them, since it is not easy to bring about change in established structures.

The apparent inability of unions and management to bring about effective change, to increase productivity in times of continuing full employment and rapid technological advance, led to such public concern for the improvement of management–worker relationships that a Royal Commission on Trades Unions and Employers' Associations was set up in 1965. At the same time the Ministry of Labour began to take a more active part in stimulating managements to try to improve their performance and, in consequence, their relationships with their employees.

This concern about management–worker relationships affects no one more closely than the personnel management specialists and we hope to explore their readiness to undertake the responsibility of improving these relationships on the job. Their activities are also likely to affect the established institutions of industrial relations and so to have an impact on those questions which are of such general public concern.

It has been suggested that the emergence of personnel management as a specialist function of management with identifiable officers at plant level has provided trade-union officers with a focus for their attention in the medium-sized and large organisations (for personnel specialists are not usually employed in small companies). The personnel specialists' availability for discussion and their development of expertise in working together with union officials have enabled work-people's representatives to clarify their demands, to determine quickly the limits within which bargaining may take place about each issue and to get speedier results. Have the personnel specialists, by their very existence, been responsible for more rapid wage drift? Have they, by urging the advantages of competing with other firms on fringe benefits such as sick pay and pension programmes, without knowing what they were doing, increased the country's inflationary problems? Have they been a conservative force in preventing change in the handling of industrial relations by emerging as upholders of established procedures when perhaps some of these should have been amended? All these questions have been asked in recent years but have not been answered. Personnel specialists, certainly, would like to think that they are making a sound contribution to good industrial relations rather than providing a channel for disruptive influences. Perhaps major difficulties arise from the general lack of understanding of what are good industrial relations, and the methods of achieving these.

Personnel specialists have, for many years, claimed expertise in building and maintaining the organisations in which they are employed. They would argue that their contribution is made at the following points:

(a) in recruiting, selecting and introducing individuals into the organisation and, by every means possible within the limits of the situation, enabling the individuals to make their optimum contribution to the enterprise;

(b) in facilitating the development of more productive working groups;

(c) in enabling the organisation to manage internal change (a process which sets up a certain degree of conflict which needs to be held at an appropriate level);

(d) in assisting the organisation to adjust to new developments in the community in which it exists—changes in the social structure, in social legislation, technological developments, market changes, and new attitudes in the surrounding society.

The personnel specialist, then, claims to have a much wider responsibility than solely that of the custodian of agreements between management and organised work-people. He is not only interested in the struggle between these two groups but in the human relationships within the organisation as a whole. It may be useful now to clarify the terms we shall use. Since *personnel management* is used to describe two separate activities, it is necessary to begin by making a distinction between them. All managers who are in control of staff must of necessity engage in personnel management. The term is also used to describe the work of functional specialists who assist other managers with their personnel management activities. It is this specific activity which we shall explore since we wish to examine the work of the functional specialists in personnel management with particular reference to their industrial relations contribution.

To describe the man or woman who carries responsibility in this occupation we shall use the term *personnel specialist*. (Personnel manager is often used to designate the head of a personnel department, but it will be necessary to consider personnel directors in more senior positions and personnel assistants in subordinate posts, so it is appropriate to use this more general description. In using the term *personnel specialist* we recognise that there is another difficulty, i.e. this phrase may be used to designate an expert such as an industrial relations or training officer with limited but specialist expertise in the personnel function. We shall hope to clarify this distinction where titles are insufficient.)

There are considerable difficulties in identifying who is a personnel specialist, for some people who would appear to be employed full-time in dealing with personnel matters prefer to regard themselves as administrators, teachers or office managers. Others who spend a very small part of their time on personnel work may have one title which they use when signing letters about personnel matters and another to indicate their other responsibilities. In a recent survey, Collins found that there were many different designations used to describe members of this occupational group.[1]

Included in the Questionnaire	Written in by Respondents
Technologists	
Personnel Director	Manager Personnel Services
Personnel Manager	Personnel Superintendent
Personnel Officer	
Personnel Assistant	
Staff Manager/Officer	Personnel Controller
Employment Manager/Officer	Staff Director
Labour Manager/Officer	Staff Personnel Officer
Appointments/Recruitment Officer	Head of General Branch (Staff Dept.)
Industrial Relations Manager/Officer	Administration and Staff Manager
	Staff and Administration Officer
Employee Relations Manager/Officer	Staff Controller
Labour Relations Manager/Officer	Head of Staff Section
Negotiating Officer	Staff Assistant
	Woman Staff Supervisor
Welfare Manager/Officer	Women's Supervisor
	Supervisor (Females)
	Establishment Officer
	I/c Salaries and Establishments
	I/c Staff Recruitment
	Industrial Relations Director
	Consultation and Administration Officer
Education Manager/Officer	Training Superintendent
Education and Training Manager/Officer	Distribution Training Officer
Management/Executive Development Manager/Officer	Training and Education Officer
Training Officer	
Technicians	
Apprentice Supervisor/Master	Apprentice Training and Recruitment Manager
Instructor/Trainer	
Training Assistant	
Safety/Accident Prevention Officer	Safety Superintendent

[1] Anne Crichton and R. G. Collins, 'Personnel Specialists: a Count by Employers', *British Journal of Industrial Relations*, July 1966.

Included in the Questionnaire (*cont.*)	Written in by Respondents (*cont.*)
Safety Engineer	Fire Officer
	Rescue Man
	Accident Investigator
Medical Officer	Safety and Fire Prevention Officer
	Safety and Hygiene Technologist
Nurse	Physiotherapist
	Chief Nursing Officer
	Ambulance Room Attendant
	Nursing Sister
	Nursing Superintendent
	Suggestions Secretary
	Pension and Insurance Officer
	Pensions Secretary
	Sports and Social Officer
	Sports and Social Club Secretary
	I/c Internal Publicity
	Internal Publicity Assistant
	Job Analyst
	Personnel Records Officer
	Hostel Warden
	Travel Officer
	Study Man (Work Study)
	Manager Administration
	Labour and Security Officer
	Welfare and Training Officer
	Training/Safety Officer

This list gives some indication of the range of work which is now being undertaken in personnel departments. Collins has suggested that it is useful to divide the occupational group into technologists and technicians (and though the borderlines are ill-defined we have endeavoured to indicate where these might lie). He defines the personnel technologists as 'those concerned with building and maintaining the organisation in a broad and general way' and the technicians as those with very limited responsibilities.

The expertise of a skilled bargainer is perhaps more obvious than the other skills of the personnel specialist. The good bargainer may be able to save his employers large sums of money by his abilities, whether in preparing briefs or in the rituals of striking the bargain where his nerve and timing may be all important. The industrial relations specialist has held high status in his occupational group since the advent of full employment, though this pre-eminence is now being challenged by those concerned with education and training who have to be admitted to the counsels of the most senior management group in order to ensure the satisfactory development of any executive training scheme. It has been argued that the personnel specialists have not, until recently, taken much initiative for forward planning in their function but have been mainly geared to fire-fighting—thus the expert fire-fighter, the industrial relations expert, has been the most highly esteemed of the personnel specialists.

The more the rest of the personnel work becomes preventive, the less easy it is to measure its effectiveness; it becomes more and more a matter of belief or conviction. Yet it is clear that manpower planning, suitable investment in training, a well-organised wage and salary structure could affect more long-term savings than the best fire-fighting skills applied by negotiators who are simply seen as custodians of the agreements. However, these are not alternatives but adjuncts. There will still be a necessity to reach agreement on terms and conditions of employment even when, or especially when, all these other personnel activities are undertaken, and it will probably become more difficult than ever to do so under the pressures of government control on prices and incomes and within the time limits thought suitable by the public for bargaining.

Our account begins in Part 1 with a general survey of the way in which the institutions of industrial relations have grown up, a description of the main contending parties: trade unions and employers' associations and the development of state intervention.

Having established the framework we then go on, in Part 2, to examine the subject matter of industrial relations expertise, the substance and procedures of collective bargaining, the tactics and strategies deployed, the relationships existing between the bargaining organisations and within each organisation.

In Part 3 we explore what facts are known about the distribution of personnel specialists in industry, commerce and the social services. Little is known about the distribution of this group and even less about the way in which they do their day-to-day work, about the discretion they are permitted and the influence which they have. (We can only conjecture that a 'professional' group with a salary range of from less than £500 to £10,000 per annum must have very great differences in responsibility or, at least, that there are great differences in the recognition of the worth of individual's contributions.)[1] We shall consider what we have been able to discover about the involvement of some personnel specialists in industrial relations; we shall try to make an examination of the present-day work of personnel specialists from writings about their activities and aspirations; and we shall enquire into the influences affecting their approach. Are they professional men? Is personnel management a distinctive and different speciality in management which needs a separate and different occupational grouping? Why are some personnel specialists anxious to identify with the specialist 'professional' group and others refuse to recognise this adherence?

In Part 4 we shall look at changes and developments in the context of industrial relations today, first in terms of raising the performance of personnel specialists in industrial relations. This necessarily involves a discussion of the training of personnel specialists to take up the responsibilities which we describe, and we propose a new tiered system of training which seems to us to be necessary. Personnel specialists alone cannot improve performance in industrial relations, so we turn next to the question of raising the standards of general management in this field. Finally, because managers cannot alone control the structure within which they operate, we examine means for the improvement of the system of industrial relations in Britain.

The book is about industrial relations and about the personnel specialists. It seemed to us that, while a lot of attention is given either to the problems of industrial relations or to those of the personnel specialist, there was a need to examine the problem of the one in relation to the other. We have relied heavily on existing texts for some of the factual material which is already available to students (about the law, for example). We have tried to take account of evidence of a survey we carried out of one in five members of the I.P.M., and which we hoped would give some measure of the involvement of members in industrial relations. We have been greatly assisted by practitioners in the field, both personnel specialists and trade union members and officers.

[1] 'Personnel Management Salaries', *I.P.M. Digest*, vol. 2, no. 11, Feb. 1967.

The book is intended for practitioners who, while expert in the arts of industrial relations, do not often have their problems analytically discussed. The book is also intended for students of personnel management and industrial relations for whom we hope it will provide a discursive and critical supplement to the factual information already available.

1 The Framework of Industrial Relations

1 Employers' Organisations[1]

Employers' associations are mysterious organisations. Their development reflects the development of the structure of industrial relations itself in Great Britain, and their present complexity is inseparable from our industrial relations system. But while trade unions in general and in detail have been the subject of considerable study, employers' associations are not often informatively discussed. The Royal Commission was set up in 1965 as the Royal Commission on Trades Unions and Employers' Associations, but it is probably regarded by the public as being concerned mainly with trade unions. The Written Evidence of the Ministry of Labour (H.M.S.O., 1965) devotes relatively few paragraphs to employers' associations and even the Commission's examination of the associations' evidence was often largely concerned with the associations' opinions about unions and the structure of collective bargaining. This emphasis is partly because recent public concern about industrial relations is really concern about the unions (rightly or wrongly). But there are deeper reasons for this inattention to so significant a part of the framework of industrial relations. As Clegg

[1] There is considerable confusion in the names of employers' organisations: some are called 'federations', others 'associations'; in some industries regional 'associations' may constitute a national 'federation'. H. A. Clegg pointed out that 'In constitutional theory a federation is a body in which the constituent authorities have "co-ordinate" powers in their different spheres', but added that this distinction was none too meaningful concerning employers' organisations. In fact the word 'association' or 'federation' should be regarded merely as a part of the title of the particular organisation, denoting no constitutional description.

suggested, they 'can easily preserve secrecy, and they have little incentive to do otherwise'.[1] They are not evangelical or proselytising institutions and they are the repositories of information collected from the independent and competing commercial organisations which compose their membership. The public knowledge has been considerably improved recently by the work of the Commission, by way of evidence given to it by employers' organisations and by the Commission's Research Paper.[2]

They are not ancient institutions, not usually as old as their trade-union counterparts. When they began to develop in the latter half of the nineteenth century it was often reluctantly and apologetically because they seemed to contradict the principles of unplanned, laissez-faire competition which were still current in industrial and commercial circles. They were seen as unfortunate necessities, 'an evil forced upon employers as the only means for their defence against the unions'.[3] So, reluctantly and defensively their numbers grew: the General Coal Masters' Association in Yorkshire in 1844, the North of England Ironmasters' Association in 1863, the General Builders' Association in 1865. Their growth was stimulated by changes in trade unionism which reflected changes in the law and a developing militancy. The establishment of employers' associations in turn led to the development of formalised procedures for the settlement of disputes, to the emerging framework of industrial relations as we know it; Clapham lists the following conciliation arrangements as examples: the Committee of Conciliation in Potteries in the 1830s, the Silk Arbitration Board in 1849, the Hosiery and Glove Trade Board of Arbitration and Conciliation 1860, and the North of England Iron and Steel Conciliation Board in 1869.[4]

The development of employers' associations and of the conciliation arrangements of which they formed such an essential part

---

[1] A. Flanders and H. Clegg (eds.), *The System of Industrial Relations in Great Britain*, Blackwell, 1956.

[2] V. G. Munns and W. E. J. McCarthy, 'Employers' Associations', *Royal Commission Research Papers*, 7, H.M.S.O., 1967.

[3] *ibid.*, p. 204.

[4] J. H. Clapham, *An Economic History of Modern Britain*, C.U.P., 1932, vol. 2, pp. 173–5.

illustrates one of Lewis Coser's propositions in discussing the functions of social conflict,[1] that one of the parties to conflict has an interest in the organisation and unity of the other side, as long as approximate parity of power has been achieved. When the early trade unions were weak the employers tried to break them; as the unions gained strength and became established the employers reluctantly organised to meet them and, by the 1891 Royal Commission, evidence was given by an employers' representative that 'organisation' on both sides was the best way of preventing strikes.[2] With the recent Royal Commission, times have changed to the extent that the Confederation of British Industry is at pains to discuss how it can best help the trade unions to develop and improve.

ORGANISATION

Employers' organisations are so large in number and diverse in structure that any generalisations about them are dangerous, but neither the subject nor the generalisations can be avoided.

The Ministry of Labour's Directory lists 1,411 employers' associations. The legal definition of a trade union under the Trade Union Act of 1871 covers both workers' and employers' organisations, but whereas most trade unions are registered with the Chief Registrar of Friendly Societies, only 81 employers' associations were so registered in 1965. Some of the recent discussion of trade-union reform has concerned a new form of trade-union registration with penalties for exclusion from the register; comparatively little seems to have been said about the registration of employers' organisations. Whether they require, or are likely, to be reformed or not, employers' organisations exist in large numbers, are important features of most industrial and commercial groups, are likely to be further encouraged by the growing complexity of industrial and employment legislation, and are central to our system of industrial relations. What are their effects and how appropriate is their structure to their considerable responsibilities?

[1] L. Coser, *The Functions of Social Conflict*, Routledge & Kegan Paul, 1956, p. 129.
[2] Flanders and Clegg, *op. cit.*, p. 204.

In terms of their size and finances, McCarthy,[1] conducting a survey of 36 employers' organisations discovered that 80 per cent of the national federations in the survey (defined here as national organisations with local affiliates or associations) and 30 per cent of the national associations (defined as organisations with no local associations) had more than 200 firms in membership, and 40 per cent of the national associations had less than 40 member firms. No federation's members employed less than 10,000 workers, and one-third of them employed more than 100,000. Sixty-four per cent of the national associations said their members employed 1,000 to 10,000 people; 17 per cent 10,000 to 50,000; and 10 per cent claimed to employ more than 50,000. Employers' organisations are financed by their member firms, usually by way of a collective levy or subscription.

An example of employers' organisational arrangements comes from the evidence to the Royal Commission of the Shipbuilding Employers' Federation.[2] The Federation was established in 1899. It does not have individual firms in membership; these join one of 17 local associations which together compose the Federation. This is an example of the typical arrangement in which local or trade associations are loosely organised in a federation; it is the federation, typically, not the association, which matters in terms of industrial relations. To take another example, the Engineering Employers' Federation is the largest in Britain; it is composed of 39 associations which comprise about 4,500 separate establishments. In the Ship-building Employers' Federation, each member association nominates representatives who, twice a year, attend the policy-making meeting, 'the Central Body'. Intervening business is conducted by an Executive Committee. Federated firms pay one subscription to the local association and another, based on the company's annual wage bill, to the Federation. The associations are autonomous and give a direct service to member firms; they offer advice and assistance on labour questions, handle negotiations with trade-union officials in the district and make necessary contacts with public bodies. The

[1] Munns and McCarthy, *op. cit.*, pp. 90–1.
[2] Royal Commission on Trades Unions and Employers' Associations, Witness: the Shipbuilding Employers' Federation, Minutes of Evidence 48, H.M.S.O., 1967.

Federation advises local associations on matters of national policy, provides information about earnings and conditions of work in other districts, negotiates with the Confederation of Shipbuilding and Engineering Unions and, at national level, negotiates with individual unions on questions affecting their members. The Federation's Executive Committee or the Conference and Works Board also hears claims, at meetings called when necessary, on which a failure to agree has been previously registered in the district.

✓The highest level of employers' organisation is the Confederation of British Industry, which was formed as the result of amalgamating the Federation of British Industries, the British Employers' Confederation and the National Association of British Manufacturers in July 1965. The C.B.I. now has the advantage of being the single authoritative representative of British industry but it functions purely as a co-ordinating body. It includes as members individual firms and associations of employers, and the nationalised industries are eligible as associate members. It has no direct control over collective bargaining and takes no direct part in the negotiating process, but as the single, authoritative counterpart to the T.U.C., the C.B.I. is becoming increasingly involved in discussions and joint investigations. There are those who advocate a more direct and formal involvement of the C.B.I. with the T.U.C. and the government, in the over-all control of industrial relations and employment policy; incomes policy, in particular, suggests itself as suitable to joint or tripartite control. Whatever the merits of this case it seems certain that the C.B.I. is likely to become more positively involved if only because of its unique and imposing position. There is a tendency for institutions which must, by virtue of their position, be consulted to find that their functions become less consultative and more authoritative; they become more powerful because they are there.

OBJECTIVES

The objectives of employers' organisations have been stated very clearly in the Royal Commission's Research Paper: 'The aim and object of all organisations is to serve the interests of their members. This involves the protection of the employer from the demands of organised labour, and also the protection of his interests in relation to government, public authorities, professional bodies, suppliers of materials and customers.'[1] The chief distinction, according to the authors, is between the idea of the organisation as a common forum for sharing views and experience and the idea of the employers' organisation as a method of achieving joint action to solve common problems. Employers' organisations, like others, often make expansive claims to be more than self-interested, defensive bodies. They now regard themselves as pursuing a higher purpose than an exclusive concern with their members' commercial interest. As the Engineering Employers' Federation puts it: '. . . Historically every other function was subordinated to the primary purpose of defending the employers against attack from the trade unions . . . [but] the Federation maintains most firmly that increasingly over the years its policies have, to a large extent, been governed by national economic considerations and, equally, that much of what the Federation has sought to do has been governed not only by sectional interest but by the economic interests of the country as a whole.'[2] It is worth quoting here the T.U.C.'s view of such altruism: 'Trade Union leaders are usually much more candid than others in recognising that their primary responsibility is to their members. It can plausibly be argued that trade union leaders should disguise the truth of this proposition and talk about "the national interest" as frequently as everybody else. The alternative, of course, is for leaders of other groups to show the same integrity as trade unionists in recognising publicly the reasons why they themselves do not pursue policies other than those based on self-interest. . . . Trade unionists . . . take a somewhat jaundiced view of those whose interests are different to their own lecturing them on their social responsibilities, with the real intention of producing a result which is favourable to their own interests.'[3]

Employers' associations now play an essential part in industrial relations but they have other functions. They are concerned to represent the interests of their member firms and the industry (the

---

[1] Munns and McCarthy, *op. cit.*, p. 5.

[2] Engineering Employers' Federation, *Evidence to the Royal Commission on Trades Unions and Employers' Associations*, pp. 33–4, published by the Federation.

[3] T.U.C.'s written evidence to the Royal Commission, p. 61.

two are not necessarily co-extensive), they may exert pressure on Parliament like any other respectable interest group and, in turn, they form useful and informed bodies for the government to consult on questions concerning their respective industries. They may provide their member firms with central services such as legal advice or advice about administrative technique or technical research; they may advise about the best appropriate consultants available to tackle a member's special problems; they may also maintain standards of fair trading and competence—this latter area of activity once included, quite respectably, resale price maintenance but, again, times have changed.

In a questionnaire survey of a one-in-five sample of the I.P.M.'s membership which we conducted in January 1967 our respondents listed the following purposes served by employers' organisations of which their firms were members:

1. To negotiate national agreements	73
2. To provide information about wages and conditions of employment	45
3. To provide information about trade and technical matters	43
4. To provide both 2 and 3 above	17
5. To interpret and advise on government policy and legislation	32
6. To settle disputes in industrial relations	30
7. To co-ordinate education and training	18
8. To advise on safety and health	9
9. To undertake local industrial relations negotiations	8

We are concerned here solely with their responsibilities concerning employment and industrial relations. This concern will not necessarily distort a discussion of the employers' associations because these responsibilities are not only common to the majority of them but they are also the chief responsibilities of many.

It is a subject of complaint in some quarters that the associations are loose-knit and have little or no disciplinary power over their members. It is difficult to see how they could have more. The commercial organisations which make up the membership could hardly be more independent, by their very nature, and they join for what the association does *for* them rather than *to* them. The advantages sometimes do not seem to be enormous or obvious. To put it the other way, when the C.B.I.'s representatives were asked by the Royal Commission to describe what a firm loses when expelled or asked to resign from its association, Mr Sloan could at first answer only in terms of an analogy which must have appeared horrifying: 'If I were told to resign from my golf club I would not show my face on the train in the morning. It is a moral stigma if you are asked to resign from an employers' association. . . . It is a very real sanction, I would have thought.'[1] On further reflection the C.B.I. representatives added some more tangible disadvantages: that it would be 'extremely difficult to persuade certain authorities that they were reputable firms' (Sir Maurice Laing) and that excluded firms would find it difficult to deal with unions in dispute because they would be unable to use the conciliation board machinery for the industry. It is a measure of the importance of the industrial relations function to the employers' association that the C.B.I. emphasised this 'loss of the agreed disputes procedure' as the most serious disadvantage of the excluded firm. But exclusion as a disciplinary measure is rare; more frequently the firm may leave voluntarily when it wishes to organise its industrial relations affairs in a manner which cannot be contained within the arrangements arrived at by the association.

Clegg has pointed out a fundamental change in their activities since the Second World War; previously organised as a defence against trade-union pressure, since 1939 the 'problem has ceased to be the need to avoid undercutting through the breaking of agreements and has become instead the need to avoid competition for bidding up rates and conditions far beyond the agreement'.[2] The avoidance of competition for labour has taken two forms, the best-known of which concerns the associations' attitudes to negotiated rates of pay. Practice in this respect varies between the employers' organisations, which negotiate rates and which attempt to enforce them on member firms as standards from which deviation is not permitted, to the negotiation of rates which are minimal and which

[1] Royal Commission on Trades Unions and Employers' Associations, Witness: the Confederation of British Industry, Minutes of Evidence 6 and 9, H.M.S.O., 1966, p. 1024.
[2] Flanders and Clegg, *op. cit.*, p. 227.

are considerably exceeded by wages paid within the member firms.[1]
Employers' organisations have been criticised on the quite contradictory grounds of contributing by their practice to an uneconomic
and non-competitive standardisation of wages which eliminates the
flow of labour to the most efficient firms and, at the same time, for
failing to enforce the discipline of standardised rates on maverick
firms which are contributing by their indiscipline to an inflationary
wage spiral. The whole issue of the employers' associations' influence
on negotiated rates of pay is embedded in the complex question of
national and of plant bargaining, a question to which we shall
return. The second form of avoidance of competition for labour is
much more covert, less open to informed discussion and less sup-
portable by evidence. It seems certain, however, that in areas of
chronic manpower shortage, employers' associations have come to
an understanding that member firms will refuse to employ labour
from other members in the same district. At best these 'no-poaching'
agreements mean that firms are not permitted to entice labour from
other employers. At worst such agreements may mean that workers
can find it difficult to seek other employment. The least dangerous
consequence seems to be that such arrangements are likely to contribute to stickiness in the labour market; the most dangerous, the
possibility, which, it is hoped, remains hypothetical, of re-
introducing what is, in effect, a blacklist.

Employers' associations have been seen at various times as
secretive and reactionary organisations, concerned sometimes to
apply the employers' power against unions and their members while
avoiding, through their comparative anonymity, the direct account-
ability of the individual firm. Clegg lists the weapons which were
employed in the past: the provision of blackleg labour, strike
insurance, the *document* (a pledge by employees not to join a union),
the *discharge note* and the *list* (a list of names of strikers whom
members of the association agreed to refuse work, usually without
reason). Clegg adds: '. . . the list remained in use for a very long
time. Evidence in 1891, 1903 and 1912 establishes this point. In

---

[1] The former, tightly controlled arrangements, are comparatively rare. In the
organisations surveyed by Munns for the Royal Commission, only the National
Federated Electrical Association controlled the wages of member firms.

fact, it may still be in use today.'[1] It is alleged that firms in membership of the Engineering Employers' Federation 'support the Foremen and Staff Mutual Benefit Society which contains a clause in its constitution prohibiting its members from belonging to a trade union'.[2] Employers' organisations, as their very existence suggests, have come to terms with trade unions, but in the field of white-collar unionisation general acceptance of the principle of union recognition has not been achieved. On 19 June 1964 the British Employers' Confederation (now merged in the C.B.I.) circulated a 'strictly private and confidential' letter (which was later quoted in *The Times*) warning member organisations of the difficulties attendant upon staff union recognition.[3] The attitude expressed in this letter has not been inherited by the C.B.I., but McCarthy concluded that the attitude of employers' organisations' officials to non-manual unionisation was that most of them 'are or would be "neutral". But a significant minority express open opposition and only a few suggest that they would encourage such a development.' Munns noted that 'employers have generally not seen any great advantage in bargaining collectively with trade unions on wage rates for these groups of workers. It seems that generally employers prefer to deal with these grades of worker either on an individual basis or on a company basis.' The major weapon of the employer against employees has been and is the lock-out; it was last used in 1967 by the Shipbuilding Employers' Federation against members of D.A.T.A.

But we should not be surprised by evidence of occasional hostility by employers' organisations towards labour, particularly those of us who argue that conflict is a reality in industrial relations and its manifestations should not be suppressed.[4] And the hostility of employers becomes less frequent and less virulent as time passes (it is a matter of conjecture whether this development is the result of

[1] Flanders and Clegg, *op. cit.*, p. 208.

[2] Notably by D.A.T.A. in Royal Commission on Trades Unions and Employers' Associations, Minutes of Evidence 36, H.M.S.O., 1967, p. 1523.

[3] The letter is quoted in D.A.T.A.'s written evidence to the Royal Commission and by Clive Jenkins in 'Tiger in a White Collar' in *Penguin Survey of Business and Industry*, 1965, edited by Rex Malik.

[4] This argument is best expressed in R. Dahrendorf, *Class and Class Conflict in an Industrial Society*, Routledge & Kegan Paul, 1959.

growing goodwill or an inevitable, but conditional accompaniment of post-war economic circumstances). In the highest reaches of employer organisations hostility has given way to an encouraging readiness of the C.B.I. to work with its counterpart, the T.U.C. The *Observer* reported on 30 July 1967 on a joint investigation of industrial disputes: 'The report will come out flatly against Conservative suggestions that local tribunals should be set up with powers to impose legal penalties on those who break procedural agreements.' The C.B.I.'s initial evidence to the Royal Commission showed a similar understanding of the role of trade unions and an awareness of the dangers of containing them by legal prescription.[1]

Few would deny that the employers' organisations are a responsible force in industrial relations and that they help to develop more mature attitudes among their members. There is less agreement, however, about whether they have contributed to effective industrial relations by virtue of the substantive and the procedural agreements to which they have been party. There are various tests, as we shall see, of what are and what are not 'effective' industrial relations. But the criticisms of the effectiveness of employers' organisations fall under three heads:

1. The procedural agreements to which they are party are the product of their own complex evolution and are now ossified and ineffective.
2. They have contributed to the proliferation of nation-wide bargains which are outmoded and which prevent the parties from making necessary innovations.
3. They have been ineffective in promoting best practice among their members as the result, in part, of their own inadequate staffing and training.

We shall look at the matter of procedural agreements in the pages specifically devoted to them. Let us examine the remaining charges.

There is no doubt that employers' organisations lend themselves to the construction of agreements on a national scale because this, in

---

[1] At the end of 1967 the C.B.I. changed its mind and its evidence and, returning to the Royal Commission, advised the advantages of stronger legal constraint.

part, is the purpose for which they evolved. They were also under trade-union pressure to move in the direction of the national bargain; the continuation of district agreements in the coal-mining industry, for example, was a source of conflict. But employers' organisations are largely defensive organisations and, like other defensive arrangements, their strength is sometimes that of the weakest member. For this reason, the pacemakers in many industries are outside their respective federations; the list includes names which are not only widely known but which have reputations for applying the best industrial relations practice—Esso Petroleum, Alcan Industries, Vauxhall Motor Company, Ford Motor Company, Steel Company of Wales, Lancashire Cotton Corporation. Critics of the federations say that this is no accident, indeed that an essential preliminary to negotiating a worthwhile productivity bargain is for the company concerned first to resign from its federation.

Employers' organisations are also apparently engaged in an examination of their structure and, particularly, that of the trade association. Both the procedure agreements and the great size of the Engineering Employers' Federation have been the subject of criticism. It has been suggested that, on both counts, a federation which incorporates the whole of the motor industry as one of many subordinate parts is hardly likely to be able to play an effective part in the contemporary industrial world. This charge is denied by both parties, the Engineering Employers' Federation and the Motor Industry Employers,[1] but we must remain in some doubt while it is apparently necessary for *ad hoc* arrangements like the Motor Industry Joint Labour Council to be established. Doubts apparently also exist within the Federation, as this letter from Philips Industries Ltd to the Royal Commission demonstrates: 'It is our view that the Engineering Employers' Federation is far too large and ponderous an organisation to continue filling what was once a constructive role. The diversity both in size of companies and interests of manufacture make it ineffective. We suggest they could with advantage be broken down into smaller groups, perhaps on an industry basis, perhaps also with regard to the sizes of member

[1] Royal Commission on Trades Unions and Employers' Associations, Witness: Motor Industry Employers, Minutes of Evidence 23, 1966, pp. 3476–7.

companies. By a fresh start in the smaller groups, professionalism might to some degree be lessened and the semantic mumbo-jumbo might be reduced.'[1] The employers argue that their own institutions have roots almost as complex and ancient as those of their trade-union counterparts and that, therefore, as much patience should be exercised while they examine their structure as is claimed for the trade unions. Whether one sympathises with this request or not depends on the assumptions one holds about the value of voluntary collective bargaining; employers' organisations are certainly an essential ingredient in it.

We are also asked to remember (fairly constantly in the first part of the Royal Commission's Research Paper) that the prime determinant of what an employers' organisation does is what its members want it to do; it exists to serve their needs and there are strict limits to the extent that it can trespass beyond the members' perception of their needs. This will not do as a general excuse, of course. If employers' organisations are judged to be at fault, the argument that they are limited by their members' perceptions is an explanation so entirely understandable as to justify robbing them of any responsibility in the future. The justification for their conduct merely demonstrates their unsuitability for an important role. The justification is based on the inescapable limitations on the employers' organisations' ability to exercise control over their members. It seems that there is not much more prospect of control over developments in the future than has been exercised in the past: 'The control of plant productivity bargaining by employers' organisations seems therefore to be even less likely than the control of straight wage increases. Not only is the vetting and authorisation of company plant or site wage increases undesired . . . but practical problems would arise in assessing the merits of a particular increase in relation to the measurements of improved efficiency.'[2]

Control seems indeed to be limited, not only by practical realities but, to some extent, by intention. In McCarthy's survey 72 per cent of national association officials and 42 per cent of national federation officials said that they made little or no attempt to influence the

[1] *ibid.*, Witness: Engineering Employers' Federation, Minutes of Evidence 20, 1966, p. 2843.
[2] Munns and McCarthy, *op. cit.*, p. 77.

industrial relations activities of members. Among local officials, 37 per cent made little or no attempt to influence members but, in engineering, 56 per cent of local officials said they tried to influence their members a lot.[1]

DEVELOPMENT WORK

But we should not hasten to judge. Employers' organisations are expanding their services and have developed more positive functions and activities. There has been an increasing concern to bring about improved managerial practice. The West of England Engineering Employers' Association pioneered the provision of work study appreciation courses. Organisations have established or encouraged the establishment of management-training centres; the former British Iron and Steel Federation's Staff College at Ashorne Hill, for example, has been regarded in some quarters as one of the best institutions of its kind in Britain.

Munns makes a great deal of the development of a more positive role. Some associations, he says, are developing a service 'to assist members who wish to improve the quality of management in their own firms, and to foster the development of good labour relations'.[2] But the actual evidence seems to be both scant and recent. The Clyde Shipbuilders' Association arranged a supervisors' training course at Strathclyde six years ago, concluded that a course for one industry was not desirable and now confines its activities to circularising members about courses available in the area. The London Region of N.F.B.T.E. has organised five one-week courses for supervisors every year for the last three years and it 'supports' external courses by circulating information and providing speakers. The F.C.E.C. 'sponsors' courses in civil-engineering management. Since 1965 the N.F.E.A. has run two-week sandwich courses in site management and 'sponsors' part-time courses at Battersea. Munns believes that 'Activities of this kind have grown in recent years and further growth seems likely to be stimulated by the operations of Industrial Training Boards'.[3] It is, of course, because of the need for stimulus that the Boards were created. He found some indications of a specialist management consultancy service in one or two cases in the

---

[1] *ibid.*, p. 97.   [2] *ibid.*, p. 51.   [3] *ibid.*, p. 52.

'trade' field but added that 'in the industrial relations field nothing on this scale yet exists in any of the associations visited, but some of the activities of association staff tend in this direction'.[1] Munns believes that the 'consultative role will be strengthened at the expense of the regulating attitude'[2] (which, itself, has had precious little effect), but the spasmodic developments that have taken place are of recent origin and have in part been the result of employers who 'have turned to their associations for advice and guidance about the operation of the Training Boards particularly in relation to the levy and grant system'.[3] Once again, in other words, the associations represent their members, do what their members want and respond to the same stimuli. This is hardly the description of organisations which may be expected to engage in innovation and development.

STAFFING

There remain questions on how the employers' organisations are and should be staffed.

It must be remembered that the employers' organisations are not controlled by their staffs of permanent officials. There is usually a structure of national, regional and specialist committees composed of representatives of member firms, elected or appointed, often in proportion to the numbers employed by the firm (or to the wages bill). The overall policy control of the Engineering Employers' Federation, for example, is in the hands of a General Council and a Management Board composed of office bearers (who are employers), elected members (from the associations) and *ex-officio*, including permanent, staff members. The specialist committees may be composed in the same way but the area of their specialism may well be negotiations. In the regions, too, policy matters and even negotiation may be the partial responsibility of employers' representatives who are part-time members of the association. The respective power and influence of the permanent and the representative members is not at all clear but it seems fair to assume that the main work of industrial relations negotiation falls upon the permanent staff, particularly in issues concerning dispute procedure and the application of agreements rather than their national negotiation. For this reason we shall discuss some aspects of what appears to be current staffing policy.

[1] *ibid.*, p. 52.   [2] *ibid.*, p. 81.   [3] *ibid.*, p. 61.

The representatives of the Shipbuilding Employers' Federation were asked by the Royal Commission[1] where the full-time officials were drawn from and whether they had any industrial relations training 'in what is after all a rather complicated subject'. The employers' representative answered that in some cases they came from industry, in others 'they advertise for a man and they interview candidates, and I think the main attribute is whether he understands human nature, whether he appears likely to be able to be on reasonable terms with his opposite number in the trade unions, whether he is a reasonable administrator'.

These, apparently, are fairly representative opinions. Munns concludes that 'Apart from the recruitment of professionally qualified accountants, lawyers and statisticians for specialist work, specialised experience or qualifications are not normally sought',[2] and that 'there is some caution about recruiting from member firms and specialised experience in labour relations is not necessarily an advantage'.[3] In terms of job specification, 'the essential thing is that he should be "the right man for the job" in terms of personal qualities and mental, physical and intellectual capacity' and that 'most of the existing staff of associations are self-taught and have learnt from experience'. McCarthy presented the following results of a survey of officials' previous jobs.[4]

Previous job as	Nat. Assn.	Nat. Fed.	Local Associations		
			E.E.F.	N.F.B.T.F.	B.F.M.
Accountant/ solicitor	11	17	33	24	8
Officials of employers' association	19	75	25	31	61
Work in the trade represented	24	8	11	10	23
Industrial relations job	11	—	14	—	—
Other jobs	35	—	17	35	8

[1] Royal Commission, Minutes of Evidence 48, 1967, p. 7903, etc.
[2] *op. cit.*, p. 64.   [3] *ibid.*, p. 70.
[4] *ibid.*, p. 99.

McCarthy concluded that 'very few had any previous experience of an industrial relations job as such. . . . It also appeared that virtually none of the chief officials interviewed had any training for their jobs other than experience'.[1] And the experience, it seems, is often at a limited level, as the representatives of the s.e.f. explained: 'A number of the local associations have recruited personnel from the yards, with experience of negotiations in the shipyards. Some indeed have been shop stewards in their day. . . . In a number of what we call the large one-firm districts, the secretary of the local association is an employee of the firm, and he has probably been employed in the time office or in the office which deals with [industrial] relations. . . .' There are two aspects of these replies which are interesting because they are typical of one approach to the problem of staffing the industrial relations function. The first concerns the employment of ex-trade-union officials, a frequent arrangement in shipbuilding, the motor industry and the coal-mining industry, among many others. Nearly 50 years ago Sidney and Beatrice Webb wrote: 'It is a unique feature of the technical officials of the Cotton Unions that they have frequently been willing to serve the industry as the paid officials of the Employers' Associations when they have been offered higher salaries. Their main duty, whether acting for the employers or the workmen, is to secure uniformity in the application of the Collective Agreements as between mill and mill; and such a duty, it is argued, like that of the valuer or accountant, is independent of personal opinion or bias, and can be rendered with equal fidelity to either client.'[2] The question of the propriety of this state of affairs, from the union's standpoint, does not concern us here. But this is a significant matter in relation to the kind of expertise which is believed to be desirable in industrial relations specialists. And this relates to the second aspect, whether it is associated with ex-union officials or not. What kind of contribution are they expected to make to their organisation's affairs?

Industrial relations expertise based on experience (either in the union or in the time office) is important, as the Webbs suggested, if the job is seen as essentially one of agreement minding. But this

[1] *ibid.*, p. 99.
[2] Sidney and Beatrice Webb, *The History of Trades Unionism*, Longmans, 1920, p. 479.

role is not easy to reconcile with innovation, because to question the existing procedures and to introduce new ones is to undermine the very expertise by which the office-holder has succeeded to his post. No-one should under-estimate the complexity of the material of which these men are demonstrably the master; the question is whether this is the kind of expertise most necessary in large sectors of industrial relations where the requirement now seems to be for adjustment and change. The experts are expert in static defence; when the front line changes their knowledge of the terrain is lost. It is because of their reliance on expertise of this sort (if on any at all) that the employers' organisations have been accused[1] of failing to exercise a positive influence either on the structure of their own agreements or on the practice of their member firms;[2] one cannot blame the staff for not fulfilling a role for which they were not appointed, experienced or trained, a role which it was not thought necessary to fulfil. The employers' organisations' industrial relations staff, may, by virtue of their experience (where they have any), be essentially defensive, but it is sometimes difficult to imagine how in the nature of things they can be anything else. We shall discuss later the close inter-relationship which must exist between the commercial, technical and social elements in business decision making, without which personnel management becomes no more than a series of *post hoc* adjustments in an effort to contain the social effects of decisions taken elsewhere. Is any inter-relationship of this kind possible for an employers' organisation which has tenuous

---

[1] 'Standards of labour management in British Industry have, in recent years received, and deserved, much criticism. Most federations and associations would regard labour management, within the limits of its rules and agreements, as a matter for its members. One or two, however, go out of their way to acquaint their members with the latest publications on matters of personnel management and with the work of the various societies and institutes concerned' (Clegg, in Flanders and Clegg, *op. cit.*, p. 229). The same point was raised in the Ministry of Labour's Written Evidence to the Royal Commission 10 years later.

[2] 'A negative management policy breeds the view that the "only way to get anything done in this firm is to stop the job". There can be strong trade unions but there cannot be good industrial relations without good employers. Employers' organisations may accept this view—but they rarely say so. They do not conduct an inquiry into malpractices nor do they criticise their delinquents' (*Trade Unionism*, published by T.U.C., 1967).

links with its members and which relate to an industry where there may be a great variety of circumstances and problems? It may be that defensive arrangements are the best that can be expected from the employers' organisations, while the more advanced and radical solutions come from the firms (the employers' organisations continuing to exercise a conservative and co-ordinating influence to ensure that no firm's solutions are achieved at the expense of the industry as a whole).

In the meantime the kind of staffing policy pursued and advocated by the employers' organisations must seem anathema to those personnel specialists in pursuit of a more 'professional' role for themselves. It has indeed become fashionable in personnel management circles to decry the promotion of old hands to responsible posts and to assume that the truly influential role can be filled only by the highly trained expert grounded in the behavioural sciences. The C.B.I.'s representatives did not agree. When asked by the Royal Commission if they would choose a personnel manager to be the director of an employers' association, Sir Maurice Laing said: 'It would depend what background a personnel manager came from and what other experience he had. If he was an expert in personnel management and did not know the general management of business, I would not choose him.'[1] Mr John Davies added: '... the whole of the tendency one would like to see emerging, and which is indeed characterised by the merger of the C.B.I. itself, is the recognition of the absolute interlock between the economic and commercial problems and the industrial relations one.' Now this does not seem to be the same point as made by the S.E.F.; it does not relate to the particular kind of expertise or lack of it to do a particular, but limited, job. What the C.B.I. representatives appear to question is the relevance of a limited specialism, however 'professional', to the co-ordination of the human, commercial and technical problems of industry. And this relates uncomfortably closely to the criticism made of the personnel 'professional' by Donald Petrie.[2] Personnel specialists have been too ready to dismiss as prejudice the objections which line management have held to giving them more influence in

[1] Royal Commission, Minutes of Evidence 6 and 9, pp. 1117–9.
[2] 'The Personnel "Professionals"—Who Needs Them?', *Personnel Management*, September 1965.

the management of the enterprise. In some cases, perhaps that represented by the views of the s.e.f., the objectives may truly stem from a limited understanding of the potential value of industrial relations expertise. In other cases, however, the objections may reflect a suspicion that the personnel specialist, in spite of or because of his professional expertise, is unable to see personnel problems in the commercial and technical context from which they arise. We shall return in Chapter 14 to the question of the industrial relations expert.

2 Trade Unions

UNION OBJECTIVES

The T.U.C. in evidence to the Royal Commission,[1] lists 10 continuing objectives to be achieved by trade unions:

1. Improved terms of employment
2. Improved physical environment at work
3. Full employment and national prosperity
4. Security of employment and income
5. Improved social security
6. Fair shares in national income and wealth
7. Industrial democracy
8. A voice in government
9. Improved public and social services
10. Public control and planning of industry.

Some of these objectives are, of course, vague, like 'industrial democracy'. Others are necessarily defined only subjectively; no-one would disagree that 'fair shares in national income' is a respectable objective but, when the process begins of determining what they should be, definitions are of no help because we are immediately enmeshed in the complexities of determining how they are settled.[2] A

---

[1] *Trade Unionism, op. cit.*, p. 33.
[2] The T.U.C. recognises this: 'The case for trades unionism as a whole is based on the assertion of rights . . . and it is equally true therefore that those whose interests and perspective is different to that of working people will quite probably take a different view', *ibid.*, p. 105.

broader definition of the functions of trade unions might be that they are concerned to advance their members' economic and social interest, that they exert an independent challenge to the authority of employers over their members and that they constitute an essential representative element in the framework of a political democracy. Of these three functions the first (which is emphasised by some people to the exclusion of the others) need not necessarily be exercised by trade unions at all. The economic and social well-being of workers can be, has been and is, admirably provided for by employers who do not recognise trade unions and by states which do not permit their existence. The defence of independent trade unionism cannot alone rest on economic terms; it must rest ultimately on the dangers of unilateral control by employers and on the weakness in the political framework of an important interest group not being independently represented. Trade unions, although they evolved as, and continue to be, largely economic associations, are indispensable on social and political grounds.

The complexities of relationship between personnel specialists and trade unions are not, however, the trade unions' biggest problem. If most people accept the account of the functions of trade unions which has been given here, that they are indispensable ingredients in the structure of an industrialised political democracy, most are also concerned over what they consider to be 'the problem' of British trade unionism. Contrasting the current attitude towards trade unions with that of the past, William Pickles wrote: 'Nobody who lived through and remembers the miners' strike and the General Strike of 1926 can fail to contrast the widespread sympathy which the miners then met among the middle classes, or the solemn enthusiasm of the ordinary trade unionist (though not of his leaders) for the General Strike, with the bitterness which greets every strike today.'[1] Trade unions in Britain are the subjects of a number of controversies which are often incoherently argued and sometimes conducted from contradictory positions. Their administration is said to be archaic and their finances inadequate for their functions; at the same time they are accused of being too powerful. They are accused of being undisciplined and irresponsible while it is also

[1] 'Trade Unions in the Political Climate', in B. C. Roberts (ed.), *Industrial Relations: Contemporary Problems and Perspectives*, Methuen, 1962, p. 36.

suggested that their associations with government are too close. It is said that there are too many of them, that they must be further amalgamated; it is also said that those that have been amalgamated are too big to be effective.

ORGANISATIONAL PROBLEMS

The reasons for the public's concern about the trade-union movement are complex. This concern seems to fall under two very general headings: the first relating to problems of organisation (under which is subsumed the number of unions, their financing, administration and communications systems); the second relating to union leadership and control, the extent to which the leaders are able to represent their members' interests and control their actions. There is general agreement that trade unions are not often well organised and administered and that they are under-financed. The criticism of their organisation relates to their number; in some industries and trades their proliferation leads to considerable difficulty in simply administering the agreements and makes it impossible for management positively to plan changes in industrial relations. There are 170 unions affiliated, ranging in size from the Transport and General Workers' Union (1,443,738 members) to the London Jewish Bakers' Union (24 members) or the Military and Orchestral Musical Instrument Makers' Trade Society (155 members).

The problems of the overall numbers of trade unions concern duplication of administrative costs, inferior central services, greater difficulty of co-ordinated policy planning; the difficulties exist largely for the trade unions themselves, and the T.U.C. has more than once pointed out the advantage of amalgamation. Amalgamations continue to take place at the initiative of unions. Hughes writes that 'there is more upheaval and re-appraisal of union structure going on via amalgamation than in any previous period'.[1] He also points to the ingenuity of the amalgamation arrangements that are arrived at and to the suitability of amalgamation as a solution to many of the unions' organisational problems: amalgamation affords the advan-

[1] J. Hughes, 'Trade Union Structure and Government', *Royal Commission Research Papers*, 5, H.M.S.O., 1967, p. 22.

tages of size while leaving the amalgamated unions free to set up an occupational group structure which continues to represent the sectional interests of special categories or crafts. Hughes suggests that many of the one-time craft unions (like the A.E.F. and the E.T.U.) are now 'open' in their recruitment rules and policy so that they can claim to recruit and represent anyone in the particular industry (engineering, in the case of the A.E.F.) while also recruiting all members of that particular craft (engineering) outside the industry. In moving towards an 'open' structure, the old craft unions, while retaining the appeal of their old craft status, are following the general unions, which are themselves 'opening' in their acceptance of white-collar workers and women. As craft and industrial barriers fall, unions of this type are likely to become bigger but they are also likely to find themselves more and more frequently in competition for membership in the same industry, company or plant. It may be that this competition can be contained by the T.U.C.'s adjudication or by agreements between the unions themselves but this will not prevent overlapping in *principle*, as Hughes accepts, between several unions in the same industrial unit.

Now the problems of union organisation become greatest for management with the proliferation of unions represented in the place of employment. There are 22 unions represented in Ford's at Dagenham, 17 in the Steel Company of Wales at Port Talbot. Order is introduced into what could be (and sometimes is) chaos as the result of the established procedures which have grown up between employers' organisations and federations of unions representing an industry, as the result of good will and a general desire to create a machinery for discussion at plant level, and as a result of the evolution of an unplanned machinery for shop-steward representation and joint discussion. The last point is so important to the practical operation of the machinery of industrial relations that it was emphasised by the Motor Industry Employers: 'Multi-Union representation within a firm and the election of Shop Stewards on a geographical basis may accentuate the problem, but we are not convinced that the amalgamation and merging of Unions, leading possibly to Industrial Unionism, will necessarily provide the right answer. . . . In other words, we believe that the integration of Shop Stewards' Committees has a greater priority than wholesale reorganisation of established Unions. The 1960 T.U.C. Annual Report (paragraph 24) itself contains one suggestion, i.e. that the National Executives of the Unions represented within factories might agree to delegate to a Joint Committee at National level responsibility for the oversight of the Joint Shop Steward's Committee concerned. Another suggestion is that the Shop Stewards, whatever their Union, should be responsible in the discharge of negotiating business to the Officials of the Union with the majority membership. Several solutions can be explored, and it is to be hoped that the attention devoted to the reform of Trades Union structure will not cause the more pressing problems of Shop Stewards' Committees to be overlooked.'[1]

There are two points of general importance in this passage. The first is that the Motor Industry Employers' scepticism about the value or practicability of industrial unionism is typical of the attitude of most informed observers, although industrial unionism seems to be regarded by the general public as the obvious solution. The coal-mining industry provides the best example of an industrial union, the N.U.M., and also provides a good example of the weaknesses involved. There are constant stresses in coal-mining industrial relations created by the under-representation of certain categories of workers, the daywagemen and craftsmen in particular. Some of the most damaging strikes in the coal-mining industry since 1945 have, for example, been conducted by a small minority (the Yorkshire Winding Enginemen) resisting representation by the N.U.M. or by a separate, but small, union (N.A.C.O.D.S.) concerned about disparities in its relationship with its giant neighbour. Quite apart from the value of industrial unionism as a pattern for all others, there are obvious practical difficulties in how it is to be achieved. Diverse forms of union organisation have been evolved to meet the different needs for representation by different categories of workpeople. People who see their interests as best represented by a particular kind of union organisation are likely to resist change in its fundamental structure.

UNION LEADERSHIP AND CONTROL

That employers should look for salvation to the shop stewards is a

[1] Motor Industry Employers' evidence to the Royal Commission, *op. cit.*, para. 50.

matter of considerable significance. To begin with, it marks a perceptive recognition that solutions of the large-scale problems of union organisation are going to do nothing, in themselves, to solve problems of overlapping and inter-union co-ordination at plant level. It also suggests a realisation that the increasing size and complexity of union structure are actually likely to exacerbate problems of union leadership and control, to increase the distance between official leadership and shop-floor interests and to stress the importance of shop stewards as real representatives of that interest.

The story of the development of shop stewards, of their disparate functions in different industries, of the different degrees to which they have been incorporated in the formal structure of the unions and the machinery of industrial relations, is well-known. Roberts described the shop-stewards' functions as falling into four main groups: union recruitment, the collection of union dues, the application of 'agreements, working practices, customs and habits within a shop', and representation of the members' interests to foremen or managers.[1] Writing in 1956 Roberts pointed out that only four of the larger unions had any provision in their rules for workshop committees of stewards from their *own* unions to be set up in the workplace: '. . . there are probably some others which have workshop committees in practice, but by and large, their formal adoption has not found favour with the unions.'[2] As to inter-union committees in multi-union plants, Roberts wrote that the problem had been tackled only in the printing, building, engineering and shipbuilding industries and that even here the arrangements made were not always reflected in the unions' rulebooks. The incidence of joint committees is not known but they are believed to be widespread, and their proliferation tends towards a further development: 'It is increasingly argued by shop stewards employed in multi-plant firms that the demands of workshop democracy and the need to develop a common response to employer initiatives require the development of regular contacts between work groups in each plant, organised on a multi-union basis',[3] require, in other words, the development of

---

[1] B. C. Roberts, *Trade Union Government and Administration in Great Britain*, London School of Economics/G. Bell, 1956, p. 69.   [2] *ibid.*, p. 71.
[3] W. E. J. McCarthy, 'The Role of Shop Stewards in British Industrial Relations', *Royal Commission Research Papers*, 1966, p. 52.

'combine committees'. And this is where approval of developments, the function of which is to fill the gap between the organisation of the union and its branch and the place of work, begins to break down. The T.U.C. approved, with reservations, the development of work-shop joint-committees in 1960 but the Written Evidence to the Royal Commission[1] is hedged with qualifications about the further developments of co-ordinated shop steward activities. McCarthy points out that one reason for suspicion is that 'common issues are debated and decided in ways that appear to assume the existence of a "self-governing organisation" in the workshop', a development which, in the extreme, is welcome neither to unions nor employers.[2] But in the background of all suspicions of the co-ordination of workshop representation, which, in the current state of union organisation, can take place only among shop stewards, is the brood-ing fear of subversion. The basis of this fear is the memory, often distorted, of the 'shop stewards' movement' on Clydeside during the First World War,[3] and the fear of Communist Party permeation to which Roberts made explicit reference.[4]

There are, however, deeper theoretical issues involved than the simple fears of surrender to malignant and secret forces, issues which concern the function of the trade-union movement and its relation-ship to radicalism. A widely accepted view of industrial conflict, represented best by Dahrendorf, is that the preferred response is 'conflict regulation', that is, 'such forms of conflict control as address themselves to the expression of conflicts rather than their causes'.[5] Conflict regulation depends upon both parties recognising the necessity and reality of the conflict; it also depends upon the organisation of conflict groups. 'Organisation presupposes the legitimacy of conflict groups and it thereby removes the permanent and incalculable threat of guerilla warfare. At the same time it makes systematic regulation of conflict possible'[6]—organisation inaugurates

---

[1] *op. cit.*, pp. 143–5.
[2] *op. cit.*, p. 52.
[3] The best account is in B. Pribićević, *The Shop Stewards' Movement and Workers' Control*, 1910–1922, Blackwell, 1959.
[4] *op. cit.*, p. 74.
[5] *op. cit.*, p. 225.
[6] *ibid.*, p. 65.

routines of conflict which contribute to reducing the violence of clashes of interest. Conflict regulation depends upon the recognition of the legitimacy of interest groups, upon organisation and institutionalisation. Dahrendorf argues that industrial conflict in 'post capitalist' society has become less violent because its existence has been accepted and its manifestations have been socially regulated. Conflict is less damaging when it is controlled within recognised channels; the alternative is damaging guerilla warfare. But we cannot expect everyone to approve of this process; we are warned of the dangers of guerilla warfare but guerilla warfare can be a most effective tactic. Similarly, institutionalisation may be seen as a very effective weapon in the opponents' armoury. Dahrendorf's argument can be turned on its head; it can describe the process by which independent and radical movements are undermined by organisation. In both the general and the particular senses, trade unionism has been accused of succumbing to just this process: 'The history of the inter-war period has, therefore, come to be seen as the history of how the trade unions started by trying to coerce the establishment and ended up by joining it.'[1] There have always been those in the trade-union movement who seemed to be almost intuitively aware of the emasculating machinery for conflict regulation in which, by the very process of recognition, they were being trapped.[2] There are two respects in which these issues are relevant here. The first concerns the significance of the shop stewards as the repositories of militancy.

Shop stewards are believed to be militant or irresponsible (the choice of words depends partly upon one's frame of reference) not because militant or irresponsible men tend to become shop stewards but because they represent the least institutionalised level of industrial relations in Britain. To the extent that they were recognised at all, they were recognised as the result of *force majeure*, because there was no integrated representation of the trade union in the work place, because the unions' organisation so often excluded the plant.

---

[1] W. G. Runciman, *Relative Deprivation and Social Justice*, Routledge and Kegan Paul, 1966, p. 122.

[2] One of the earliest statements to this effect was 'The Miners' Next Step', published by the unofficial reform committee, Tonypandy, 1912. One of the more recent is V. L. Allen's *Militant Trade Unionism*, Merlin Press, 1966.

The representation provided by shop stewards was non-formal in that it escaped close integration in the hierarchy of the trade-union movement; it filled a 'gap in the bottom of the executive system' of the unions. The success of the system of industrial relations in institutionalising and regularising the machinery of conflict control, missed out the shop stewards, who were both driven to engage in guerilla warfare (lacking the organisation for any other kind of conflict) and who therefore fulfilled the function of providing a channel for militant action which was denied elsewhere. Such a channel is likely to be unimportant when the unions themselves are in touch and in sympathy with shop-floor aspirations, but there are times when this is unlikely because of the very extent to which the unions have been incorporated in the fabric of the state. The Shop Stewards' Movement flourished when the government, with trade-union approval, had legislated against strikes.

The recent attempts to legislate for incomes control might have been expected to produce a similar result because, with important exceptions, the unions supported government policy and the T.U.C. established its own voluntary machinery for the notification and examination of pay claims. It was predictable, therefore, that militant reaction which could not find expression through official channels would, once again, be led by the shop stewards; if union leaders cease to represent those for whose interests they stand, then conflict is likely to break out which the leaders will find difficult to control. But this did not happen. Although certain unions (notably including clerical unions like A.S.S.E.T., D.A.T.A. and N.A.L.G.O.) have resisted incomes control, there was no marked outbreak of official or unofficial reaction elsewhere.[1] The simplest alternative explanations are that either incomes policy is widely accepted and understood among the rank and file or the government's economic policy of retraction in producing 560,000 unemployed in September 1967 independently pre-empted the possibility of industrial conflict.

Despite this evidence to the contrary, shop stewards continue to be regarded as a disturbing threat to the peace. The reaction fits neatly into Dahrendorf's theory; both the T.U.C. and the employers are concluding that the shop stewards must be included in the framework, that once they are incorporated in the system, guerilla warfare

[1] The situation has changed since time of writing.

is less likely. The fact that employers are moving in this direction partly explains the current emphasis on plant bargaining; the paradox is that, as the result of the very success of institutionalising union leadership, the leadership has in some industries been incapable either of representing or of controlling at shop-floor level, so the employer is driven to come to terms with those who do represent in the hope that they too will follow recognition with respectability. The trade unions are presented with a graver problem. The growing integration of shop stewards might have a considerable effect in changing the familiar structure of British trade unionism. We have seen McCarthy's comments on the problems of 'self-governing organisations', and while the T.U.C. is receptive to the usefulness of educating shop stewards (the willingness of the T.U.C. itself points to the problem: 'education' is always purposive and can be part of the apparatus of regularising other people's conduct) it is alarmed at the prospects of the shop stewards institutionalising themselves. Unhappy about the development of multi-union joint plant committees ('they always present a challenge to established union arrangements'), the T.U.C. is most disturbed about 'attempts to form a national centre or to call national conferences of stewards irrespective of the industry in which they work. The aim of the sponsors of this . . . type was to usurp the policy-making functions of unions or federations of unions. Unions have been advised to inform their members that participation in such bodies is contrary to the obligations of union membership.'[1]

The continued development of plant bargaining and any restriction of trade-union representation, whether it comes from incomes control or from changes in the law, is likely further to encourage the growth and importance of the shop steward, and this is likely to do more to alter the structure of British industrial relations than many more carefully planned changes. Whether such a development would lead to a more militant unionism is entirely speculative but we should remember that critics of British trade unionism include those who accuse it of having been so completely institutionalised that it now contributes neither to its members' interests nor to improving the economic performance of industry.

[1] 'Trades Unionism', T.U.C. written evidence to Royal Commission, *op. cit.*, p. 143.

The development of 'parallel unionism' at the work place and by a network of unofficial joint committees is regarded as a threat to the existing institutions of trade unionism and as a threat to the control which they are expected to exercise over their membership. We have suggested that their very attempts to exercise control (at the behest of a government with which they have strong ties) has increased rather than diminished the extent of this threat. We have also suggested that improvements in the organisation and administration of the unions may also do nothing to decrease the threat of 'parallel unionism'. There seems no way out of the dilemma. There is certainly no likely solution as long as we continue to regard 'parallel unionism' as irresponsible and dangerous and fail to see the function which it is fulfilling. There are only two possible long-term directions in which we may look for a solution. The first and least likely is that the unions move nearer to representing the aspirations and interests of their members. This means dismantling our expectations that they should be, primarily, responsible and controlling organisations; it may mean coming to terms with a greater degree of official militancy and it may mean re-examining the long-cherished (and undoubtedly influential) political affiliations of the trade-union movement. The second and more likely direction is that parallel unionism will be accepted and encouraged. This may mean, as the term suggests, the ultimate emergence of two trade-union organisations. The existing official structures would continue as an organisational rump, exercising general co-ordination of social and economic policy and acting as an important political pressure group. The negotiating structure would be the result of further developing the emerging network of joint plant and industrial committees. These have already demonstrated (in the face of considerable hostility) remarkable flexibility and survival power in their ability to cut across the complexity of plant, industry, trade and occupational differences. The increasing importance of plant and productivity bargaining, the renewed examination of industrial democracy and the perception of the Motor Industry Employers' comments, all, from different directions, suggest that the recognition and fruitful development of parallel unionism might become a reality. If it came about, nothing would represent a more far reaching change in the character of British trade unionism.

RELATIONSHIP WITH GOVERNMENT

Institutionalisation has come about partly because of the mechanisms for controlling industrial relations evolved by employers and the unions, partly because of the relationships which have developed between the unions and the state. We began by suggesting that one of the functions of trade unionism was the independent representation of an important interest group in a political democracy. It is not our business to discuss political theory, but some of the ways in which this representation has been achieved are distinctive and feed back into the area of industrial relations.

The trade-union movement has always enjoyed a special relationship with the Parliamentary Labour Party but two changes have altered the significance of this relationship. The first concerns the significance of the Labour Party itself. When the Party provided a continuous opposition, the trade unions could afford to regard it as a political or pressure-group extension to their own industrial activities, but once the Party became associated with the government of the country the relationship was bound to affect the nature of the unions' industrial activity. Union influence on the Labour Party was bound to become 'responsible' once the possibility existed of the Party forming a government and of its policies being translated into statutes. The second change is not entirely distinct from changes in the status of the Labour Party but it more directly concerns changes in the fundamental strategy of the unions. Until 1920 unions were concerned with the achievement of two sets of objectives: economic (better pay and conditions) and ideological (changing the structure of society). But the defeats of the engineers, the railwaymen and the miners and the culminating disaster of the General Strike had the result that 'the forward movement of the unions was stopped and they had to fight to preserve the most important of the improvements in the working conditions which they had secured at the end of the war. Any such bold demands as nationalisation and workers' control had, for the time being, to be dropped.'[1] Although Pribićević argues that the *idea* of workers' control was never dropped, it cer-

---

[1] B. Pribićević, *The Shop Stewards' Movement and Workers' Control*, 1910–1922 Blackwell, 1959, p. 4.

tainly dropped out of the programme of practical objectives. The Mond–Turner talks of 1928–9 were taken as evidence of a new spirit of reconciliation and collaboration in industrial relations and when the unions could once again afford to concern themselves with wider objectives it was the milder Morrison concept of state nationalisation which re-emerged. Not only were the unions' objectives changed, the means by which they determined to reach them were different. Syndicalism and associated doctrines had concerned radical programmes to be achieved by revolutionary or at least industrial action. The failure of the General Strike is generally taken to be proof of the ineffectiveness of direct industrial action on a wide scale (in fact, it was hardly a fair test since the strike was a desperate reaction following some five years of retreat). After 1926, not only were the unions' programmes ideologically milder, the unions decided to pursue them via the House of Commons and the constitution; the unions' objectives were now compatible with political influence peacefully applied and the decision to seek political influence itself modified the objectives by reference to what was practical politics.

It may be that trades unions' special relationship with the Labour Party has helped in establishing the considerable apparatus by which the movement is now consulted by government.[1] The relationship may also have constrained the unions to the extent to which they were free to represent the interest of their members by more familiar methods, particularly at times when a Labour government held office.

The section of the trade-union movement which has not been constrained by any ideological association with government is the white-collar group, which is one of the most puzzling of the contradictory features of British trade unionism. Still dismissed by many 'old' unionists as bourgeois, unfraternal and effete they represent the most unfettered opposition to income control and they are the only sector of significant expansion in union membership. But G. S.

---

[1] For descriptions and discussions of the relationship between unions and state see: B. C. Roberts, *Trades Unions in a Free Society*, Institute of Economic Affairs, 1959; D. F. Macdonald, *The State and the Trades Unions*, Macmillan, 1960; W. Pickles, 'Trades Unions in the Political Climate', in B. C. Roberts (ed.), *op. cit.*

Bain has shown that the expansion of white-collar unionism is not the simple success story that some people have believed it to be.[1] While manual employees have declined in number (from 14,776,000 in 1931 to 14,020,000 in 1961) white-collar workers have increased from 4,841,000 to 8,480,000 in the same period. Bain points out that 'The American economy has already reached a point where the white-collar employees outnumber the manual employees and if present occupational trends continue in Britain, this point will be reached here during the 1980s.'[2] In recent years the growth in trade-union membership has slowed down and the density of unionisation has dropped from 45·1 per cent in 1948 to 42·6 per cent in 1964. The relative stagnation in union growth has occurred partly because of a decline in the numbers of manual employees, particularly in those areas (coal-mining, textiles, railways) where unions were best organised; expansion in numbers has taken place, on the other hand, in areas of traditional union weakness, professional services, insurance and distribution. Union membership has not expanded fast enough among white-collar workers to keep pace with their increasing members: '... despite all the recruiting activity of white-collar unions during the post-war period, the real membership strength of white-collar unions in general is roughly the same today as it was in 1948, while the real membership strength of manual unionism and the trades union movement as a whole has actually decreased.'[3] There are many reasons for the difficulties of the white-collar unions: the vigorous opposition to their recognition by some employers and employers' organisations, the difficulty of organisation in establishments with small numbers of clerical employees, the fact that the sectors of fastest expansion in white-collar employment (which include female employees, clerical work in manufacturing industry and scientific and technical work) do not coincide with the sector of greatest white-collar union strength (public employment). But this is a story of relative failure only: the expansion of trade unionism has depended and is likely to depend

[1] (a) 'The Growth of White-Collar Unionism in Great Britain', *British Journal of Industrial Relations*, September 1966. (b) 'Trades Union Growth and Recognition', *Royal Commission Research Paper*, H.M.S.O., 1967.

[2] *ibid.* (b), p. 12.

[3] *ibid.* (b), p. 29.

still further on white-collar unionisation keeping pace with, or getting ahead of, changes in the composition of the work force.

In the meantime, argument continues over the significance of the growth of white-collar unionism, its likely results for the trade-union movement in general and its consequences for the employer. It is the last relationship which concerns us most closely. Union recognition both encourages and is encouraged by a readiness to introduce order, rationality and comparability into wage and salary payments and into other conditions of employment. Employers have enjoyed what they have considered to be the loyalty of their staff employees (a feature which the employees are beginning to believe has cost them money) and total freedom to be 'flexible' in the rewards and punishments which they have administered to individuals. As bureaucratisation increases, comparisons between similar work loads become easier; the work of personnel departments is itself in part concerned with establishing fair comparisons and, when the situation arises in which the work is evaluated rather than the worker, it becomes easier for unions to negotiate on an impersonal basis. This process, which has made the clerical worker more suitable union material than in the past, is now extending to the professional ranks. Professional associations, particularly those concerned with employees in large and public places of employment (like the health service), are apparently less exclusively concerned with the traditional aspects of professionalism as they become more concerned with the negotiation of the terms and conditions of employment of their members. It has been suggested elsewhere that the unions of professional employees have more in common with the traditional manual unions than either have with the non-professional white-collar unions, since both the professional and the manual unions often share ideological objectives, although the content of the ideology is different. The non-professional white-collar unions, on the other hand, are unencumbered by ideology, and are, as far as their membership is concerned, instrumental, a means to an end of getting more money or pursuing the differential of income which they once enjoyed.[1] This explains the militancy of unions like A.S.S.E.T. and

[1] G. Routh concluded (in *Occupation and Pay in Great Britain*, 1906–1960, Cambridge University Press, 1965) that 'During the half-century, the only big changes have been the decline in the differential for professionals, clerks and

D.A.T.A. in negotiating for employees who were once believed to enjoy a special association with their employers. For the other unions, ideology can intervene, by an association with a government promoting incomes control in the case of the manual unions, by a reluctance to strike in the case of professional employees (like teachers) still imbued with a sense of service. It is the clerical and technical unions which are ready to engage in business unionism and ready, like their American forerunners, to engage in aggressive conflict with employers, not in spite of but because they share their employers' philosophy.

The employers, and particularly the personnel managers, are currently able to adopt a more unambivalent attitude of hostility to the white-collar unions than to the manual unions. The manual unions have largely won their battles for recognition (although there are still significant pockets of dispute) and are now facing the more sophisticated problems which recognition and institutionalisation bring with them. The white-collar unions are still engaged in the recognition struggle, so that it is still possible for employers to regard them as they would have regarded unions in general 50 years ago; employers can generalise about the value and importance of trade unionism while excepting the white-collar unions from their benevolent approval. The comparison exposes much of the confusing morality with which personnel specialists often disguise their role as representatives of the employer. Managers accept the unions, as Dr Johnson said of the universe, because they would be fools not to. But the permanent position of the unions cannot be taken for granted and the white-collar unions represent a sector in which the struggle is on. The *Daily Telegraph*, commenting on G. S. Bain's recommendations for assisting the unions to overcome obstacles to recognition (obstacles which he doubted the ability of white-collar unions to overcome alone), asked why trade unions should expect or deserve the assistance of society and government in guaranteeing

---

foremen between 1935 and 1955 and for skilled manual workers between 1913 and 1924. The fall in the relative position of the professionals was substantial and affected both men and women: 1955 found them at between 60 and 70 per cent of their relative position of 1935. Between 1955 and 1960, however, they showed some gain.'

their existence.[1] We should not expect an objective answer to this question from managers because they will operate within and come to terms with the situation that exists, although they may resist the extension of this situation to areas in which they have an advantage. Personnel specialists, to the extent that they are effective managers, represent interests and occupy roles different from those of union leaders; they will claim affinities because it is part of their tactics to do so, because competence requires them to understand union leaders and because their relationships, even of conflict, must persist in time. But personnel specialists are interested parties in the relationship and we should not look to them for a defence of the unions—we should indeed be suspicious when they make it. The answer to the *Daily Telegraph*'s question must rely on social and political considerations concerning the importance of the unions to society, not to the employer.

[1] *Daily Telegraph*, 18 July 1967, leader.

3 The State

It has become commonplace to observe that British industrial relations is dominated by the voluntary principle. The view that industrial relationships are best ordered by the parties concerned has, it is said, been shared by governments; although governments have intervened, their intervention has always been apologetic, minimal, half-hearted. Voluntarism has had several practical consequences. The principle of intervention only in the last resort has meant that what little apparatus exists for government intervention in industrial disputes can be operated only after existing domestic procedure has been exhausted so that the disputing parties have nowhere else to turn. In the second place government machinery for regulating wages has also been a last resort to the extent that it existed only in trades where the parties were incapable of making their own adequate terms. More general government intervention has been excused only at times of grave national emergency; in normal times we have relied on the expertise and good faith of the parties, the employers and the unions. If we are to rely on them, then they need not be expected to be too precise in the kind of rules they lay down for ordering their affairs; if the community is to trust them, it follows that they must trust each other. The importance of mutual trust manifests itself in vague, general, procedural rules and unwritten understandings which, although an administrator's nightmare, work because they are flexible and comprehensive—they work as long as and because the parties share a basic understanding and trust. Because they have to be built on trust they have another advantage, they are adaptable to a variety of situations; if they were not built on trust they would become more and more rigorous, precise and restrictive. The end of the road would be a degree of legalistic formality which, while it might never be sufficiently particularised for each distinct set of circumstances, would be too particular to allow effective and flexible control.

Nothing seems better to illustrate Marshal McLuhan's view, that we invariably grapple with contemporary problems by trying to apply last century's concepts, than our attitude to industrial relations. We are all of us, apparently, supporters of the voluntary principle. The supporters include advocates of fines against strikers, of legal enforcement of collective agreements, of wage freezes, of incomes policies, of penalties against illegal wage claims.

Flanders has defined voluntarism more closely than most. It is, he says, composed of three features: a preference for collective bargaining to state regulation of wages and conditions of employment, a preference for non-legalistic collective bargaining, a preference for complete autonomy in relations between the bargaining parties.[1] 'Of these three', he adds, 'it is only the third which must now be unreservedly consigned to the rubbish bin of history.' This gets nearer than most other statements (in print, at least) to qualifying the acceptability of the voluntary principle. (Its implications, in fact, go further than its intentions: if a preference for autonomy in the relations between the bargaining parties is to go into the rubbish bin, then there may be precious little left worth salvaging. If this third principle goes, how can it leave undamaged a preference for 'a non-legalistic type of collective bargaining' and for 'collective bargaining to state regulation as a method of settling wages'?)

So, before we begin trying to reconcile our undying commitment to voluntarism with the times in which we live, it may be worth examining the amount of the voluntary principle which is already left to us. How far are we committed to the voluntary principle?

Voluntarism is not a birthright enjoyed by Britons from time immemorial. Sharp, discussing the Arbitration (Masters and Workmen) Act, 1872, wrote: 'The Act is interesting as a last attempt to devise a universally applicable means of settling disputes with a legal sanction . . . between 1872 and 1896 the emphasis shifted from

[1] A. Flanders, *Collective Bargaining: Prescription for Change*, Faber, 1967, pp. 34–5.

compulsory arbitration under state supervision to settlement by conciliation between the parties with the state bodies as agencies of mediation and assistance only.'[1]

The facilities which exist for 'mediation and assistance' are provided under the Conciliation Act of 1896, the Industrial Courts Act, 1919, and to a limited extent under the Terms and Conditions of Employment Act, 1959. The Conciliation Act of 1896 removed all existing provisions for compulsory arbitration and gave discretionary powers to the Board of Trade (now, to its successor in this respect, the Ministry of Labour) to provide a variety of responses to a dispute between employers and employees. It could enquire into the causes and circumstances of the dispute, it could take steps to enable the parties to meet, it could appoint conciliators on the applications of either side and, after taking account of the existing machinery of conciliation within the industry, it could, on the application of both parties, appoint an arbitrator. Reference of disputes to state arbitration agencies requires the consent of both sides and may not be made by the Minister of Labour until the industry's procedure has been exhausted.[2] Arbitration awards are not binding although findings of the Industrial Court, once accepted or acted upon by the parties, are said to become part of the contract of employment. Under Section 8 of the Terms and Conditions of Employment Act, 1959, the Industrial Court may be required to adjudicate on a 'claim' by a representative organisation that the recognised terms or conditions of employment established in the industry are not being observed, but this provision, by definition, lies outside the scope of procedure agreements between the parties. Government conciliation is carried out under the Act of 1896 and the Industrial Courts Act, 1919. The Ministry of Labour, nationally and in the regions, provides both an industrial relations advisory service and a conciliation service. In the use of the conciliation service the emphasis has always been that the machinery existing in the industry should have been used and

---

[1] I. G. Sharp, *Industrial Conciliation and Arbitration in Great Britain*, Allen & Unwin, 1950, p. 289.

[2] The T.U.C. has requested the re-introduction of legislation requiring a modified or unilateral form of compulsory arbitration in which either party could demand reference of a dispute to the Industrial Disputes Tribunal. These arrangements, under the Industrial Disputes Order, 1951, ended in 1959.

exhausted before the Ministry's conciliation officers could engage the parties in joint or separate discussions. The Ministry's confused role during the prices and incomes standstill and other recent developments have led some people to question whether this non-interventionist relationship can last.

It is these particular pieces of legislation and the way in which they surround the use of government conciliation services with qualifications which has led to the conclusion that British industrial relations is characterised by the principle of voluntarism. The government is empowered to act only to a limited extent and then with apparent reluctance; industry's own procedures are to be preferred where they exist and have not been exhausted.

The government's attitude to the settlement of disputes has, therefore, come to be seen as typifying its attitude to industrial relations. The generalisation may not be justified. To begin with, the attitude of the state to the settlement of disputes has not been consistent over time, is not entirely consistent now and, by reference to statute law, is not entirely clear. At times of national emergency governments have introduced compulsory arbitration and restricted the freedom to strike. The Treasury Agreements and the Munitions of War Act, 1915, provided compulsory arbitration and made strikes, in effect, illegal. In 1940 the Conditions of Employment and National Arbitration Order made strikes an offence. A state of war is obviously an emergency but there are peace-time conditions in which governments have considered emergency measures necessary. In response to the Triple Alliance the provisions of the Emergency Powers Act, 1920, although accompanied by denials of 'any infringement of the formal right to strike . . . were remarkably wide and established a firm base on which to organise the breaking of big strikes'.[1]

The Trade Disputes Act, 1927 (repealed in 1946) declared a strike illegal if it had a purpose other than the pursuit of a trade dispute in the industry or trade in which the strikers were employed and if it was designed to coerce the government 'either directly or by inflicting hardship'. The most recent example, and perhaps the most generous definition of an emergency which has been taken to

[1] K. Knowles, *Strikes—A Study in Industrial Conflict*, Blackwell, 1952, p. 107.

justify intervention is, of course, the powers provided for under Part IV of the Prices and Incomes Act.

This may suggest that, far from the voluntary principle being the normal standard, it represents a state of affairs which can be permitted to continue unless and until the government decides either that the unions have gone too far, or that there is a serious threat to the community from some other quarter. As the government is almost the sole judge in what it interprets to be an emergency, the voluntary principle becomes, as some commentators are now describing it, a luxury which we may be able to afford only when times are good and the unions are quiet.

Apart from the sudden intervention of the state in response to conditions which it chooses to define as emergencies, there are continuing powers available to the state which could be used to destroy the voluntary principle. Whole sections of the working community have limited access to the right to strike. Acts of 1875 and 1919 make it a crime for any worker in water, gas and (later) electricity undertakings 'wilfully to break his contract of service having reasonable cause to believe that the consequences will be a substantial deprivation of the supply'.[1] The law also confines, to varying extents, the rights of the police, aliens and seamen. One of the most general potential restrictions appears in the Conspiracy and Protection of Property Act, 1875. The Act was hailed as a triumph for the T.U.C., and has been described by Wedderburn as inventing 'a golden formula which became the bedrock of British workers' rights to organise and take effective industrial action'.[2] But Section 5 imposes criminal liability on a worker who breaks his contract believing it likely 'to endanger human life or cause serious injury to property'. In his evidence to the Royal Commission, Wedderburn suggested that this section is of no importance as long as no new extensions are put on 'serious injury' or 'property'. To the layman, however, the likelihood of strikers exposing 'valuable property whether real or personal to destruction or serious injury' would seem to be always present in a strike, and would, indeed, appear to be the very intention and purpose of the strikers. Section 5 might well be one of the many existing pieces of legislation which

[1] K. W. Wedderburn, *The Worker and the Law*, Pelican, 1965, p. 276.
[2] *ibid.*, p. 222.

lies dormant and which does not matter. But it would require, perhaps, the confluence of three sets of circumstances to reawaken interest in it: change in the economic circumstances of society, change in its political attitudes and a judge with decided views.

The intervention of the state has taken place not only by way of restrictive or potentially restrictive legislation. By far the biggest intervention and perhaps the most serious consequences for 'the voluntary principle' has come by way of nationalisation. This intervention has not generally been seen as a threat to the voluntary principle because it has, in the main, restricted the freedom of management and encouraged the position of the unions; it is, nonetheless, an example of massive state intervention in the industrial relations of industries employing two million workers.

State arrangements in the nationalised industries take several forms. In the first place the state, in the nationalisation statutes for the respective industries, has done what it can to translate the moral imperative to be a good employer into a legal requirement in the industries' management. 'In the legislation nationalising the coal mining, civil aviation, transport, electricity, gas and atomic industries, a statutory obligation has been imposed on the Boards responsible for operating the industries to enter into consultation with the workers' organisations as to the establishment and maintenance of joint machinery for the settlement of terms and conditions of employment, and for joint consultation on matters of common interest.'[1] The principal effect of nationalisation has therefore been to require trade-union recognition and effective collective bargaining by law. As these two points were discussed at some length before the Royal Commission, as being ways in which the voluntary principle should (or should not) be qualified, we can see that the state has already gone some way in the direction of positive intervention: 'Nationalisation has meant that the works committees or their equivalent in the individual establishments have been compulsorily established, instead of made dependent for their existence on the goodwill of the employer.'[2]

Nationalisation has had more detailed results. In the coal and gas industries the element of compulsory arbitration in the settlement

[1] *Industrial Relations Handbook*, p. 68.
[2] H. Clegg, *Industrial Democracy and Nationalisation*, Blackwell, 1955, p. 67.

of disputes is the result of agreements between the respective unions and managements, but in the Atomic Energy Authority it is the Act itself which requires 'the establishment of machinery for the negotiation of terms and conditions of employment including reference to arbitration in default of settlement'.[1] The same condition is set out in the Electricity Act, 1947. While the Royal Commission has been exercised over the question of whether collective agreements should be given the force of law, arrangements in the Health Service have, since 1951, been governed by regulations which 'provide that, if wages and conditions are agreed by a negotiating body and approved by the Minister, then the wages and conditions of the staffs covered by that agreement shall not be otherwise than as provided by the agreement'.[2] In the case of the re-nationalised steel industry, statutory prescription has gone further than the 'normal' requirement to recognise, to bargain and to consult; the regional boards must contain two representatives of the employees as full members of the boards.

Nationalisation has also had a considerable effect on the pattern of industrial relations in Britain, apart from the direct consequences of statutory provision. One of the more arguable and paradoxical effects has been on the unions concerned in the nationalised industries. Knowles discussed the implications of nationalisation for the unions and the considerable difficulties which might lie in the way of their choosing to strike; he suggested that 'whether the new sanctions of Trade Unionism will prove as effective as the older and cruder weapons depends ultimately on the political powers available to the workers, i.e. on the Social Character of the State itself'.[3]

A much more obviously discernible result of nationalisation is the development of distinctive employment policies which are not statutorily required. There is little doubt that managers of industries which are nationalised undergo a considerable change (despite the old charge that the face behind the desk is the same). The direct line from the board to the shareholders is removed and the choice for nationalisation has often fallen on industries with a strong element of public service. Managers are quickly made aware (if only by the

[1] *Industrial Relations Handbook*, p. 73.
[2] *ibid.*, p. 99.
[3] Knowles, *op. cit.*, p. 93.

vacillation of government direction) that they are no longer appraised simply by reference to commercial criteria but that they must also pursue (with varying energy at different times) the economic well-being of the country and the social good of their employees and their dependants.[1] They are led to believe that they must be, among other things, good employers. It is this general requirement rather than statutory provision which has led to the high standards in many aspects of nationalised employment policy. In the case of sick-pay arrangements, for example, a report in 1964 concluded that 'White-collar workers generally and all workers in the public sector are well covered, and most of the workers without any cover are manual employees in private industry.'[2] A report on dismissal procedures in 1967 stated that 'though formal internal procedures are fairly widespread among large firms and general in the public sector, in a very large number of firms (including the vast majority of small firms) they do not exist'.[3] It is probably true that if the standard practice of the nationalised industries had been more widely imitated, the Redundancy Payments Act and the Industrial Training Act would not have been necessary.

It is not, of course, simply that managers become more well-intentioned when their industries are nationalised. There are several explanatory features including sheer increase in size, increased public attention, the increased interest of M.P.s and the legally under-written relationship with the unions. One other explanation which concerns us particularly closely is that nationalisation is invariably followed by the increased centralisation, co-ordination and standard-isation of personnel policies. The most obvious example lies in the closer control of locally determined wage rates, but there is also a vast extension in the provision of national joint agreements and unilateral national interpretation and directive on every conceivable aspect of personnel policy. This activity cannot be conducted with-out considerable analysis and administration; it requires the develop-

---

[1] One of the clearest and most rational statements of the distinction is made in 'British Railways Main Workshops. The Handling of a Major Reduction in Labour Force', British Railways Board (mimeographed), 1965.

[2] *Sick Pay Schemes*, Report of a Committee of the National Joint Advisory Council on Occupational Sick Pay Schemes, H.M.S.O., 1964, p. 44.

[3] *Dismissal Procedures*, Report of a Committee of the National Joint Advisory Council on Dismissal Procedures, H.M.S.O., 1967, p. 51.

ment of large and effective personnel departments. Nationalisation has, at least, created the requirement for personnel departments operating at an administrative level of effectiveness.

It would seem, therefore, that nationalisation, whether by intention or not, directly or indirectly, has had a very considerable influence on the pattern of industrial relations in a large sector of employment. Much that has been the subject of contention before the Royal Commission, the enforced recognition of unions, the enforcement of collective bargaining, the legal status of collective bargains, is already accomplished fact in one or more of the nationalised industries and services.

What price voluntarism now? The law as it exists is complex and confused. There is no general agreement among the lawyers about basic questions such as the legal status of strikes or of the contract of employment. The legal status of strikers, for example, seems obscure. There is no recognition in law for a contract of employment to be unilaterally *suspended* by strike action and it is therefore open to the employer to take action against strikers for breach of contract. What seems to prevent a more general recourse to the law by employers is not the law itself (several such actions have been taken in recent years) but the technical difficulties of assessing damages and a realistic respect for the power of trade unions and the long-term damage which may be done to industrial relationships. The law, even where it is regarded as safe, can be suddenly reinterpreted by an eccentric decision of the judiciary (as in the case, some have said, of the House of Lords overthrowing the Appeal Court judgment in Rookes *v.* Barnard). Elsewhere the law appears to carry sufficient existing provisions on the statute book for any semblance of voluntarism to be destroyed. And voluntarism has been destroyed at times of national crisis. Between such crises we live with a formidable apparatus for determining incomes by Wages Council, for protecting the health, safety and welfare of employees, for restricting the hours of work of women and young persons. But we have always excused these interventions as exceptional to the general voluntary principle, as providing only minimal protection. We now see the Ministry of Labour, the traditional upholder of neutrality, appointed under the Prices and Incomes Act as watchdog and security agent to the Board for Prices and Incomes. The voluntary principle has by now been loaded with so many massive qualifications and exceptions that it has virtually disappeared. It remains as a tired cliché which is used to serve two purposes. The first is as an excuse for non-intervention in disputes in which the government has no hope of acting as mediator but must (when public opinion sanctions intervention and when one of the parties is on the point of collapse) join finally as an interested party. The second use of voluntarism is as a tattered but respectable old standard under which practically any recommendation for change can be made to sound reputable. We shall return to the prescriptions for change in the State's relationship to industrial relations in Chapter 16.

In the meantime we might describe the industrial relations affairs of Britain as chaotic rather than ruled by the voluntary principle or indeed by any other principle. The statute law, both recent and in terms of its more archaic survivals, contains elements which are in flat contradiction. (Governments have treated different sectors of industry in entirely different ways.) Judges have made decisions contrary both to each other and to the public intention. Sections of employees have been chosen for minimal protection, and protection has been afforded generally over certain specific rights, but no coherent pattern emerges over the reason for such choices. In collective bargaining over disputes there has been a general reluctance to intervene between the parties, though this reluctance has been swept away in times of crisis and can no longer be reconciled with the apparent determination of governments to control incomes. To say that our industrial relations system is characterised by chaos is not, in itself, to criticise it. Observers, domestic and foreign, are often lost in wonder because, despite or because of its irrational complexity, it works.

That it works is not due to subtleties of law or cunningly drafted agreements or masterly statesmanship. It works almost entirely because the parties want it to. More specifically it works because of three features. The first is that society seems to be becoming less and less ideologically divided; there is disagreement over means, less value-disagreement over ends.[1] This means that there is more

[1] The decline of ideology is a familiar theme. Lichteim pointed out (*Marxism in Modern France*) that most people mean by it the decline of left-wing ideology. This is fair comment. We are not suggesting that ideology has declined in importance but that there is less conflict over ideology—perhaps because one set of ideological values has triumphed.

cohesion, a greater area over which discussion is possible. The second is a consequence of the first. If there is less ideological division between sections of society, then they are not likely to continue to suspect each other of seeking long-term secret and subversive goals; their behaviour is less likely to be suspected of being indirect. In short, they trust each other. In practice, mutual trust has been greatly aided by the fact that industrial relations has been conducted by a body of men of a semi-professional nature, who share understanding, technique, language and, often, common experience. This is not all gain; one result has been the development of mutual trust, another has been the conservatism of British industrial relations.[1] The third feature, which grows out of the others, is a preference for practical solutions to urgent problems as opposed to theoretical and predictive systems. In the language of Karl Popper[2] this means a preference for piecemeal social engineering over historicist, long-term, solutions. In practice this preference means loosely worded agreements, flexible arrangements, a tendency to avoid the force of precedent (except in shop-floor bargaining where precedent often means what the power situation permits as precedent rather than an iron law of precedent). None of this can be described as the rule of the voluntary principle, because none of it is consistent. The only principles which seem to be consistently present are those of expediency and practicability.

It might appear that the outcome of this discussion should be to suggest that our industrial relations are so self-sufficient and pragmatic as to be immune from any changes which could be brought about by the state. This is not so. The state could introduce changes which might change the relative power of any of the parties to the system. Change could also introduce a new element of ideology which might have an effect on the delicate network of trust and confidence on which the system so heavily relies. And adjustments in the economy, and in production patterns, finally seem to make change in industrial relations inevitable.

It may be, in fact, that the state's greatest influence results from its activity in the general environment of industry and social policy rather than in industrial relations as such. The state is extending its

---

[1] We return to a discussion of this problem and its causes in Chapter 7.

[2] K. Popper, *The Poverty of Historicism*, Routledge & Kegan Paul, 1957, ch. III.

influence over education to influence over industrial and management training. The state is influencing the distribution of industry and is beginning to come to terms with manpower redeployment and occupational change. The Ministry of Labour has added to its functions of employment, welfare and conciliation new long-term activities concerned with manpower forecasting.[1] Other government agencies, like the Training Advisory Service, are providing a complete and proficient consultancy service. The Ministry of Technology collects and disseminates information to raise the level of performance. The Industrial Reorganisation Corporation enables the state to intervene directly so as to rationalise the organisation and structure of particular enterprises or even whole industries. The best particular example of this, almost unnoticed, influence which is going on while our attention is diverted by noisy debates about more obvious interventions, could turn out to be the Prices and Incomes Board. The Board hits the headlines because of its immediate responsibilities in relation to collective bargaining, but its real contribution may turn out to be the patient, critical, analysis which it is applying to problems like the application of job evaluation or to the problems existing in a whole industry and its accompanying institutions.[2] It may take a long time but at the very least the state's activities in these fields seems certain to illuminate areas of ineptitude which have too long been sheltered from the informed attention of the public, of trade unions, or of commercial competitors. In the long run, better performance may do more to change the practice and the problems of industrial relations than many more dramatic proposals for intervention.

[1] In particular the work of the Manpower Research Unit. Manpower forecasts are also being produced by industrial Economic Development Councils.

[2] See for example, *Pay and Conditions of Service of Engineering Workers*, National Board for Prices and Incomes, Report No. 49, H.M.S.O., December 1967. In the report the Board promises more detailed proposals for 'ironing out inequities ... and anomalies in company pay structures' (p. 42).

2 Industrial Relations Expertise

4 The Substance of Agreements

Trade-union representatives, personnel specialists and negotiators operate within a network of constraints, rules and procedures of varying degrees of formality. It has been usual, since Dunlop,[1] to regard this network as an 'industrial relations system' which is differentiated (after Parsons) by reference to four basic functions:

1. Adaptation—in which rule-making relates the participants to changes in technology and the market.
2. Goal gratification—in which the survival or stability of the system contributes to the attainment of the participants' goals.
3. Integration—in which shared understanding and ideology contribute solidarity among the system's participants.
4. 'Latent-pattern maintenance and tension management'—the function of preserving the values of the system against cultural and motivational pressures is provided by the role of the expert or professional in all three groups of actors in the system.[2]

The groups (workers and their organisations, managers and their organisations and government agencies) interact within an environment composed of three inter-related elements: the technology, the market and the power relations of the larger community. Dunlop examined the important determinants within each of these elements. Thus, in the technical context, the following characteristics influence the activity of participants:

1. Fixed or variable work place

[1] J. T. Dunlop, *Industrial Relations Systems*, Holt, 1958.
[2] *ibid.*, p. 30.

2. Relation of work place to residence
3. Stable or variable work force and operations
4. Size of the work group
5. Job content
6. Relation to machines or customers
7. Hours of work.

In terms of market and budgetary considerations, Dunlop distinguished between:

1. Competitive position and budgetary control
2. The scope of the market or budget
3. Market or budget homogeneity among enterprises
4. The size of enterprises
5. Secular expansion or contraction
6. Characteristics of the labour force
7. Labour-market stringency
8. Ratio of labour costs to total costs.

There is a danger, in describing an industrial relations system in terms of a network of rules, of implying a greater degree of formality and precision than in fact exists. But Dunlop's analysis brings out the importance of seeing, at the centre of the system, the actors (workers and unions, employers and their organisations, and the state and its agencies), each in pursuit of different objectives and each interacting within a framework of constraints and limitations provided by the environment within which they operate. The objectives which they seek and the extent to which they pursue them are influenced by the realities of the situation in which they live, realities concerning task, costs, markets and social power. Recognition of the reality of this complex inter-relationship avoids the danger of falling into a kind of human relations isolationism.

It has become the practice also to distinguish between two kinds of arrangements in industrial relations: *substantive arrangements* which 'establish norms or intentions in the form of specific conditions of work' and *procedural arrangements* which 'exist to adjust differences in the making of substantive rules and the relationships between the parties'.[1]

[1] A. I. Marsh, 'Disputes Procedures in British Industry', *Royal Commission Research Papers*, 2, H.M.S.O., 1966, p. 2.

We are concerned for the moment with rules, more or less formal, which have been arrived at by collective bargaining and which are the subject of collective agreements between employers and trade unions. Substantive agreements may be concerned with the remuneration for work, hours of work, the quantity of work to be done, the manning to be allocated to work, the environmental conditions of work, specific categories of labour to be employed, job security and compensation for loss of work, job entry, discipline and discharge. Some of these elements may also be the subject of procedural agreements and the division between substantive and procedural rules is not always clear. Confusion sometimes arises because of the process of evolution to which industrial relations systems are subject; a matter which is acknowledged to be the subject of 'managerial rights' at one stage of development may come to be regarded, as the result of a developing 'union challenge to management control', as the proper subject of joint negotiation at the next. Discipline may be written into the substantive agreements but a dismissal deemed by the unions to be unfair may result in grievance bargaining through procedural channels.

British substantive agreements are said to be almost unique in that they are open-ended; they do not operate for a prescribed period of time, although there are now exceptions to this rule in cases like the three-year agreement of December 1964 in engineering and the Electricity Supply Industry agreement of 1963.[1] In the majority of cases agreements, once they are reached, operate until they are superseded as the result of negotiations following a union claim which may be made when the union decides to make it. Substantive agreements may be arrived at between an employer and union at plant level, at district level or nationally, or they may be arrived at by negotiation between a complex of unions (for example, the Confederation of Shipbuilding and Engineering Unions) and of employers (the Engineering Employers' Federation). There are two almost traditional features of substantive agreements concerning rates of pay. The first is that, where they have concerned wages, they have concerned very little else. They have laid down, for the

---

[1] The exceptions are growing. There were 43 long-term agreements drawn up between January 1963 and February 1965 (Prices and Incomes Board Report, no. 49).

occupations and territory concerned, rates of pay in terms of time worked or work performed but they have not been concerned with related impediments or aids to production and earnings. National wage agreements have, it is true, often contained goodwill clauses in which the unions pledge co-operation in removing restrictive practices or in accepting work study in return for the negotiated increase in wages. But generalised statements of good intention have come to be regarded as worthless, not because the unions are dishonest in their intentions when accepting them but because unions are not executive structures and the commitment of the leaders, however sincere, cannot be communicated as commands to the rank and file. It reveals a surprising misconception on the part of managerial negotiators that such clauses were ever considered either as proper subjects for national negotiation or as compensating concessions for a wage increase.

The second typical feature of British wage-agreements is that, in some industries, they have become increasingly irrelevant either to the earnings of workers or to the labour costs of employers. Taking 1955 as the base year, the Ministry of Labour has calculated the movement in manual workers' weekly wage rates and average weekly earnings as follows:

	Weekly rates of wages	Average weekly earnings
1955	100·0	100·0
1956	107·9	108·0
1957	113·4	113·0
1958	117·5	116·9
1959	120·6	122·2
1960	123·7	130·1
1961	128·8	138·0
1962	133·6	142·9
1963	138·4	148·9
1964	144·9	161·8
1965	151·2	174·8
1966	158·2	185·0

The Ministry calculates the percentage change in wage drift (the difference between average hourly earnings *excluding* overtime and average hourly rates of pay) over the corresponding month (October) in the previous year as:

1953	+0·3
1954	+0·7
1955	+1·6
1956	+0·6
1957	+1·0
1958	—0·3
1959	+1·5
1960	+1·8
1961	+0·5
1962	+0·2
1963	+1·3
1964	+2·4
1965	+2·2
1966	+0·9

The growing disparity between nationally negotiated wage rates and actual earnings results broadly from two ingredients in earnings which are not normally the subject of wide negotiation: overtime payments (excluded from the above tables) and the payment of allowances (for working, for example, with difficult material or in a dangerous or unpleasant environment) and, secondly, incentive payments which are frequently determined within the plant on a piece or group incentive basis. Nationally negotiated rates in substantive agreements are often relevant to reality only as a fall-back rate which production workers may be 'guaranteed' in special circumstances which prevent them 'making bonus' or as determining the actual earnings of less fortunate categories of 'non-production' workers whose output may be difficult to measure. The situation causes concern, partly because it is inflationary (the difference between rates and earnings is not necessarily in itself inflationary, it is simply more difficult to control), partly because it distorts traditional or planned differentials between craftsmen and time-rate men on the one hand and payment-by-results workers on the other. The National Coal Board, for example, made successive and unsuccessful attempts over the years to correct the growing imbalance between low-paid daywagemen and high-paid piece-workers; they finally reached the point, in 1964, of asking the National Union of Mineworkers to correct the situation, and the union called in consultants. This is an interesting and rare example of a trade union engaging consultants on an industrial relations problem, but it is even more significant as an implicit confession by management that it was no longer in control of its wage-payment structure.

Alternative solutions to this problem are sometimes suggested. The first and best-known is to claim that nationally negotiated wage rates are becoming increasingly anomalous particularly where, as in the metal trades, they are conducted on a wide, multi-industry basis. The recommended alternative is to develop some form of plant bargaining which may or may not include productivity bargaining. The advantages of a development of plant bargaining are that it may:

1. Encourage management to a more positive and effective control of plant earnings by removing attention from illusory national rates.
2. Be a more precise response to the effort and manning requirements of the plant and to its cost structure.
3. More effectively commit plant union representatives to the control and implementation of agreements.
4. Help consolidate the position of shop-floor representatives and shop stewards.

If plant bargaining is extended to include productivity bargaining, then further advantages are said to accrue; in particular, negotiations are no longer narrowly confined to wages issues but involve both unions and management in a more comprehensive and realistic engagement in problems of manning, training and employment.

Productivity bargains have received a great deal of publicity and are the latest in a succession of panaceas which have been recommended since 1945. They contain several real advantages over the national agreement: they are negotiated at plant level and thus require the commitment of the union officials or shop stewards who will be responsible for their operation (or demolition); they are able to reflect the requirements of the situation at the plant; and they are more likely to avoid entrenched obstacles in remote parts of the industry. The overall advantage is that a plant productivity bargain can be related to the technical, commercial and social situation of the plant; the bargain is bespoke to the plants' requirements. There may also be secondary advantages: productivity bargains may provide an opportunity to buy out certain accumulated restrictive practices from the trade unions. This secondary advantage should not be seen as central to the productivity bargain and they have been criticised for enlarging its importance. The buy-out of the rule book is, or should be, a once-and-for-all operation, but it may result in what appears to be disproportionately high wage increases, as between the union which is still reactionary enough to have something to sell and the employer still inefficient enough to have something to buy. Employers often make these criticisms of productivity bargaining, but they are criticisms of a secondary characteristic and do not touch the principle of plant as against national bargaining. But popular as the move to plant bargaining currently is, employers' representatives are not prepared to admit that national bargaining has no advantages while plant bargaining has all. In their evidence to the Royal Commission[1] the C.B.I.'s representatives voiced several of the general suspicions about plant bargaining: that it was comparatively easy to solve the problems of one firm in this way but that an employers' organisation must have regard to the industry as a whole and, here, the plant bargain could give rise to expectations of wage increases which were inflationary and which could not be supported in some parts of the industry. There are further complexities which make easy acceptance of the plant bargain dangerous. It may provide the astute union with the opportunity to win an advantage in one firm which is then applied across the industrial board; a C.B.I. representative claimed that this very process had led to an increase of wage costs of 20 per cent in 12 months in shipbuilding, a claim which led a member of the Commission to wonder whether it is 'not better to stick with your restrictive practice at this rate'. A productivity bargain often represents a new frontier agreed between manager and unions; a union may be able subsequently to cross this frontier by patrol activity at various points. The effect of these isolated incursions may be to reintroduce the restrictive practices or allowance payments which had been bought out in the productivity bargain, so that the stage can gradually be set for another productivity bargain.[2] Productivity bargains thus imply a heavy

[1] Royal Commission, Minutes of Evidence 6 and 9, 1966, pages 240–5.
[2] There were guarded allegations before the Royal Commission that this kind of process has been going on at Fawley, the archetypal British plant productivity agreement (p. 257). The allegations were denied by the Esso Company in a letter to the Commission: 'no new crop of restrictive practices has grown up since our 1960 agreements' (p. 267).

responsibility to exercise strict control in policing the agreement; this responsibility for control can sometimes lie heaviest on the level of management least capable of carrying it and susceptible to the greatest pressure to abandon it, the supervisors.

Representatives of employers' organisations are probably right to examine critically the easy appeal of the productivity bargain and they may be right, consequently, in rejecting the implied criticism that their commitment to national agreements is a weakness.

From their own evidence the employers seem to be well aware of the problems and to be concerned to examine ways in which national agreements can be arrived at that lay down general principles but leave the consequential details to be agreed at plant level, the local agreement finally being examined at national level to ensure that it does not violate national principles. The re-examination of national wage agreements and structures takes one of several forms.

The simplest is that there is more wrong with the procedures and systems which produce national wage rates than with the principle of national negotiations. This argument implies criticisms of the major federations of employers and trade unions and of the existence of negotiating structures which can incorporate as subsidiary, ill-represented parts, the whole of the British motor industry. It is not national wage agreements which are wrong, it is wage agreements inappropriate to the industries they cover which lead to trouble. This is the kind of criticism about which the C.B.I. is no doubt concerned, and we shall return to it in the next section because it really concerns a discussion of procedural agreements.

A second approach to the problem of national substantive agreements is to accept that they must be related to the continuing necessity for allowing flexible differences at plant level between different work, different workers or different plants by reference to principles which cannot be laid down for an industry at national level. There seem to be two quite different schools of thought which are searching for the same kind of solution but for different reasons. The first is value-free and is concerned with introducing effective wage payments methods for their own sake. It may be represented to some extent by the N.C.B.'s new dual structure (national day-wage and regional power-loading agreements; the previous arrangement was national day-wage and coal-field chaos among piece-workers), and by I.C.I.'s agreement which seeks agreement in principle at national level while plant implementation waits upon specific agreement at plant level. The electricity-supply industry has also experimented with a more all-embracing national agreement. The second body of opinion which advocates a tandem wage structure does so for more obviously ideological reasons, accepting the necessity for some overall national control but trying to relate it to a degree of plant flexibility and freedom of adjustment because this is believed to be good. One reason for this view is as an attempt to come to terms with the wages implications of social planning and incomes control. It is also suggested that wages policy which is based upon arrangements and negotiations at plant level is likely to encourage the growth of shop-floor representation and that this development is desirable in terms of encouraging industrial democracy. One of the more recent schemes of 'two-tier' bargaining was set out by Ross and involved a relationship of two constituent elements in the wage-packet: a guaranteed and nationally negotiated minimum and a plant supplement which varied with the productivity of the plant.[1] There are elements of such a two-tier structure in German industry where works councils are legally permitted to conclude agreements about supplementary wages as long as they are permitted to do so by the wider collective agreement.[2] There are several converging reasons for trying to work out the relationship of national rates and plant supplements. In the first place P.B.R. payments are likely to become more and more inappropriate as highly mechanised or automatic processes are extended, so that P.B.R. cannot continue to be regarded as a substitute for national rates. In the second place a growing number of observers are concluding that if industrial democracy is to be meaningful it must be achieved by way of the framework of collective bargaining, but no one has yet suggested how 'pressure from below' can be reconciled in practice with commercial or political control on wages from above.[3] In the third place it can be argued that if income control is agreed to be necessary then it must

[1] N. Ross, *Workshop Bargaining, A New Approach*, Fabian Tract no. 366.

[2] A. Sturmthal, *Workers' Councils—a Study of Workplace Organisation on Both Sides of the Iron Curtain*, Harvard, 1964, p. 62.

[3] See A. Flanders, *Industrial Relations—What's Wrong with the System?*, Faber, 1965.

be achieved by taking into account rather than ignoring, shop-floor pressures and interests, because if it does not it will either fail, or it will succeed at the expense of a representative and independent trade-union structure. Finally, however valuable plant productivity bargains are going to be, it is difficult to see them proliferating plant by plant, industry by industry, without some attempt to exercise comparability and control either by employers or by unions; once this effort is made it implies the existence of criteria for comparisons and suggests therefore a relationship existing between plant bargains and national standards.

Plant bargaining currently fits rather unhappily into the existing structures. The general tendency, as the result of centralising the institutions of industrial relations, has been the gradual diminution of district rates in favour of a national pattern. The Prices and Incomes Board, for example, observes that, in the engineering industry, 'the negotiation of district rates and conditions is a function now almost completely obsolete'. The process has been hastened by the traditional enthusiasm of trade unions for national standards. Plant bargaining not only interrupts this tendency, it threatens to reverse it. There are suggestions that the conditions existing within the plant are not the only criteria during plant productivity bargaining but that there is increasing pressure from union negotiators to have regard to a district norm, particularly after an influential plant productivity agreement has been signed with an important employer within the district.

The existing structures, both of collective bargaining and of the law, are largely concerned to protect minimum standards. The existing structures have been constructed partly as the result of trade-union pressure for national protective standards (by agreement or by law). Plant productivity bargains are difficult to accommodate in the structure because 'plant productivity bargains are easier to achieve than national productivity bargains and stand a greater chance of being effective';[1] plant productivity bargains, in a sense, represent a move in a direction opposite to the whole recent development of industrial relations. It is not surprising that we are only beginning to be aware of the problems to which they may give rise.

[1] Jones and Golding, *Productivity Bargaining*, Fabian Research Series, 257, p. 23.

One problem concerns the extent to which the terms of a productivity bargain are exclusive alternatives to other agreements reached within the industry; can the unions 'make a traditional type application for another increase in wages during the lifetime of the productivity agreement?'[1] When the question was raised at Fawley the result was a small increase extra to the productivity bargain, but Jones and Golding state that most recent productivity bargains specifically exclude additional wage increases during the period of the agreement.

It may, therefore, be possible to control the effects of comparisons between plant and national agreements as long as control can be written into the plant agreements themselves (as Jones and Golding suggest is now the case). But control may no longer be confined to the agreements if there is the possibility of recourse to law. There is already some evidence that this probably exists. Section 8 of the Terms and Conditions of Employment Act, 1956, survives so as to provide some guarantee that the conditions of employment which are general in an industry can be enforced for a group of employees in that industry. Section 8, once again, protects minimal standards. But what is the area of employment conditions by which comparisons are to be made? There are at least two possibilities by which Section 8 might be invoked against the spirit and purpose of productivity bargains. In the first case it could be argued that an agreement made in an industry becomes general for employees in that industry and *must* therefore be applied to employees covered by a productivity bargain in an isolated plant within the industry. Such a case is not likely to concern manual employees where negotiated rates are expressed on a time-rate basis (the rate is likely to be exceeded by earnings specified in the productivity bargain). But negotiated agreements for clerical workers are more usually expressed as *increases* which are to be paid. If the increase is general to the industry, is it to be applied to those subject to a productivity bargain even when they have achieved terms more generous than those prevailing generally? The second case concerns the swings and roundabouts nature of productivity bargains. They are able to provide unusually high earnings because some work practice or arrangement has been sacrificed by the employees in the bargain.

[1] *ibid.*, p. 16.

But what if it could be established that the particular practice or arrangement was general to the industry?

There is thus a potential threat to the purpose of productivity bargains which seek to establish their own rules and arrangements relatively independently of any outside comparisons with the industry as a whole. The degree of independence is, in fact, their chief advantage. The paradox is that an employer may leave his association in order to achieve the independence necessary to conclude a productivity bargain only to find that his arrangements are subject to the comparisons with the association's terms and conditions from which he had hoped to escape. Leaving the employers' association is of little account if the law continues to enforce the association's conditions.

This is perhaps an extreme (but not hypothetical) example of the conflict of purpose between the plant productivity bargain and the protective structure on which it has been superimposed. Such conflicts are inevitable between 'progressive' agreements and 'defensive' law. Before we start prescribing hasty amendments to the law we should remember that large sections of the community might once again be grateful for the existence of devices to protect national minimum standards. In the meantime there are important questions of definition to be answered.

Whatever the means used to arrive at substantive conditions there are certain over-riding considerations which shape the intentions of those who hold ultimate responsibility for them.

Management's contribution to the planned pattern of substantive arrangements might be said to be influenced by several considerations as to the objectives of wage and salary planning from the employers' point of view. These factors do not take into account the constraints which are introduced by collective bargaining; they represent the managerial intentions of substantive arrangements. The factors would include:

1. Cost effectiveness, the general consideration that management's intentions in a payments policy should be met at the lowest real cost to the firm. This does not imply the payment of the lowest possible wages; if an employer decided, for example, to outbid its competitors for labour or to buy out union membership, it would be committed

to a high-wage policy, but it would still wish to pursue this policy at the lowest possible cost to the firm. This general requirement has detailed implications in the provision of incentive payments. It suggests that wage costs should be effective in that they should not be incurred without forecasting the return to them.

2. Wages payment policies should be appropriate to the technical factors of the work performed. The most obvious example of inappropriateness is the payment of incentive rates for work which is machine-paced or in which there is an element of hazard. There is a suspicion that in many jobs management does not know the component factors for which wages and salaries are being paid. One criticism of some complex forms of job evaluation is that they serve to conceal the factors which are most important to the job's performance. Job evaluation often merely provides a heterogeneous collection of historical, environmental, psychological and technical ingredients, each of which is accorded some arbitrarily determined financial aspect. Just as the task determines what is to be done it also determines some approximate guidelines about the way in which it should and should not be paid. But technical considerations may be quite irrelevant in determining how much it should be paid.

3. Business factors obviously influence gross totals of wages costs. They also influence the internal construction of wage and salary structures. A complex, multigrade structure is expensive in terms of the number of monetary differentials which must be maintained. A highly 'flexible' structure is also likely to be expensive; some wage structures are administratively more costly than others. A firm may temper the cost effectiveness of its payment policy by what it can afford in the manner of payment. These considerations are influenced not only by the profitability of the enterprise but by its cost structure and the proportion of wages cost to total. In an extractive industry like coal-mining where wages costs are about 60 per cent of total, there is both a greater need to be precise about wage payment policies and less possibility of being flexible than in light engineering, where the proportion may be 10 per cent, or in chemicals where it could be even lower. High capital costs, on the other hand, may lead the investors and the board to insist on hastily concluded wage agreements and on continuous concessions to the unions in order to keep the plant operational, particularly at periods of heavy market demand.

4. Wage payment policies affect and are affected by the groups to which they are applied, so that social factors are important in determining wage and salary structures. Group incentives can solidify or disrupt the harmony of informal groups and this might be used competitively or may produce accidental conflict. The diversity of salaries or the length of salary bands may be influenced by the proximity of the employees who are subject to them and by the effectiveness of the informal communications system. Wage and salary policies may run into difficulties if they do not reflect in differentials, differences in status which are perceived by group members, particularly if those difficulties are not foreseen.

5. Related to social factors, but distinct from them, are considerations of justice and equity. To some extent it is dangerous and improper for management to conclude its position on moral questions before its judgment can be questioned in collective bargaining, but management will be constrained by considerations of what is just and equitable in the matter of payments. This is a complex subject which we cannot discuss here in detail; suffice it to say that the extent to which managers try to do what is 'right', not because of but sometimes, in spite of union pressure, is not always recognised. It may be worth adding that the extent to which managers are subject to moral pressure may have nothing to do with the increasing influence of professionalisation, nor with the development of business ethics, but may simply result from managers having a moral sense which they share with everyone else as members of the community. Personnel specialists may well have a professionalised ethic but this is an encumbrance of which they are apparently trying to rid themselves.

6. Payment policies need to be an appropriate and relevant instrument of the employer's general employment plans and forecasts. The most obvious example is the extent to which it is forecast that the organisation is subject to change. Rigid, inflexible wage and salary structures may be appropriate to business conditions which are relatively static, but the need for technical or commercial adaptation is almost certain to require payment adjustments or a payments policy which is capable of containing adjustment. A detailed example could be found in the manner in which job descriptions are written: a detailed and exhaustive account of the

job's ingredients may be valuable until circumstances change; if change is predictable, then a looser description of the job's distinguishing features (more particularly of the definitive features which *financially* distinguish it) may be more valuable. Wage and salary structure must also relate to employment and promotion policies, to whether, for example, they hinder or facilitate job rotation, lateral transfer, career planning and retraining. Wage and salary policies may also contain built-in strategic decisions about the extent to which they will reward experience and motivation or merit and ability; the particular 'mix' may reflect whether the structure is regarded as contributing in itself to a positive employment policy or whether it is seen as facilitating and not hindering the deployment of employment policies by other, non-financial means.

7. A purely negative consideration is that the payment policy should not be a cause of conflict in itself. This precept may read like a truism but there is no doubt that a significant cause of industrial disputes has sometimes been carefully constructed by management in the shape of the wage structure. Turner, Clack and Roberts after discounting most of the generally accepted explanations of labour unrest in the motor industry concluded that one of the causes (along with the procedures, which we shall discuss in the next section) was wage payments which both fluctuated violently (a final line worker's 'normal' earnings of £23–£24 in 1962–3, actually ranged between £13 and £31) and which appeared to show no tendency for earnings to rise (because rate increases were offset by overtime reduction and because 'any rising tendency is largely concealed by week-to-week variations in pay received'[1]). A well-known cause of industrial disputes has been the imbalance in wage structures caused by the effect of bonus payments on traditional differentials. There can also be more subtle effects of wage structure on disputes or on morale. Salary scales and ranges which are too short may, particularly for 'career grades', create a sense of bitterness at the lack of progression and at the apparent failure to reward developing experience and judgment.

8. A new factor influencing the determination of payments policy is government control and influence. Until recently this concerned

[1] H. A. Turner, G. Clack and G. Roberts, *Industrial Relations in the Motor Industry*, Allen & Unwin, 1967, p. 162.

only the payment of wages in government contracting firms, the payment of minimum wages in industries governed by Wages Council and the varying influence of the several exhortations to observe a pay pause, guiding light, plateau or freeze. The Prices and Incomes Act, 1966, however introduced a new element of compulsion to observe incomes restraint and the establishment of the Prices and Incomes Board led to criteria to be applied to increases resulting from productivity bargains.[1] The severer restraints have been removed but the government's interest in income control and in payment policy is likely to be a permanent feature of the scene in future. Incomes policy apart, some 20 per cent of the working population is now in some form of government or state-industry employment and so will continue to be subject to fairly direct government influence.

We have been concerned, so far, only with the wage element in substantive agreements. This emphasis to some extent reflects the degree to which bargaining effort has been concentrated in Britain on maintaining and improving wage rates and earnings, to the comparative neglect of welfare provision and the improvement of conditions of work.

Reid and Robertson have commented that until recently 'Trade unions almost completely ignored sick pay, redundancy payments and pensions, and those schemes which did appear were introduced by employers either unilaterally or with the passive consent of the unions.'[2] The necessity for legislation (Contracts of Employment Act, 1963, Redundancy Payments Act, 1964 and Industrial Training Act, 1965) has been cited as evidence of this neglect. Reid and Robertson explain it by suggesting that unions have a natural preoccupation with achieving improvements in wages until a 'threshold' level of adequacy has been reached, when they can afford to make other, rather more luxurious claims. These authorities also point to the methods of social progress favoured by British trade unions, which emphasise state provision of welfare benefits and which even

[1] Seven criteria were set out in the 23rd Report of the National Board for Prices and Incomes and were re-defined in the Board's Report no. 36, *Productivity Agreements*, H.M.S.O., 1967.

[2] G. L. Reid and D. J. Robertson (eds.), *Fringe Benefits, Labour Costs and Social Security*, Allen & Unwin, 1965, p. 30.

see improvements in employer provision as likely to weaken the case for better state benefits. The complex structure of collective bargaining and the different interests of different workers in different unions may, they suggest, also explain the lack of a unified drive for welfare improvements. Another reason for trade-union in activity is that 'pension schemes, sickness benefit, company subsidised facilities, even in some cases longer holidays, have until the very recent past been introduced unilaterally by the employer. Trade unions' reactions ranged from mild interest or indifference to hostility if there was a suggestion that the employer was attempting to wean allegiance from the union to the firm.'[1]

The likelihood of a widened frontier of collective bargaining, whether for ideological reasons or at the initiative of management in productivity bargains, will probably immerse the unions in interests and objectives no longer confined to wages. Many unions are already changing their approach, and the T.U.C. is reminding its members of the leeway that remains to be made up and that the failure to negotiate in this area has left British employees comparatively ill-served. The provision made by governments since the war and the current concern about levels of poverty is beginning to suggest that state provision will never catch up with social need. Continental and American experience also suggests that the dangers of producing a cowed and subservient work force have been exaggerated; indeed it seems likely that union restraint in Britain has resulted in a work force which has lost on all grounds, as it is neither particularly sturdy and independent (measured by its strike record) nor is it particularly affluent in terms of real income.

[1] *ibid.*, p. 317.

5 Procedures

Procedural machinery is concerned with 'the making, application and interpretation of substantive agreements, and the processing of grievances'.[1] The Ministry of Labour estimates that there are over 500 separate pieces of negotiating machinery. The Ministry's *Industrial Relations Handbook* gives a descriptive account of the procedures operating in the main employment groups. There are comparatively few underlying rules or principles which could be said to be common to most British procedural arrangements. Marsh seems to suggest that there are four such principles: 'procedure should be exhausted before either party is free to take unilateral action'; 'when decisions have been arrived at genuine attempts should be made to apply them'; 'issues, other things being equal, should be settled at as low a level in procedure as possible'; a preference exists for general procedures, 'all-purpose arrangements, to be used flexibly as particular situations arise and as commonsense seems to direct'.

Distinctions are possible between kinds of procedural machinery, although distinctions applied to complex social phenomena always tend to be arbitrary. But we can roughly distinguish according to the nature of the activity encompassed by the procedural machinery and by reference to the structure of the machinery (in particular, whether it is self-governing or subject to external control). In terms of the nature of the activity, it is usual for American discussions to distinguish between procedural arrangements which are concerned with contract negotiation, which results in substantive agreements, and

[1] A. I. Marsh, 'Disputes Procedures in British Industry', *Royal Commission Research Papers*, 2, H.M.S.O., 1966, p. 4.

procedural arrangements which concern contract administration, the settlement of grievances often arising out of differences in interpretation of negotiated agreements. We see, once again, the danger of confusion arising between the use of the terms 'substantive' and 'procedural' agreements. The distinction may be made more clearly by regarding 'procedural' as referring to process while 'substantive' refers to subject matter or content. Procedural agreements represent the process by which the terms and conditions of employment are arrived at; procedural agreements also represent the process by which differences and grievances over agreed terms and conditions of employment are settled. Procedural agreements are therefore closely concerned with the settlement of wages and conditions but they are not the same as agreements about wages and conditions, and they are about other things as well.

The useful American distinction between contract negotiation, sometimes called legislative activity, and contract administration, or judicial activity, is less frequently applied in Britain. This is partly because British agreements are not quite contracts in the American sense and because, more significantly, judicial activity is less appropriate to much of British industrial relations. The procedural agreements of a sector as large as the engineering industry, for example, are still dominated by the concept of 'managerial rights'. The resulting system of what Marsh calls 'employer conciliation' is one in which employers' panels rather than joint committees decide the justice of procedural claims, panels which have to meet on an *ad hoc* basis 'because if this were not so, they would take on a joint standing character which would compromise managerial rights'.[1] In addition to systems of employer conciliation, whole areas of employee relations may be subject to the arbitrary decision of employers which may be challenged as the result of decisions taken on the basis of relative power and opportunity; in this context the application of the notion of judicial activity may be particularly out of place. But the extension of national ownership has led to the development of more formalised rules and to procedures for management's authority to be checked 'legally' within the framework of more comprehensive procedural agreements. This development, together with a changing climate of

[1] *ibid.*, p. 12.

opinion may make the distinction between contract negotiation and contract administration more meaningful in Britain.

As far as the structure of procedural machinery is concerned, the greatest variations are about the handling of matters in dispute between the parties rather than in the negotiation of substantive agreements. Marsh distinguishes between conflicts of interest and conflicts of rights, which, he suggests, are more amenable to judicial treatment[1]: 'Conflicts of right are said to arise when a dispute concerns the meaning of an existing agreement. It is assumed that what has to be decided are the rights and obligations of the parties to the agreement, and it seems plausible to argue that such disputes are suitable for resolution by some process of judicial or quasi-judicial decision. In contrast, conflicts of interest are said to arise when there is no existing agreement which can be appropriately applied. . . . Since there are no established rights to be interpreted it is assumed that these disputes involve the power relations of the parties and their collective interests. For this reason they are thought to be less suitable for resolution by judicial or quasi-judicial techniques.' In other words, conflicts of interest tend not to take place within procedural channels because the existence of procedure suggests that such conflicts have been regularised and finalised, so that future conflicts will either take place within procedure and be about rights or they will be explosive and wreck the procedure.

It is obviously not only the distinction between substantive and procedural agreements which is sometimes confusing; the terminology is also confused in that various authorities tend to use their own terms. The following table is intended to help to distinguish between the various processes, the relationships between them and the terms that are often used to describe them. It is not intended to imply a clear and precise distinction between, for example, regulated and non-regulated adjustments to conflict, or between substance and procedure. Thus, industrial disputes are obviously appropriate not only to D.4 (in the table) because they may also be used as instruments in *regulated adjustments* and they may also be allowed by the

---

[1] *ibid.*, p. 16. This is not, in fact, what he writes. He actually puts things the other way around, that conflicts of interest are more amenable. But the lengthy footnote to p. 16 (quoted above) seems to make it quite clear that this is a typographical error.

METHOD OF CONFLICT ADJUSTMENT

	Regulated adjustment to conflict			*Non-regulated adjustment to conflict, or conflict suppression*
	A	**B**	**C**	**D**
1 Source of conflict	Substantive matters	Application of substantive matters	Questions concerning adherence to an application of procedure	Absence of procedural rules through imposition of managerial rights or through employer conciliation or scope of procedure too limited
2 Conflict type	Conflict of interest	Conflict of rights	Conflict of rights	Conflict of interest
3 Appropriate form of conflict settlement	1. Substantive agreement 2. Procedural agreement for settling differences over substantive agreement	Negotiations within procedural channels, mediation, or arbitration within agreements	Negotiation within procedural channels, mediation, or arbitration, or recourse to law	Power confrontation, intervention of third parties, legislation by government
4 Instrument	Bargaining and/or trial of strength	Procedural agreements	Procedural agreements and/or third parties	Industrial disputes
5 Process (terminology)	Contract negotiation Collective bargaining Legislative activity	Contract administration Grievance bargaining Judicial activity	Judicial activity	No process
6 Result	Substantive agreements	Re-defined substantive agreement	Clarification or re-definition of procedure	Violence of conflict likely to increase until both parties see some advantage in more conflict regulation

procedures. Again, the distinction between *regulated* and non-regulated adjustments to conflict is none too precise in practice; the over-regulated approach to industrial conflict (in which any possibility of strikes is completely outlawed by the procedures) may, as we shall see, lead to effects similar to those resulting from conflict suppression.

Differences in the structure of procedures broadly concern their length, the number of procedural stages and the devices which are incorporated to deal with unsettled questions. The length of the procedure and the number of stages are very closely connected. In the engineering industry a question in dispute must be raised first with the foreman, then with the shop manager, then at works conference (at which stage the local union official and the employers' association may enter), then at a local conference and finally at a national or 'central conference'. In shipbuilding, yard and district questions are referred when there is failure to agree, from a yard conference to a local conference to a central conference, and there is final provision for a general conference although this last stage appears to have fallen into disuse. Procedural agreements frequently contain time limits for the discussion of questions at each stage.

The passing of unsettled questions up through procedure serves several functions. It prevents the necessity for a dispute following a failure to agree at the level at which the question was raised, by providing the alternative of further levels for negotiation. It helps to remove the most tendentious questions (those on which failure to agree is most likely) from the arena in which feelings are highest, it gets the question away from the work-place and thus promises greater objectivity. It helps to ensure that a question which contains a principle of wider implication than to the place of work where it arose, is discussed at an appropriate level. The process necessarily takes time—often, it is said, too much time. Thus 'the average time between the first raising of an issue to formal Procedure and its disposal (or recording of failure to agree) is over seven weeks for all engineering cases and more than thirteen weeks for car firm references. A case which proves difficult, however—involving, say, an adjournment at Works or Local level and final reference back from Central Conference—would average seven months in general and eight months in a car plant issue.'[1] And, Turner, Clack and Roberts tell us, the situation is getting worse. The procedure is being used increasingly, disposal rates are falling as the number of references increase and the frequency of constitutional strikes which take place after procedure has been exhausted is getting higher: one per year in the 1950s, 44 in 1964. Procedures are said to be unsuitable in some cases, and their unsuitability can take one of two different forms. We have already noted Marsh's comment on the preference for general, all-purpose arrangements, for a procedure which must be used for all negotiating purposes so that a procedure which may be suitable for the protracted settlement of substantive arrangements may also have to suffice for the settlement of much more urgent questions concerning work-place arrangements, discipline or dismissal, questions 'which are normally decided, albeit within procedure, after a demonstration of strength by workers in the form of unconstitutional action'.[2] The second sense in which procedures may be unsuitable is that they may not be designed for the industry or sector of an industry to which they are applied. Turner, Clack and Roberts make this point convincingly for the motor-industry: 'One reason for the high strike-proneness of the car firms and of the federated firms in particular, seems to be that the present organisation, attitude, agreements and conciliation procedure of the employers' association provide no effective basis for the settlement of the major issues in dispute between the firms and their workers.'[3]

One important respect in which procedural agreements may differ is in the arrangements which are made to deal with unsettled questions or matters over which a failure to agree has been registered. Marsh distinguishes between the use in procedures of arbitrators, mediators and conciliators, 'arbitrators usually acting to impose a binding settlement upon the parties when they have finally disagreed, mediators intervening and attempting to produce a formal plan for adjusting the viewpoints of the parties, and conciliators suggesting ways in which they might come together'.[4] The arrangements for reference of questions outside the procedural system may differ in

[1] Turner, Clack and Roberts, op. cit., p. 255.
[2] A. I. Marsh, op. cit., p. 18.
[3] Turner, Clack and Roberts, op. cit., p. 258.
[4] Marsh, op. cit., pp. 6–7.

several different ways. To begin with, the decision to refer a question to arbitration (or to mediation) may follow automatically on a failure to agree and this decision to refer may be binding on both parties. Alternatively the decision to refer to arbitration may require the agreement of both parties. In the second place the decision to refer to arbitration may come at different points in the procedural hierarchy or, as in the engineering industry, it may not come at all; there is no provision here for the settlement of questions where there is a failure to agree other than to throw them back to the bottom of the procedure or to leave the parties free to act as they will. In the railway industry reference of questions to the Railway Staff National Tribunal (the awards of which are not binding) must follow unsuccessful attempts at their resolution elsewhere within the agreed procedure. There is a third possibility represented by the arrangements in the coal-mining industry and in the boot and shoe industry: here the procedure need not be exhausted before a question is referred to arbitration, reference to arbitration can be made at various levels providing the parties agree that the question concerns issues appropriate to that particular level. In the third place the decision of arbitrators may be binding on both parties or it may be dependent for its acceptance on the agreement of the parties to the arbitrators' findings. Dahrendorf presents (with acknowledgements to W. E. Moore and Clark Kerr) a tabulation of the possible forms of conflict regulation which rely on third parties:[1]

Type	Invitation of third party	Acceptance of third-party advice	Description
A	None	None	Conciliation
B	Voluntary	Voluntary	Mediation
C	Voluntary	Compulsory	⎱
D	Compulsory	Voluntary	Arbitration
E	Compulsory	Compulsory	⎰ (suppression)

Kerr suggests as the consequences of third-party intervention in industrial conflict, that it reduces irrationality, contributes to the exploration of various possible solutions, assists the parties to

[1] Dahrendorf, *op. cit.*, p. 227.

retreat gracefully from previous positions and raises the costs of continued conflict.[1]

The fourth respect in which arrangements for settlements outside the procedures vary, concerns who does the settling. We can broadly distinguish between arrangements which continue to be domestic (although they rely on 'outsiders') and arrangements which are made by the state. In the domestic arrangements an arbitrator or a panel of arbitrators or a tribunal may consist of persons outside the industry but chosen or approved by the employers' side and the unions' side within the industry. These people may be academics, lawyers or people experienced in industrial relations in other industries or who have retired from employment in the industry concerned. Domestic arrangements overlap with those of the state to the extent that the parties to a procedural agreement may choose to incorporate within the agreement reference of unsettled questions to one of the state's agents. Facilities are provided under the Conciliation Act of 1896 and the Industrial Courts Act of 1919. Procedural agreements may make provision for reference of unsettled questions to the Industrial Court. The Minister of Labour may, in any case, refer unsettled disputes at the request of the parties to the Industrial Court or to arbitrators appointed by the Minister or to an *ad hoc* board of arbitration.

The arrangements which are incorporated within industry's procedural agreements are the subject of some controversy. It is obvious, for example, that the kind of arrangements (if any) that are made for arbitration, will affect the length of time taken to settle questions. It is also suggested in some quarters that the provision of domestic arbitration arrangements and, preferably, the provision of binding arbitration arrangements, is to be welcomed because it represents finality in an otherwise interminable wrangle. But arbitration as a simple device to end industrial conflict has become suspect, partly because it was believed to contribute to the inflationary settlement of wages disputes (thus leading to the suspicion that arbitrators did little more than reflect the power balance of the industrial environment in which they operated), partly because arbitration can represent an artificial element of finality in what should be a flexible

[1] C. Kerr, 'Industrial Conflict and its Mediation', *American Journal of Sociology*, November 1954.

process of adjustment which needs to incorporate an element of conflict.[1] It has been suggested that automatic reference to arbitration, with awards binding upon both parties, both introduces a deceptive appearance of order and represents an unacceptable infringement of the unions' right to strike. It is significant that the coal-mining industry, the procedures of which contained just such watertight arrangements, was not noticeably successful in avoiding disputes; the likeliest consequence of such arrangements was that they substituted unofficial for official disputes. It may be that the possibility of allowing official disputes would have contributed to a lower total dispute level in the industry. It may therefore be dangerous to criticise the procedural arrangements in the engineering industry merely on the grounds that they are insufficiently decisive.

The weakness concerning the inappropriateness of general procedures to specific and more urgent questions would seem to be comparatively easily remedied. In some industries there are subsidiary procedures for dealing with disciplinary questions, or special procedures may be constructed for a particular purpose at a particular time. It is obvious that any appeal procedure which follows dismissal should be arranged quickly and should lead to a final decision which is binding (but procedures can never, of course, be regarded as the final remedy; an aggrieved party which feels sufficiently strongly on a question will strike, and even attempts at introducing legal sanctions have not worked in preventing it). The introduction of the coal-mining daywage structure in 1955 was so considerable a revision of previous arrangements that it could be expected to be submitted to considerable stress; the consequential disputes were dealt with by a specially constructed procedure for negotiating and settling grievances arising out of disputed assimilation of jobs to the new daywage grades.

But the existence of such special purposes is not typical. The reliance on general procedures may be an aspect of the imprecision which Marsh describes as characterising British procedural arrangements; the procedures which exist may be laid down as the result of custom and practice rather than being codified. The Shipbuilding

[1] These questions are discussed by McCarthy in 'Compulsory Arbitration in Britain', in 'Three Studies in Collective Bargaining', *Royal Commission Research Papers*, 8, H.M.S.O., 1968.

Employers' Federation, describing how a union may raise a question directly with the S.E.F., added 'Although there is no agreement directly covering the matter, it has been accepted for years.'[1] Some of the parties covered by procedures may be parties by custom rather than by agreement; neither the A.E.U. nor the Boilermakers have ever entered the shipbuilding main procedural agreement 'although they do in fact on many occasions follow the procedure for avoidance of disputes'. In the practice of negotiation there are many examples of corners being cut and the more ponderous dictates of the procedural law being avoided. In many cases there is no procedural law at all. Marsh writes that there are probably 'more establishments in which domestic procedures work by custom and practice than by agreements which have a written format'.[2] Where procedures exist and are formal they may be subverted with the goodwill and connivance of both sides, by continuous and informal consultation during a dispute and by the deliberate contravention of the rule that no negotiation should take place under duress.[3] One of the parties, on the other hand, may break or be accused of breaking with procedure and this question may itself become a matter for dispute (in these circumstances the employer usually has the advantage in that breaches of procedure carry no threat unless they are challenged by unions, and it is usually the employer's interpretation of terms which applies while matters are in dispute). Procedure may also be used in bargaining tactics where formal adherence to procedural rules may be used to delay the progress of negotiations. All these instances presuppose at least that the parties know their procedure but there are cases in which there seems to be great uncertainty about what the procedures are or about whether they are being observed. In the motor industry procedure requires that formal reference from the plant management concerned should be not the company's head office but to the local engineering employers' association and thence to the Engineering Employers' Federation itself. . . . Even in some big recent

[1] Royal Commission, Minutes of Evidence 48, 1967.
[2] Marsh, *op. cit.*, p. 18.
[3] Clack suggests (*Industrial Relations in a British Car Factory*, Cambridge, 1967, p. 46) that 'informal procedures would often be conducted more expeditiously and with a greater sense of urgency at such times'. Marsh agrees that 'The use of the technique of no negotiation under duress is in fact a tactical matter. . . .'

stoppages, it has been unclear whether the company concerned or the employers' association was handling the matter at issue.'[1]

Procedures, then, tend to be general, flexible or vague, as the T.U.C. describes them: 'In Britain, considerable emphasis is placed on flexibility in procedures. . . . Great emphasis and great weight can therefore be placed on the importance of procedures only if these are drafted with sufficient flexibility for people to use discretion and common sense in interpreting them.'[2] Marsh also emphasises the reliance on personal relationships and on close understanding between employers and full-time trade-union officials—a reliance which strains relationships between workplace representatives and managers who work at the level where the practical issues of job regulation are most urgent. The close understanding does not imply co-operation; negotiators may use their understanding to win advantage from the rudimentary procedures within which they operate. The negotiators (union or employer) tend to resist outsiders' recommendations that the procedures should be made more precise, rigorous and legal. No procedures, they argue, can be sufficiently comprehensive to deal with the complex and subtle differences which separate one plant or company from another and, if they were, they would be too rigid. They claim that, in any case, any system of industrial relations must rely on the basic goodwill of the participants and that our system does no more than make explicit recognition of this fact.

It emphasises the importance of the actors in the situation and of their mutually related roles. But they may be required to play their parts at two levels which are difficult to reconcile. As participants in and maintainers of this system their own experience and the 'flexibility' of the system may both be admirably situated to mutually supporting roles and to the continuance of the system without too much stress. The incidence of industrial disputes in Britain is comparatively low for an industrialised community, but it has been suggested that it may be as low as it is at the cost of not initiating or containing a sufficiently high rate of change or of growth. Stability and harmony is not the only requirement of an industrial relations system. Marsh concludes that procedures are easiest to

[1] Turner, Clack and Roberts, *op. cit.*, p. 258.
[2] 'Trades Unionism', *op. cit.*, p. 114.

operate, amongst other things, when there is least technical change, markets are steady and there is the greatest degree of predictability. The principle participants in operating the procedures are interested to some extent in a steady state because they (certainly management's representatives) are judged to some extent by the absence of conflict. When the procedures are such as to rely heavily on the understanding and personal relationships of the parties, then the parties are particularly likely to be locked into the system, operating and rewarded for their skill in its technical intricacies and their subtlety in commanding its nuances.

But driven within the system (partly by role expectations and partly by the nature of the system) they are not likely to be successful on the second level of performance which is increasingly required of them, that they should innovate, 'negotiate positively', examine the system 'objectively'. As experts in the maintenance of the system we may be asking the impossible of them. Marsh's description of the procedural arrangements in the building industry might well be applicable to others: 'joint sponsorship, development and policing have produced, among full-time officials at all levels, a high sense of involvement and mutual understanding. In a situation of this sort those concerned are not ready to find faults with what has been built up with so much care; nor are they anxious to indulge in experiment.'[1]

A growing amount of criticism is being directed at British procedural arrangements. In particular, 'engineering procedure has been subject to more censure than any other in Great Britain. It has all the characteristics most likely to attract criticism: a controversial past, a questionable present and an uncertain future. Yet in a formal sense it has also been extraordinarily resistant to almost every development in thinking about industrial systems which has taken place for the past half century.'[2] The trouble is that it is difficult to formulate and codify these criticisms in a rational way because what is effective procedure in one industry may be ineffective in another. In applying critical criteria to disputes procedure, the variables to be taken into account must include consideration of market, tech-

[1] Marsh and McCarthy, 'Disputes Procedures in Britain', *Royal Commission Research Papers*, 2 (Part 2), H.M.S.O., 1968, p. 57.
[2] *ibid.*, p. 31.

nology, history, profitability, the internal structure of unions and employers' organisations and the diversity of products and labour. There are no simple prescriptions for ideal procedural agreements.

Any attempt at generalisation is dangerous but it might be possible to point to some of the weaknesses and strengths which exist. Marsh suggests that there are two major tests: that the procedures should be *acceptable* to the parties and that they should be *appropriate* in that they should 'reflect the actual levels of decision-making and regulation within a particular industry'.[1] Criticisms of existing procedures often concern their appropriateness in that they are said to impose a national uniformity on plant, company and even industrial diversity. Marsh tentatively suggests that joint conciliation is to be preferred to employer conciliation and that standing arrangements may be better than *ad hoc*. It might be possible to go a little further. We can probably generalise about the extent to which arbitration should be incorporated in procedural agreements. It has always seemed reasonable that questions concerning the interpretation of existing agreements (substantive or procedural) should be subject to final decision by arbitration in that this represents a 'judicial' activity over 'conflicts of rights'. Arbitration as a voluntary commitment in the procedural agreement might also be reasonably extended to disputes which are concerned, not only with the clear interpretation of existing rules, but to those questions which concern discipline and dismissal, in that these questions seem particular to a quasi-judicial process rather than the power adjustment which is inseparable from substantive bargaining. Stieber has pointed out that, in the United States, 'while contractual commitments to arbitrate rights disputes have shown a steady increase during the last twenty years—from 73 per cent in 1944, 83 per cent in 1949 and 89 per cent in 1952—arbitration clauses covering interest disputes, which were never very common, have become even less popular during the last decade.'[2]

It is not only the single issue of arbitration which depends upon the nature of the dispute to be settled but the whole framework of

[1] *ibid.*, p. 6.
[2] 'Grievance Arbitration in the United States: an Analysis of its Function and Effects', p. 5, in 'Three Studies in Collective Bargaining', *Royal Commission Research Papers*, 8, H.M.S.O., 1968.

procedural arrangements themselves. What shapes the structure of procedure is thus not only the nature of the industry on which it is imposed but also the nature of the dispute which has to be handled. It is not enough to discuss only the kind of procedural agreement that suits an industry; the discussion should concern also the nature of disputes, because the extent to which the procedure fits or is appropriate depends upon a cross-reference of environmental conditions and of the kind of issues which have to be processed. The features which will emerge in a particular industry will determine the number of distinct procedures, the extent (if any) to which they will incorporate arbitration, the number of stages and the speed at which the stages are traversed.

6 The Conduct of Collective Bargaining

There is a growing literature in Britain on practically every aspect of industrial relations except the actual conduct of negotiations. There are several reasons for this neglect. The subject is difficult to research because managements are understandably concerned to preserve the secrecy of what takes place in negotiations. There is a much smaller area of government and of legal intervention in Britain than in the United States, so that there is also less research material in the way of published verbatim accounts of submissions before arbitrators. A widespread belief also exists in Britain, that negotiators' skills cannot be taught; this might indeed be one of the few managerial fields which is still believed to be the province of those born with inherited aptitudes aided by experience. The practice of collective bargaining *is* difficult to teach, but the difficulties are probably exaggerated. The same underlying explanation may apply both to the neglect of teaching and to the neglect of research. There is a sense in which the practice of collective bargaining is not a respectable field of study. The study is necessarily close to the art or science of winning in a conflict situation which has, in Britain, overtones of social class and political ideology. Teaching effective performance seems to carry Machiavellian implications and a downright commitment which academics would prefer to avoid, at least overtly. In the United States, where collective bargaining can be regarded as a much more value-free aspect of business enterprise, there are not the same inhibitions. American texts and, no doubt, American teaching programmes, set out surprisingly frank expositions of techniques which might not even be confessed to being practised in

Britain.[1] It is difficult to excuse the neglect of collective bargaining behaviour in any study of industrial relations because the deployment of the bargainers' skills may, in itself, be an important element in the bargain; as Stevens puts it, 'Although negotiation reflects and transforms the basic power relationships inherent in the situation, we should recognise that "negotiation power" is a type of power in its own right. Negotiation power, *per se*, comes from facility and shrewdness in the execution of negotiation tactics. . . . Negotiation power, along with other kinds of power, determines the final result.'[2]

Another reason for the comparative neglect of collective bargaining and negotiation, other than as a study of its institutions and evolution, is that the study has not yet coalesced into a discipline conducted within one, coherent, theoretical framework. At least five analytical approaches have been made to the subject. The first concerns the economist's attempt to analyse the components of wages. The second, a sociological approach, is an attempt to explain negotiations in terms of institutions' application of power in the conflict over limited resources. The third concentrates on social psychological manifestations of, and explanations for, conflict in negotiation. The fourth sees the parties to negotiating situations as members of small groups and attempts to apply the analysis of group psycho-dynamics to their situation. The fifth, in which there has been a recent vogue, explains negotiations in terms of games theory and applies mathematics to their analysis. At the present stage of development it seems as well to be unhindered by academic demarcations in a discussion of the subject.

Stevens defines collective bargaining as 'a social-control technique for reflecting and transporting the basic power relationships which underlie the conflict of interest inherent in an industrial relations

---

[1] For example, 'Fear of the loss of wages can be worked on by the employer by means of communications to the employees at the plant and by letters or bulletins to the wives and families at the homes. . . . This form of pressure tends to undermine the morale of workers and lessen their desire to be on strike. It is intended to force the workers to bring pressure on the union to reach a settlement as quickly as possible'—Maurice S. Trotta, *Collective Bargaining: Principles, Practices, Issues*, Simmons–Boardman, 1962, p. 83–4.

[2] C. M. Stevens, *Strategy and Collective Bargaining Negotiation*, McGraw-Hill, 1963, p. 2.

system'.[1] He goes on to stress that collective bargaining is a mixed relationship containing elements both of co-operation and of competition; other writers have also noted that, however conflicting the relationship of collective bargaining is at any one time, it carries the implications that both parties wish the relationship to persist in time. There are other, subtle ways, as we shall see, in which time introduces itself to an analysis of collective bargaining as an additional and confining dimension; collective bargaining is a Heraclitan process which cannot be frozen so as to be observed at any one point. The mixed elements of co-operation and of conflict are incorporated in a definition by Walton and McKersie who see labour negotiations as an example of social negotiations (there are frequent contemporary analogies in the American literature between collective bargaining, the civil rights struggle and international relations) and who define it as 'the deliberate interaction of two or more complex social units which are attempting to define or redefine the terms of their interdependence'.[2]

The application of games theory to explain collective bargaining may not be as strange to the negotiators as it often is to outsiders. Perhaps this is because there is, to practitioners and observers of the art, a game-like atmosphere of unreality in which negotiations are conducted, a sense in which the negotiations appear to be conducted at a level and by reference to rules which sometimes seem to have no reference either to the real positions of the parties or to the outcome. The game model which negotiators sometimes see as closest to their activity is the fixed-sum situation in which one party wins to the extent that the other loses. But this is too simple because there are certainly negotiation situations in which both parties may win and others in which both may lose. Stevens prefers to describe 'the conflict-choice model' in collective bargaining as an 'avoidance-avoidance' situation in which, after a union claim the employer faces initial alternatives which are equally distasteful to concede a costly claim or face a costly strike. In an 'avoidance-avoidance' situation the preferred course for the employer would simply be to walk away, but he cannot escape, because of the

[1] *ibid.*, p. 2.
[2] R. E. Walton and R. B. McKersie, *A Behavioural Theory of Labour Negotiation*, McGraw-Hill, 1963.

mixed relationship which exists with the union, so he is forced to bargain.

It would be dangerous to generalise over the whole field of collective bargaining because it contains sub-processes 'each with its own function for the interacting parties, its own internal logics and its own identifiable set of instrumental acts or tactics'.[1] We shall, therefore, look at the conduct of negotiations under three headings: distributive bargaining, formal, non-bargaining relationships, and internal (or intra-organisational) adjustments. The second part of this framework, internal adjustment, is particularly important in the present context because it brings out an important but often ignored aspect of negotiations, that they do not simply take place between two solid organised and unitary structures. This aspect is also important to our particular purpose here because we are concerned with industrial relations and with the personnel specialists as representatives of employer organisations in collective bargaining. Before going on to the discussion of collective bargaining under these three headings it must be admitted that this categorisation, like most others, is, in some respects, too simple. The existence of an issue usually implies some difference between the values of the parties.

However, value differentiations can be carried to a point where the bargaining to which they give rise can hardly be regarded as distributive; they concern rather the conflict of basic ideologies. When this occurs the conflict, as Coser suggested, tends to be bitter and disruptive. There is an element of ideological conflict in many confrontations of unions and employers, which characterised the coalfield disputes up to 1926 which were largely concerned with issues of nationalisation or worker control. Disputes of this kind are now rare but an element of ideological conflict must enter into the relationships of what are essentially two different types of organisation; business organisations as Etzioni describes them, basically remunerative organisations, and trade unions which he describes as mixed

[1] *Ibid.*, p. vii. Walton and McKersie set up the following distinctions: distributive bargaining, integrative bargaining, attitudinal structuring and, finally, intra-organisational bargaining. For several reasons we have rejected this framework; attitudinal structuring, for example, may be associated both with distributive and with integrative bargaining. The distinction between distributive bargaining and integrative bargaining also seems to be questionable.

remunerative-normative organisations. One possible view of the evolution of the British system of collective bargaining is that it has progressively reduced the element of ideological conflict; integration and mutual recognition has converted conflict between the parties into disputes over objectives which are mutually understood, objectives capable of joint negotiation rather than simple aggression.

DISTRIBUTIVE BARGAINING

Walton and McKersie define distributive bargaining as the 'system of activities instrumental to the attainment of one party's goals when they are in basic conflict with that of the other party'.[1] It may be useful, although an over-simplification, to regard distributive bargaining as taking place in three stages: the preparation for bargaining (including the determination of negotiating objectives and the assembly of the agenda), the actual process of negotiations and, finally, their termination (by an agreement, by breakdown, by a strike or a lock-out). The first and third stages are the ones most capable of rational analysis.

Preparation for Bargaining

In the preparatory stage, the most familiar technique in determining negotiating objectives is commonly supposed to be the horse-trade situation in which the parties both claim and offer the impossible, expecting a mid-point settlement; 'the large-demand rule provides that the initial bargaining demand and counterdemand are in excess of the least favourable terms upon which each party is willing to settle, and in excess of what each expects the agreed-upon position to be. Both parties know this.'[2] But the initial positions are not arbitrarily selected. Long-term considerations set limits to the 'basic area of interdependency' and set the extremes beyond which either party might prefer to end the relationship rather than settle. Technical, commercial and marketing considerations will influence the initial bargaining postures adopted, and may even influence the choice of the bargaining opponent; one American bargaining strategy adopted by British white-collar unions is to choose pace-

[1] *ibid.*, p. 4.
[2] Stevens, *op. cit.*, p. 33.

setters to negotiate with rather than to bargain on an industry-wide front. Such a policy of *bumping*, of choosing the targets one-by-one rather than striking over the whole industry-wide field, has at least two advantages as a union strategy. It enables strike-pay to be financed without exhausting strike funds because the strike can be paid for by men who are still at work. It also has the advantage, which must have a peculiar appeal to socialist union members, of relying on the more cannibalistic characteristics of free-enterprise; the individual firm chosen for a strike suffers both from what the union is doing to it and from what its employer-competitors are doing to its share of the market.[1] The parties are often regarded as determining target points (which may be the initial claim and counter-claim) and resistance points (beyond which negotiations may give way to other forms of conflict). A major recent criticism of British industrial relations has been that the targets are invariably determined by the unions, which thus have the initiative. The common assumption is that management has lost control of industrial relations to the unions, which have captured the initiative by the frequency and size of the claims they decide to make. It may come as a surprise to managers to learn that union members frequently complain in precisely the same terms, that the unions are entirely controlled by the strategies and initiatives of management. We will suggest later that this mutual despair amongst the membership of both organisations is because, to some extent, neither is in control. Control often resides within a comparatively small group of professionals, the negotiators on both sides who, while they do not enter into a strategic conspiracy for the control of their organisations, certainly exercise an influence which resists the creation of a strategic initiative elsewhere. We call this influence *aspirational rigidity*; it may help to explain the feeling of bewildered impotence which seems to be shared by so many of the non-professional (in a negotiating sense) members of organisations, both union and managerial.

[1] This is not a new strategy. Knowles quotes the *Banker* of April 1946 which describes shop stewards in the strike-bound Cossor firm as exhorting Philco workers to work harder so as to bring the Cossor company to heel! Knowles suggests that the bumper strike goes back at least to 1821 (*Strikes: A Study in Industrial Conflict*, Blackwell, 1952, p. 12).

Even when responding to a claim management sometimes seems singularly vague about its own target and resistance points. There may be two explanations for such uncertainty. The first is that management may be so inept that it really has not costed the claim or its implications, calculated its response to the claim or determined its own limits. The second explanation is that management must inevitably appear vague about its proposed resistance and settlement levels because the process of negotiation is largely concerned with adjusting the opponents' subjective judgment about one's own objective position. There may even be circumstances, as we shall see in discussing processes of internal adjustment, when the negotiators do not themselves know the points at which their organisations may settle or break-off; this state of affairs, too, can arise either from ineptitude or from subtle judgment. Walton and McKersie suggest that a long history of negotiation and of familiarity make it more likely that the real expectations of the parties will be known to each other: 'the resistance points of parties will tend to be compatible if each party has a relatively accurate picture of the other's utilities. . . . When there are well-established traditions and role requirements for each of the negotiators and when the specific pressures bearing on them are generally known, the negotiators tend to enter bargaining with more or less consistent expectations about each other's utility function.'[1]

This suggests an approach to the determination of objectives which is sometimes advocated in Britain, the presentation of negotiating claims as targets which are also, in effect, resistance points. This approach is more widely known in the United States as 'Boulwareism'. It represents proposals by management which appear, on the face of it, to be take-it-or-leave-it terms. But Boulwareism is not presented as an aggressive negotiating technique so much as a positive managerial attitude which is an alternative to horse-trading. Management's proposals must, it is said, be preceded by careful analysis and must represent a genuine attempt to offer what is right, fair, and what will be seen to be fair. To the extent that the proposals represent a genuine statement of management's true position they must be un-negotiable; management's first offer is a statement of management's final position. This is really non-

---

[1] Walton and McKersie, *op. cit.*, p. 44.

negotiation, as Stevens points out. It is not so much a bargaining technique as a philosophy of management which depends upon open lines of communication to the employees; 'it is, in a sense, an appeal directly to the employees which can by-pass the unions.' Whatever the ethics of this approach, it depends heavily on its own previous success to prevent the reintroduction of an element of real negotiation.

An approach related to Boulwareism, but distinct from it, is the union buy-off intended to make the union redundant. This requires the employment by management of industrial relations officers with experience and with ears close to the ground. Their function is to anticipate the next set of union claims (and the union's realistic settlement objectives) so that they can be met by management before they are made by the union. The intention may be either to weaken the position of an already recognised union or to make the union seem irrelevant to a partly non-unionised work force. In the second variant, the employer must demonstrate that his terms and conditions of employment are at least as good as they would be if the plant were unionised. The first variant (again exempting its ethics from discussion) can hardly be supported on the grounds which are frequently used to defend it; it is never an example of enlightened management policies towards trade unions.

Approaches like Boulwareism and the union buy-off both depend in the ultimate on the absence of labour militancy and organisation over the whole labour front. Industrial relations may well be passive in one sector simply because there is violence in another part of the front. Thus it is always possible that the peace which reigns in a non-unionised plant or company is made possible by good employment conditions which are set by reference to a standard of acceptable conditions achieved in another part of the industry, perhaps as the result of considerable conflict with the unions through collective bargaining. The importance of violence in another part of the front may simply be in establishing standards for the 'enlightened' employer to meet or surpass, but the employer deceives himself if he believes that the standards are established independently of union operations, even though the unions are not represented in his own plant. An analogy on a wider scale to peace being dependent on violence in another part of the front emerged from the racial conflict in the United States in 1967. When Detroit had been disrupted by racial strife, community leaders in Chicago confidently asserted that they would not allow similar disruption to take place in their own city because they were embarking on a programme of civil improvement. Their assertion was justified, but it is likely that conflict in Chicago was avoided largely because it had occurred in Detroit. The situation in Detroit demonstrated both the urgent need for reform and perhaps also the directions in which it should take place.

The preparation of the agenda for negotiation is important not only because it sets the arena for negotiation—but because the agenda itself may be a part of negotiating tactics. Items included in the initial agenda may be subsequently taken out as trading items; they may be included with the intention of trading them for negotiated advantages. Even when they are not included or excluded as a matter of tactical advantage, an agenda may be deliberately composed of a mixture of strong and weak items. Because of the mixed and on-going nature of the negotiating relationship, effective relationships may be difficult to maintain if one side consistently wins its cases. One experienced management negotiator has said that he would be worried by consistent successes in a negotiation session (particularly conducted before arbitrators) and that it is a long-term advantage to lose some cases; judgment comes in selecting the cases to be lost.

There is another aspect of the preparatory stage of negotiations which seems to have escaped comment. This concerns not so much the targets that are arrived at or the agenda items submitted, but rather the non-targets or the items which are consistently left out. Negotiators, particularly those who are employed virtually full-time in the role, seem to settle into a mutual, professional acceptance of each other's standards and expectations. There are certain things that are not asked for and certain things that are not said; if they are said it is as a deliberate tactical irritant rather than as a serious negotiating objective. This aspirational rigidity on both sides may have contributed to the conservative acceptance of practices and standards which have long been criticised from outside, but the criticisms are usually rejected as naïve by the insiders. It is easy to account for aspirational rigidity: negotiators must co-exist; one sometimes suspects that the relationships which connect across the negotiating boundaries are stronger than those tying the negotiators to their own organisations. There is a point beyond which negotiators seem unwilling to embarrass their opposite numbers. There may be sound functional reasons for this mutual respect; Stevens suggests that, although both parties may begin with a constraint to participate in the bargaining situation, the very real tensions in the bargaining relationship may well lead to 'various forms of aberrant behaviour' and to breakdown. There may, therefore, be a common interest in keeping tension down to a given level of effectiveness.

The Process

The objectives of negotiations, however precisely calculated, are often shifted in the actual process of negotiation; indeed the purpose of distributive bargaining is largely to adjust the expectations and intentions of the other party. Quite apart from the impact of the tactics employed by the parties, it has also been suggested that the role of the negotiators and the nature of negotiations changes with time. Thus Douglas suggests that in the initial stages the principal role of the negotiator is as a delegate of his organisation and that, particularly from the union side, the opening passages of negotiation may be taken up by ritualistic attacks upon the employer. Such attacks can have little effect upon experienced opponents but they may strengthen the resolve of union observers as well as strengthen the intra-organisational position of the union leader. The union negotiators may later return to this role as a compensating show of strength for accepting a relatively unfavourable position. Stevens distinguishes two distinct stages in the negotiating process. In the first stage the emphasis is on the costs to the other side of maintaining its own position; thus the union will try to convince management that refusal to adjust its position will certainly result in a strike, and the union will emphasise the costs of the strike to the company. The employer's equivalent tactic is to emphasise the damage resulting from acceptance of the union's target: that it will bankrupt the company or the whole national economy and the union members will be unemployed. In the second stage there is a more collaborative and less belligerent attitude as each party begins to stress the low costs to the other of moving to its own position; the union underlines the belief that higher wages will not mean higher costs because the members' hearts will be so overflowing with love that productivity will rise, absence reduce and so on.

American writers on the negotiating process emphasise the time element to an extent which it would be dangerous to imitate here. This is because many American contract negotiations must be completed by the time the contract runs out, so that negotiations often take place toward a deadline and thus there is therefore considerable emphasis on the shift in positions to be expected (and played for) at the eleventh hour. In British negotiations there is rarely an eleventh hour. One party may well announce a deadline but, where there is unilateral rather than a collectively imposed time constraint, the deadline can also be unilaterally removed. So the union may give notice of the intention to strike but strike notices can always be withdrawn; the deadline in British industrial relations is, therefore, much more a part and parcel of the negotiating process as one of the tactics which may be employed. Deadlines may be real (objective) or tactical (subjective); they are a part of the 'bluff' or 'not bluff' apparatus. The belief in the reality of the deadline imposed by the other side will be influenced by its behaviour in previous situations. The National Union of Railwaymen, for example, has frequently imposed a strike deadline but it has been withdrawn so often that it must now be approaching the point when it needs actually to strike if only in order to maintain the value of the deadline tactic.

The analysis of evidence leading to judgments about the real intentions of the opponent is part of the infinitely subtle skill used by the experienced negotiator, a skill which, more than any other aspect of his job, justifies the contention that negotiation cannot be taught. Some of the evidence is relatively hard and obvious: the previous performance record in like situations, the strike fund of the union or the market situation of the company. But other evidence of intentions may be revealed in the negotiating situation itself. American writers mention the importance of non-verbal signals, the absence of comment or rebuttal which allows one party to proceed without the commitment of the other. Peters and Walton and McKersie stress that these signals, whether they be nods, grunts or silences, are a form of communication which are clearly understood within the context and that it is important to the maintenance of the bargaining relationship and to good faith that they should not be ssed to imply commitment which is later rescinded ('we never said hat'). The negotiating game, in other words, must be played ccording to rules which are internally consistent.

The process consists of shifting the respective positions of opponents, positions which are announced as being immovable but which re known by all the parties to be movable. The initial positions are invariably unacceptable to both parties; more specifically, each party would prefer the worst that its opponent could do rather than accept its initial bargaining position. The initial positions are adopted s a preliminary to discovering, through negotiations, a range of preferences which is acceptable, in varying degrees, to each party. The range of acceptable preferences is called by Stevens the *contract zone*, a *manifest* contract zone when communications are clear and he zone is perceived by both parties. Walton and McKersie term he range of acceptable preferences the *area of interdependency* which 'stems from two sources: market rigidities and jointly created ain'.[1]

The process of moving each party away from the unacceptable initial positions into a range of acceptable preferences and finally to n agreement is the result of the interaction of two sets of factors—situational conditions and process conditions. The situational conditions are the facts which make up the environment within which negotiations take place: the actual costs of a strike, wages costs, market position, requirement for manpower, cost of living, government policy. The process conditions are the influences which the parties can bring to each other within the negotiations: the force of rational argument, the relationship between the negotiators, the xtent to which their pronouncements are acceptable, their skills in djusting each other's position. It is the interaction between these internal and external factors which contributes to the appearance of unreality which often surrounds the negotiating process, for the observer might conclude that settlement depends on the internal factors, whereas there is an obvious and important determinant imposed by the reality of the world outside. One important element is he relative power of the participants in what is a struggle for power, but an analysis of negotiation in these terms alone would be misleading.

[1] *ibid.*, p. 19.

It would also be misleading clearly to separate situational condi tions and process conditions and to discuss the influences of each o the negotiating process as independent determinants. There is a overlap between the two sets of conditions because, while som situational conditions are apparent to both parties (they are objec tively perceived), some others, although equally real, are communi cated to one party by the other (they are subjectively perceived b one). These situational factors therefore become a part of the proces and one party has to exercise judgment as to the extent to which the are in fact situational or in part a process tactic. Information or th absence of information becomes critically important, as Walton an McKersie point out: 'It is not necessary for the objective condition to change; it is only necessary for the perception of these condition to change in order for a negotiator to alter his position. In contrac negotiations objective knowledge virtually never becomes complete.' Purely process skills are often successfully employed to make th opponent reveal more of his own information about situational con ditions. One, usually unsuccessful, tactic is the finesse, when a part 'reveals' inaccurate information about situational conditions: 'W know you made £100,000 profit on this product last year', in th hope that the information will be corrected, 'That is not true, w only made £80,000.' Another tactic listed by Walton and McKersi is that of 'exaggerated impatience' when one negotiator may appea to be heading too rapidly to the final stages which 'may force th inexperienced negotiator (his opponent) into prematurely revealin the bargaining room he has allowed himself.' Another tactic may b to use evidence from the situational conditions or even to arrang for the evidence to appear; union negotiators may regret the out break of unconstitutional strikes while negotiations are in progres but use it as evidence of the almost uncontrollable militancy of th men on this issue. An extension of this tactic is to arrange a rea commitment to outside situational conditions: the deadline strike o an announcement by directors that the plant will be closed. Outsid commitment is a dangerous device if it is employed only as a proces tactic, and may lead to the paradoxical position of one party pro ducing casuistic arguments to help to unhook its opponents from commitment which must be jettisoned.

[1] *ibid.*, p. 60.

A whole range of legitimate tactics are also employed to adjust the attitudes of opponents. This is the area in which *attitude* adjustment must be seen as instrumental to the negotiating process. The tactics which are most usually commented upon here are various rattling devices from personal abuse to time-wasting and irrelevant argument, not used (as they often are) accidentally, but in a deliberate attempt to provoke some kind of breakdown which will reveal more situational information. The opposite device may be more effective, to produce an attitude of such geniality, sweetness and light that the opposing party reveals all, or more, in a sudden outflow of mutual partnership. An aspect of this tactic is for the negotiator clearly to recall the distinction between his own major negotiating objectives and subordinate tactical advantages; he may therefore concede one tactical victory after another in the hope that he is softening his opponents' attitude; the negotiator who vigorously chases every tactical rabbit on the other hand may find himself both losing a sense of direction and hardening his opponent's resolve to win the final battle. A device which may be used in the large negotiating conference where delegation confronts delegation is the appeal to the least experienced member. One negotiator in our experience used to address the union observer from plant level, who was normally expected to be silent at high-level negotiations; he did it by reference to the unimpeachable principles of industrial democracy: 'it is surely important that the men's voice should be heard here'. Yet another tactic which the writers have seen employed was used as a first move by a union negotiator, so early that negotiations had hardly begun. He opened by asking whether it was management's intention to meet the union's claim. Management's negotiator, who was experienced but not devious, replied that it was not their intention to do so, an understandable reply because their refusal to meet the claim was the reason for their commencing negotiations. The union negotiator then threatened to walk out because there seemed little purpose in negotiating with such intransigent opponents. The tactic was deployed with several purposes: to shock management into the revelation of situational information, to create a nervous and/or conciliatory mood in which real negotiations would begin. Needless to say, it was a tactic which could be used only once.

These and many other devices may be used by negotiators as part of the process in which they are involved. They may be appropriate to the purpose at a particular time but they are often, of course, unsuccessful; they may result in counter-tactics and in unplanned responses. One result may be the generation of considerable tension between the parties. The tension may, as Walton and McKersie told us, contribute to some kind of negotiation breakdown. One or both parties may, in such situations, use various devices which are intended not to achieve advantage but to regain an atmosphere in which effective negotiations can be resumed. There may therefore be several phases in negotiation, quite apart from the periodic variations which Stevens described; some phases will be characterised by tactical deployment, others with attitudinal construction or repair. It is some of these latter phases which sometimes give negotiations the appearance of time-wasting as one or the other party goes back over ground which is familiar in order, for example, to reduce tension in preparation for a new phase to begin. In this sense attitudinal adjustment is subordinate to the main negotiating process.

Terminal Stage

Negotiations usually end in agreement. How this agreement is arrived at is a mystery which no discussion of situational and process conditions or of tactics really helps to solve. The agreement, in contract or substantive negotiations, will normally not coincide with the target claim nor the resistance points of the parties; to say that it emerges from a 'manifest contract zone', an 'area of interdependency' or a range of acceptable preferences does not help to determine how a particular point is selected for agreement. It may be that situational conditions almost entirely determine, within gross limits, what is to be agreed, while the final fine adjustments are the result of process skills exercised by the negotiators. They certainly dare not engage in open communication with each other about their real intentions during the closing stages of negotiation, for to show readiness to accept a position is to accept it. Conversely, if they show readiness to move away from a previously prepared position they have as good as abandoned it. Stevens puts the final dilemma as 'How may a party announce his equilibrium position without prejudice?' or 'how to "come clean" without prejudice'.[1] His own

[1] *op. cit.*, p. 104.

solution to this subtle problem rests on the use, once again, of sign language which may suggest that progress is being made towards an acceptable point by 'small, revocable steps' taken without formal commitment. Another device he cites is the use of off-the-record meetings outside negotiations. This particular convention must be one of the most puzzling to outsiders; when it is used the negotiators may temporarily drop their negotiating roles to give each other more information about their respective positions than could otherwise be exchanged. The convention normally extends to an understanding that what is said 'outside' negotiation will not be quoted 'inside' it, even though the same people are present. It is easier to assess the influences on the final agreement in deadline negotiations than in others, but there is a general sense in which *all* substantive negotiations take place against a deadline background; they must be concluded or terminated because important considerations await the outcome. They may be broken off when it becomes apparent that, far from reaching an agreement, the parties are not negotiating within a contract zone. Grievance negotiations, on the other hand, may continue as long as one party harbours a sense of injustice and continues to believe that something can be done about it (unless there is special, finite procedure). Grievance negotiation may be less time-constrained because a set of conditions, usually those imposed by management, prevails until they are overthrown by negotiation; the parties do not have to move to any new situation because there is a status quo, but the reversal of the status quo means often a quite opposite state of affairs. In substantive negotiations, on the other hand, one of the parties has expressed dissatisfaction with the prevailing conditions, and there is a gradation of settlement points which is easier to attain and failure to achieve settlement costs money.

When negotiations do not result in agreement the particular consequence of breakdown depends upon the procedures and the intentions of the parties. The procedures may dictate that unsuccessful negotiation should give way to submissions before arbitrators, in which case the styles and tactics of the parties usually change, partly because the choice of tactics is often limited by the existence of more formal 'rules of evidence'. In other cases, breakdown may be followed, by custom or by mutual choice, by continued discussion before conciliation. In other cases one of the parties may decide to extend negotiations to the application of overt power in order to shift its opponent's position; there will be a strike, go-slow, or lock-out. The most extreme of these measures represents a degree of commitment which is rarely entered lightly. Invariably, once the commitment is made, the act of commitment will alter the target and resistance points of one or both parties so that negotiation, when it is resumed, will do so in a different context. In many cases the strike as a negotiating weapon resembles the un-logic of the ultimate deterrent; it is effective because it is not used. But the dilemma that follows such a paradox is that it ceases to deter as belief in its use generally fades.

The situation can, of course, get out of control. More precisely, it can drift towards a situation of 'endemic conflict' which Turner, Clack and Roberts suggest as existing in parts of the motor industry in which 'disagreement, mistrust and detailed aggression or defence have become acquired attitudes'.[1] In such persistently hostile relationships collective bargaining is more likely to terminate in strikes than in agreements, or, alternatively, the employees strike first and talk afterwards. This situation, once it develops, tends to perpetuate itself and is difficult to break. There are several reasons for its emergence as a pattern of relationship. Turner, Clack and Roberts conclude, ominously, that 'such endemic conflict situations can only be securely resolved by the separation of the leading personalities from them'. It is usually the men's leaders who are most removable and the result is usually their dismissal. This was the final outcome of the Ford dispute in 1957, and of the Barbican-Mytten dispute in 1967. The inference is that a clash between personalities often explains conflict of this kind. This is no doubt true but there are other, more structural explanations.

One union leader who observed the Ford dispute at first hand has suggested that the bitterness of that particular conflict resulted, in part, from a breakdown in the communication code of collective bargaining. We have previously discussed the importance to bargainers of familiarity with each other's methods and expectations, the subtle but real significance of non-verbal signals and the meanings which phrases are commonly taken to imply without being

[1] *op. cit.*, p. 289.

stated. The dangers of misinterpretation are greater where there are, perhaps, 30 unions representing employees in the same plant. The dangers of failure to read the code can also be increased as the result of mergers and take-overs. In these circumstances allegations of deceitfulness and bad faith may be explained by a single failure of communication.

A more frequent reason for the break-away from control of industrial relationships is a sudden change in the strategy of one of the parties, which results in the expectations of its opponents becoming mistaken. This occurs when, for example, a soft line by management gives way to a hard line. The difficulties of readjustment to the opponent's position are added to new difficulties and uncertainties over communication—'do they mean what our experience tells us they used to mean, or do they mean what they say they mean?' This situation can arise over the way in which the strike threat is deployed. An employer may have acquired a reputation for being easily coerced by the threat of a strike during bargaining (perhaps when the market situation justified easy capitulation to pressure). But times or intentions may change. The workers, on the one hand, may continue to refuse to believe that the employers mean to weather out a strike, so that they are almost forced, bewildered, over the brink. The employers, on the other hand, must demonstrate the seriousness of their position and must demonstrate it as quickly as possible, with the result that they may move from laxity to intransigence. Meanwhile the workers, continuing to believe in everything that their previous experience has taught them, continue to hope that additional pressure will do the trick. In this way the whole situation rapidly spirals out of control. Workers apply massive power to win tiny adjustments, managers become immovable over small concessions because it is no longer the value of the concession which is in question, it is the clear demonstration of the meaning of a new vocabulary. In either case the instant response to conflict is the application of power; in other words, the parties have ascended, quickly and innocently, to a new platform of endemic conflict. The only way out may indeed by the separation of the parties concerned, not because of their personalities, but because they happened to have been around when words meant different things. New personalities are necessary because they need to come fresh to the battlefield, unencumbered by previous learning. But it is a particularly bitter conclusion that men have to be sacked by management because they cannot unlearn a role that management has taught them.

But these are special, if not entirely unusual, circumstances. In more normal relationships, the strike as the terminal stage of negotiations can have advantages.

Quite apart from its tactical or strategic importance, the strike may facilitate the progress of negotiations. Marsh has exploded the myth of 'no negotiation under duress' as being in itself a negotiating posture. Negotiations do go on while strikes are in progress, but they are often conducted outside the negotiating framework, informally or before third parties. In this way alone, the strike may lift discussions to a new level of reality. Walton and McKersie list three positive by-products: they may be long-term investments, they enhance the credibility of future strikes; they may increase the internal solidarity of the striking party (cf. Lewis Coser); they may clear the air, 'provide a foundation for building constructive relationships'. Most commentators seem to show a genteel avoidance of one obvious advantage and purpose of the strike: it represents the ultimate recourse to the arbitrament of power without violence which is permitted in free societies for the settlement of issues over which man's interests are deeply concerned. It is this, surely, which makes strikes sometimes inevitable, even good.

7 Internal Adjustment

Negotiators represent their respective organisations in the bargaining process that takes place between them. But the negotiators are seldom free agents; they are constrained by the organisation they represent and they, in turn, may influence their organisation. This is what we mean by internal adjustment. It is the most neglected aspect of what is, in Britain, a neglected field, but from our point of view intra-organisational bargaining is most significant because it particularly concerns the negotiating role of the personnel specialist and because it illuminates the distinction between short- and long-term objectives, between tactics and strategy.

The simplest and clearest representation of the total negotiating situation, which also took account of the area of internal adjustment, would be one in which the function of negotiation was separated from the function of determining negotiating goals (see chart, below). There may be some usefulness in a model of this kind but unfortunately its simplicity is deceptive. It may represent, to some extent, internal adjustments which take place between the respective levels in the hierarchy on each side; it may also represent the symmetry which often typifies the relation of one set of goals to the other, but the distinction of function and role is much too precise to resemble reality.

On the union side, for example, the actor in the negotiating role may also have been instrumental in achieving the agreement of his annual conference and his executive to policy formulations which he largely constructed himself. Even so, he or his executive may not have found the passage easy and he may have engaged in a great

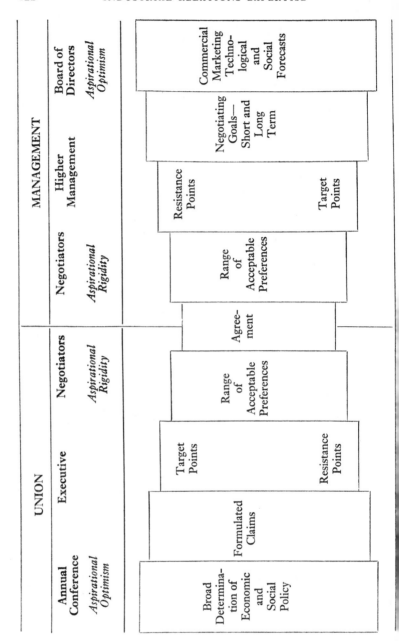

deal of 'intra-organisational bargaining' on the way; it may be that his own objectives will have been changed as a result of the process. The power of the respective parties to the 'bargain', within the union, will depend in part on the union's own constitution and structure and on external constraints (from the market, the economy, the labour composition of the union and from technology). So, although the process of internal adjustment may have been very important in determining the final negotiating brief given to the union's negotiators, we cannot clearly separate the role of negotiator from the role of policy formulator.

On the management side the division of functions is sometimes easier to see. This is particularly so where negotiations are conducted by personnel and industrial relations specialists. However, they are often conducted by higher management or by members of the directing board. When they are not, senior managers may exercise the right of sudden intervention.

The final postures of the negotiators on both sides are determined by a complex process of pressure and counter-pressure exercised within their respective organisations.[1] How and why are these pressures exercised, more particularly on management side? In the first place why is it so often thought necessary to create a division of functions for negotiation on the management side when this division is not so obviously present on the union side?

The most obvious reason is that the trade union is much more of a negotiating institution than is management; negotiation is a central activity for the unions while for management it is at best an activity secondary to its main purpose, and at worst it is dysfunctional to the pursuit of its purpose. Negotiation also requires knowledge, sometimes of a mass of complicated agreements and procedures, and considerable skill and judgment which, it is believed, can best be applied by specialists. 'The vast majority of managers', wrote Flanders,[2] '. . . prefer to have as little as possible to do with labour

---

[1] This whole discussion rests on an assumption of rationality: that the various actors engage in purposive behaviour based on intelligent analysis of the situation surrounding them. This assumption is not always justified: negotiating postures and responses are sometimes adopted as the result of hunch, chance and guesswork.

[2] A. Flanders, *The Fawley Productivity Agreements*, Faber, 1964, pp. 251-2.

relations, and are as a rule quite willing to delegate for most of the time to a personnel manager or department' or, he added, to 'let the unions act as the "managers of discontent".'[1] There are other less obvious reasons for the division of functions. We have already described the phenomenon of aspirational rigidity by which the very success achieved by the operators of a system tends to limit their expectations of what can be achieved from the system. Aspirational rigidity means that those who determine long-term objectives and strategic goals should be different from those responsible for negotiating their achievement. The separation of functions, even when it is made, does not guarantee that long-term objectives will be determined. This is because management often fails to distinguish between the determination of objectives for negotiation and their actual negotiation; management may believe that those who are best at negotiation are therefore those most likely to determine their own objectives. The converse of this position is that senior management is so ill-informed about industrial relations that it is quite incapable of determining rational objectives or that it fails to determine objectives at all.

A good example of the consequences of the conflict between aspirational rigidity and aspirational optimism and of the failure of internal negotiations between these extremes comes from recent evidence about employers' organisations. They are accused of being insufficiently innovative, and of being bound by the system within which they operate. Their excuse is that they can do only what other members require them to do. But it seems that this is a situation about which few of their officials claim they *want* to do any more. They consistently seem to fail to clutch at the available straws. Only 22 per cent of officials in McCarthy's survey said their associations could do with more money, and 'Few officials could name functions which their organisation ought to perform but which they were prevented from carrying out because of a lack of resources.'[2] Less

---

[1] There seems to be some support, surprisingly, for the union substitution for personnel department functions in Turner, Clack and Roberts (*op. cit.*). It suggests a serious misreading of the scope and functions of personnel management as being confined to the welfare and grievance representation of employees. If this interpretation is correct, their view is about 30 years behind the times.

[2] *op. cit.*, p. 92.

than 29 per cent of national officials and 15 per cent of local officials said they had insufficient influence over members; in engineering, only three per cent of local officials said they had insufficient influence. Only 32 per cent of national officials and only 19 per cent of local officials wanted to see any change in the system of national negotiations or in procedures for settling procedures. Half the national officials said there were no particularly time-wasting practices or inefficient labour practices in their industries.

The point of referring to the evidence here is not to argue that employers' organisations are staffed by complacent people but that, given the negotiating function of their organisations, they are inevitably locked into the system and contained by aspirational rigidity. Employers' organisations thus provide an excellent if extreme example of the consequences of functional specialism in collective bargaining. It suggests the total unreality of expecting them both to operate the system and to change and improve it. It is not only their power but their expectations which are necessarily limited, and they are not even influenced by the processes of internal adjustment which are usually present in a managerial structure.

The managerial structure of a business enterprise is not so specialised, of course, but it is convenient to stick to our model to the extent of assuming that the negotiating and the objective-determining functions are carried by separate individuals, because in this way we can identify as interaction between role-holders what would otherwise have to be explained as the balancing of factors within the same individual. Even in the most authoritarian organisation the determination of strategic targets, of what should be achieved, will obviously be tempered by what can be achieved. In other words the actual strategy of bargaining programmes will itself be the result of interaction, and adjustments within the organisation. The shape of the bargaining programme may well reflect the relative weight, importance and status of the respective parties to the process of internal adjustment, the senior managers and the specialist negotiators. There may, of course, be external pressures which adjust the shape of the intra-organisational bargain. An internal situation in which strategic aspiration is too high may have the missing internal corrective of aspirational rigidity replaced by external adjustment from the union in the actual negotiating process. For this reason, aspirational rigidity should not be dismissed as obstructive conservatism: it represents the realistic expectations of practical men and is a prelude to confrontation with reality outside the confines of the business enterprise. But too much respect for aspirational rigidity and for the realistic expectations of experts may mean that there are no strategic objectives at all, that the enterprise staggers from one crisis to another, managed by industrial relations rather than managing them.

The forces which are represented in this model of the total bargaining relationship are shown as existing in a simple rather than a complex relationship. To this extent the diagrammatic representation on page 122 is an over-simplification; it accounts for the interaction of symbolic abstractions rather than men, it explains the inter-relation of actors carrying single roles. In a managerial organisation reality may mean that the same man is both managing director and negotiator. The distinction resulting from our explanation is more serious on the union side, for here the relationships which are unexplained are structural rather than accidental. Earnings are often made up of nationally negotiated minimum rates and plant-negotiated bonus rates. In the national bargaining and political structure the national union official is the professional (influenced by aspirational rigidity), while the shop steward is almost indistinguishable from the lay member (influenced by aspirational optimism). In the plant or company bargaining structure the same explanation can be brought to bear, but it now defines the shop steward as the professional bargainer (influenced by aspirational rigidity) while the lay member is the rank-and-file worker (influenced by aspirational optimism). In other words, this account sets out to explain influences in any *single* bargaining relationship; it cannot be applied to the whole, complex structure.

These forces are crudely represented in the model set out on page 122. The union and the management structures are represented as being engaged in an agreement. The agreement partially coincides with a range of acceptable preferences, or a contract zone which exists for each of the parties but which is not known to the other. As we approach the disengaged extreme of both the union and the management organisation, the aspirational optimism of the controllers of the organisation pulls the objectives for negotiation away from practical reality. As we get nearer to the point of engagement these disengaging forces are corrected by the organisation's experts who introduce the corrective of predicting practical and attainable targets; the experts introduce aspirational rigidity. The particular negotiating strategy of an organisation may reflect the dominance of one extreme of influence or the other. The complete dominance of the organisation's disengaged extreme may have one of several effects: negotiating breakdown, continual dispute or the desperate acceptance of unplanned and improvident agreements as the only apparent alternative to achieving objectives which were always impossible (total war may, paradoxically, result in total capitulation). The complete dominance of the negotiating experts, on the other hand, may mean that negotiating strategies are virtually determined by the other side. The consequences here are likely to be insufficient adaptability and insufficient relationship between negotiated agreements and the commercial, technical and social circumstances in which the organisation operates. It may be to introduce a confusion of analogies, but when a car is driven by its road wheels it is out of control; it is under control when the motive force of its engine is geared down to control the speed of its wheels. It is also worth remembering that friction, internal and external, is essential to the process.

How does one party to intra-organisational bargaining influence the other? Walton and McKersie give a partially helpful account of 'tactics for achieving intra-organisational consensus'. They list six such tactics:

1. The negotiator can avoid incompatible expectations from the beginning by preventing the principal's expectations from hardening until after the opponent's (the union's) position is apparent to him.

2. The negotiator can attempt to persuade senior management to revise its expectations after they have been developed.

3. The negotiator can structure or manipulate the bargaining situation so that the inducement to alter expectations arises from the situation itself rather than from his own arguments.

4. The negotiator can modify the principal's expectations so that

he is prepared to accept a lower level of achievement after the fact of the lower level having been achieved.

5. The negotiator can disguise or exaggerate the actual level of achievement in order to minimise the dissatisfaction experienced by the principal group.

6. By tacit bargaining: 'the negotiator can engage in tacit bargaining as a way of explaining to his opponent that his behaviour is not to be taken seriously.'

This account is only partially helpful because the whole emphasis is on 'how the negotiator copes with . . . conflict within the group'; it is not concerned with how senior management exerts pressure on the negotiator. One suspects that this latter aspect of the problem of intra-organisational bargaining is the most serious one in Britain. From our questionnaire survey of personnel specialists the impression emerges of two levels of bargaining, the one between negotiators and the unions, the other between the negotiators and senior management. We asked:

'If your department carries the major responsibility for conducting higher negotiations, are targets determined for you by higher management at the outset?'

The reply:

Industrial	Yes	109
	No	43
Staff	Yes	84
	No	44

And we asked:

'Are limits determined by higher management beyond which you may not go?'

The reply:

Yes	92
No	15
Sometimes	75

106 respondents had discretion in the conclusion they could negotiate towards, 24 were given no discretion and 53 were given discretion sometimes.

We asked for example of limits; we have selected the following from 38 responses:

'The Board may agree an increase of, say, 4 per cent and give one discretion to go to 4½ per cent or perhaps 5 per cent without referring back. It depends on circumstances, but I invariably have some latitude.'

'In the negotiations of a critical price a top limit of 5 per cent was set. I exercised my discretion by exceeding this limit by a further 1½ per cent in order to achieve a settlement. It was not possible to achieve Board approval for the extension—my decision was endorsed by the Board.'

[There are limits set on] 'any item likely to increase production costs and thereby reduce slender profit margins and/or competitive pricing. In practice, higher negotiations are rarely conducted without several adjournments, giving ample opportunity for discussion with higher managements and limits may be changed according to the progress of the negotiations.'

'This is a matter of teamwork amongst management. A good team, closely in touch, knows how far it can go. Usually I can decide domestic problems (i.e. within the two companies and three factories in my authority) but not those which will have repercussions in the other group units.'

'(1) Before entering into negotiations at 'regional' level we normally seek the authority of the Board to negotiate what we think is right.

(2) Downwards, we will limit management to a predetermined prepayment for a given amount of work in specified conditions. We then allow a negotiating margin of 5 per cent, i.e. plus or minus 2½ per cent.'

Some of these comments suggest a penumbra of imprecision within which the negotiator is expected to reach a settlement, even a tacit expectation that he may settle beyond the given, prescribed limit set by senior management. It is as though our description of the target and resistance points in negotiations between management and unions also applied to the intra-organisational bargaining between management and negotiator. It certainly suggests the existence of a control zone, or a range of acceptable preferences between the aspirational rigidity of the negotiator on the one hand and the aspirational optimism of management on the other.

The analogy between the actual negotiating process and the intra-organisational negotiating process goes further. We noted the importance of limited information and incomplete knowledge to the conduct and tactics of negotiation; limited information is also important in intra-organisational negotiation. Walton and McKersie suggest that limiting the information available to the negotiator is relevant to the actual tactics of negotiation between management and unions. Negotiators ignorant of their own organisation's total situation cannot reveal information about it to their opponents, so the organisation may 'compose the committee of people who obviously cannot reveal clues, because they themselves do not have significant knowledge of their party's resistance point. In fact the chief negotiator may be such a person.'[1] This 'calculated incompetence' is another functional reason for the division of roles between management and negotiator. There are other respects in which the negotiator will be unaware of his organisation's commercial situations and plans.

His different perception of the goals to be achieved is explained not only by his ignorance of the total situation, nor by aspirational rigidity. Differences will also result from the formal institutionalisation of negotiation which results in the existence of negotiators with a specialist role. These secondary characteristics are by-products of the negotiator's role rather than characteristics which are essential to its performance. Management at the enterprise-directing level may be concerned primarily about costs; management at shop-floor level may be concerned about avoiding interruptions to production; personnel specialists and negotiators tend to worry about consistency and the consequences of precedents which will dent the uniform application of agreements. These differences in perspective become more rigid and formalised when roles are carried by functional specialists who are members of their own department. Interdepartmental conflict is familiar to any student or member of large organisations. For members of the personnel department this may mean that the members believe that, if only the rest of the organisation would respect and listen to 'the personnel point of view' industrial relationships would become more harmonious or effective This belief may be the result, in some instances, of a more total

[1] *op. cit.*, p. 68.

understanding of the situation than is possessed by line managers; in others it may result from a less complete understanding. In grievance bargaining, for example, personnel department negotiators may have to let down foremen or supervisors who have mis-interpreted agreements or misapplied company policy; the damage done to formal authority is a necessary cost in maintaining control, consistency and trust. In other circumstances the personnel depart-ment may itself be in a position equivalent to the foremen, with the relatively narrow perspective. This may occur because the criteria which determine whether a negotiating issue should be won or lost by management (although the verdict is rarely as conclusive as those terms suggest) are not entirely internal, and do not relate only to the justice and rightness of management's case. In these circum-stances it may be the bewildered personnel department which is let down by management which may be pursuing a relatively soft line ('the present commercial circumstances mean that in no circum-stances can a strike be contemplated') or a relatively hard line ('the present dispute at the present time offers the opportunity of re-asserting strength which we have been unable to demonstrate in previous commercial circumstances'). There are other less dramatic but more frequent occasions on which personnel departments may resent the apparent lack of managerial understanding of sound in-dustrial relations principles. A minor grievance adjustment conceded by management may terrify the personnel specialist's sense of pre-cedent. This kind of conflict often occurs over marginal cases (substantive agreements over pension rights, for example, usually lay down precise definitions which invariably exclude some deserv-ing hard cases) in very large organisations in which the personnel department has been largely responsible for the bureaucratisation of consistency; when they do occur, the amount of public concern they generate may result in senior management's over-ruling the person-nel department's correct interpretation, and the costs to public relations may well be less than the precedent costs to the mainten-ance of the agreement. This kind of thing makes personnel specialists very angry, but it makes foremen very angry too.

In these intra-organisational or inter-departmental conflicts it is very difficult to arbitrate about who is right and who is wrong. It would certainly be naïve to generalise about such issues by concluding that the personnel viewpoint should be upheld on all personnel issues. All that can be hoped is that the respective cases, for short-term and long-term considerations, are put and that decisions taken are informed and purposeful. There is then, yet another analogy with the negotiating situation proper; conflict of interest, whether it be inter- or intra-organisational, is best accommodated when its parties are represented in overt exchange. But it would be stretching the analogy too far to suggest that at this level, too, conflict should be institutionalised. Personnel departmentalism has no doubt contributed to a stratified separation of interest and perspective. Line managers have been criticised for their lack of understanding of industrial relations expertise (see Flanders), but personnel specialists have also been attacked for their professional isolation from business control (see Petrie). The very engagement of personnel specialists means that they are required to develop an expertise in operating a system which will inevitably limit their perspective by what we describe as aspirational rigidity and by the acquisition of characteristics secondary to the performance of their role. The dilemma is that they should make their specialist contribution without being dominated by it and that managers should hear it without being deafened. Perhaps the dilemma must exist and cannot be resolved; inter-organisational conflict is, after all, now accepted as being unavoidable and functional.

8 Formal Non-Bargaining Relationships

Employers and workers engage in relationships outside the bargaining process. These are often not the subject matter of industrial relationships because they concern work and communications. But the institutions of employers and workers also engage in relationships outside bargaining; they consult and confer, sometimes in a spirit of co-operation, sometimes about subjects in which they have a common interest. This different kind of relationship has encouraged some observers to distinguish between formal relationships which are competitive on the one hand, co-operative on the other. Thus Walton and McKersie set up 'integrative bargaining' as a separate and distinct framework from 'distributive bargaining'. They define integrative bargaining as 'the system of activities which is instrumented to the attainment of objectives which are not in fundamental conflict with those of the other party and which therefore can be integrated to some degree. Such objectives are said to define an area of common concern, a *problem*.'[1] This definition, in conjunction with their definition of distributive bargaining, implies the existence of two separate sets of relationship existing between management and unions: the one concerned with matters of common interest (problems), the other with matters over which interests will differ (issues). Now this kind of dualism closely parallels the practical distinction in British industrial relations between two distinct sets of industrial relations machinery: the one, collective bargaining, dealing with 'issues'; the other, joint consultation, dealing with matters in which there is believed to be a common interest with

[1] *op. cit.*, p. 5.

'problems'. This outlook is coming to be regarded as outmoded and seems to be as open to objection in theory as in practice. For this reason we have chosen the clumsier title of formal, non-bargaining relationships to describe relationships between management and workers which are outside distributive bargaining. One of these non-bargaining relationships is joint consultation.

The negotiating procedures of Britain evolved, in general, to meet the needs of the developing representative institutions of employees and employers. The consultative machinery, on the other hand, grew as the result of the recommendations of government and the employers from above. Machinery for joint consultation, along with extensions to bargaining machinery, was recommended by the Whitley Committee in 1916–17. The recommendations were made against a background of considerable industrial unrest and even greater public concern. They were made also at a time when employee demands were more ideologically militant than they have ever been since, because the demand then was often for some degree of worker or joint control. To some union leaders, therefore, joint consultation has always been regarded as a palliative, as an employers' device to cajole employees into more profitable co-operation and to deter them from militancy.[1] Encouraged by government, by the statements of well-intentioned employers and by the management teaching of the time, joint-consultation arrangements flourished. But the private reports of disillusionment amongst the practitioners on both sides at last began to be reflected in academic studies until finally even the Ministry of Labour seemed to jettison joint consultation. The evidence of our own investigation suggests that personnel specialists, at least, are still convinced of its value: out of 328 respondents, 227 thought joint consultation a useful adjunct to bargaining, 28 gave qualified approval, eight mentioned improved communications, and only 24 thought it a waste of time (39 did not reply). There may be special reasons for the personnel specialist's almost isolated approval; as the traditional intermediary he may, for example, find the opportunity to bring employers and

[1] For example, '... Whitley Councils and the other forms of industrial conciliation were steadily set up to sap the strength of the shop steward's movements and the other demonstrations of rank-and-file militancy'—Arthur Horner, *Incorrigible Rebel*, MacGibbon & Kee, 1960, p. 45.

employees together in a relatively uncharged atmosphere facilitating to his own role.

The reasons for disillusionment about joint consultation or, at least, for its failure to live up to the extravagant promises that were made for it, are familiar.[1] Prominent among them is the fact that management's intention (often reflected in the constitutional rules) to confine discussion to 'matters of common interest' has resulted in a discussion of the trivial and the insignificant only, and a consequential managerial concern over the 'apathy' displayed in the consultative process. This is what bedevils any attempt to divide the subject matter of industrial relations into 'issues' and 'problems'. 'Problems' are so often the problems of management while the problems of the employees, once presented to management, become 'issues'. Management is concerned about the removal of impediments to production and profit—matters, it believes, which must surely be of mutual interest. But the impediments may be differently regarded by men whose jobs have been progressively de-skilled or whose crafts have been gradually diluted. Skills are expensively acquired. The possessors of skills may continue to believe that they should be rewarded in some way for the costs of acquisition even after the skills have ceased to be required. What concerns the employees and their representatives is the matters that relate them to the work environment in which they will often have a different frame of reference from that of the employer.

For this reason the separation of issues and problems and the construction of separate negotiating systems either theoretically (as in Walton and McKersie) or practically (as in joint consultation) is suspect. There is also a sense in which it seems nonsense to talk about 'integrative bargaining', in that bargaining surely concerns the settlement of differences (which continue to separate the parties) while to move towards integration suggests some other process which, if entirely successful, implies, in absolute integration, the disappearance of parties or factions able to bargain at all. Joint consultation was no doubt intended to be an integrative device. There are several others.

Most of them relate to a style of management behaviour rather

[1] They are set out in H. A. Clegg, *A New Approach to Industrial Democracy*, Blackwell, 1960, and in *Joint Consultation in British Industry*, N.I.I.P., 1952.

than the detailed programmes of negotiation because the tactics of integration are often admitted to be in an 'antithetical relationship' to the quite different tactics of distributive bargaining. Although we have questioned the wisdom of talking in terms of 'integrative bargaining' it remains true that in certain circumstances, distributive bargaining can be subordinated to the process of integration. This may be one of the cases in which there is a hierarchy of negotiating objectives and in which negotiation is used to pursue non-negotiating goals; the negotiators may be required, for example, to achieve targets lower than those within their abilities in order to achieve another and quite different goal.

Harbison and Coleman have distinguished three types of union–management relationships as 'bench marks on a kind of continuum of collective relationships'.[1] They are: armed truce, where major objectives are in conflict, collective bargaining is largely a negative process for settling differences and unions are tolerated; working harmony, based 'as much upon hard-boiled realism as it is on mutual confidence and trust', but in which collective bargaining is a means of working together; union–management co-operation, 'in which the parties through joint-action attempt to reduce unit costs of production, increase efficiency, and improve the competitive position of the firm'—this is a rare relationship which the authors describe as existing only in small companies or at times of crisis. The categorisation is not exhaustive; Harbison and Coleman refer to 'open conflict' relationships which they say often occur in the early stages of negotiation, but, as we have seen, Turner, Clack and Roberts suggest a pattern of 'endemic conflict' existing in parts of the motor industry which would seem to be a type of relationship persisting in time.

It has been suggested that the quality of union–management relationships depends not only on the maturity and judgment of the actors in their various roles, nor entirely on the effectiveness of the procedures and systems which exist, but is also considerably influenced by the technology of the industry. Thus Joan Woodward has suggested that the pressures and tensions created by mass-production processes may be much greater, in industrial relations terms, than those associated with process production. This 'explana-

[1] Harbison and Coleman, *Goals and Strategy in Collective Bargaining*, Harper, 1951.

tion from the technology' is currently often quoted as justification for a 'socio-technical systems' approach to industrial relations problems. But Turner, Clack and Roberts question its application or relevance to the motor industry; if valid, they ask, why should one car firm's record be much better than another, or better at one time than another, or why should one nation's car industry be significantly different from others? Similar explanations stemming from the production process were used to 'explain' the coal-mining industry's unfortunate dispute record, but the explanation could hardly account for violent differences in disputes between collieries within the same coalfield. This is not to say that technological considerations are irrelevant in determining the relationship characteristics of a firm or industry; rather it suggests, once more, the complexity of this matter in which relationships will be determined by a number of factors of varying weight, some of which may be mutually cancelling, and some mutually supporting. This is why there is no determinancy or absolute predictability about the analysis of industrial relations problems. Some of the broad boundaries are set by influential environmental factors like market, production process and physical environment, but further analysis uncovers other and finer influences—the procedures and system of management, management and communication structure, social influences—until we are finally left with the subtle adjustments resulting from the interaction of one personality on another. The problem of understanding these influences is twofold: in the first place we have to list the influential factors; in the second place we have to measure their respective influence. The problem of measurement is enormously complicated by a methodological difficulty: how can we arrive at comparisons of the importance of respective influential factors when the measurement of each factor is carried out by analytic tools appropriate only to that factor but which can not be applied to others? For example, a calculation of the influence of the market might be carried out by an economist, while an analysis of the influence of personality might be made by a psychologist; what kind of final measurement of respective influences can be expected to emerge when the methods of analysis are not interchangeable and when the analysis itself is not presented in standard terms? And we have left out of account the imprecision of the analytic tools which exist in the various disciplines. It is problems like these which raise doubts about the wisdom of the social scientist's repeated assurances that he is about to achieve a breakthrough when his assertions can be accurately measured and his predictions made finite. For the moment it would seem better for us all to make the modest claim that we are trying to understand and to discuss rationally an extremely complex area.

Although, by discussing industrial relations, we are bound to concentrate on management–union relationships we must also remember that a discussion of integration cannot be exhausted by any summary, however full, of the possible relationships existing between management and unions. A whole range of relationships exists between employer and employee independently of relationships between employers and unions. We can best illustrate the extent of this range by describing the conditions existing at each extreme. At one end is the employer who would claim that his employee relations had transcended the stage of any kind of distributive bargaining. Such an employer is usually large and successful and aims to apply the most advanced and sophisticated techniques available in the field of personnel management. The range of integrative devices open to him would include co-partnership, profit-sharing (now rather suspect in terms of its effectiveness), collective goal determination, the Scanlon plan, joint appraisal programmes and staff status for all. Such an employer would also set out to be a 'good' employer because of the familiar happy identification made between moral and commercial interest; it's good to be 'good' and it pays to be good. He has got to be good, in fact, because he must demonstrate that the level of integration or togetherness at which he aims provides terms and conditions of service at least as comfortable as those provided in other firms which engage in distributive bargaining. There is little doubt that sophisticated and integrative programmes of employee relations have contributed to reduced industrial conflict. Suspicion of their ultimate validity rests on three premises: that the standard of acceptable terms and conditions, which may be exceeded, is set by distributive bargaining elsewhere, so that integrative arrangements must always be exceptional (peace in one sector as the result of warfare in another part of the front, as we described it previously); that the value of industrial harmony and of the avoidance of conflict may be falsely enlarged;

that authority, however benign its manifestations, is unilateral and unchallenged and therefore more entrenched than where it is manifest.

At the other end of the range of employee relations outside the field of collective bargaining is the absolute autocracy of the dominant management which has never allowed the unions in, or which has ousted them after a bitter but decisive conflict and which employs techniques that are anything but sophisticated. This is the kind of employee-relations pattern which may be found among small employers, often employing a majority of female workers, sometimes in areas where there is no great tradition of trade-union organisation or militancy. The employee-control devices are paternalist or negative in the sense that they rely either on personal loyalty or affection, or on the issuing of orders and the application of sanctions. They may sometimes rely on a particularly dysfunctional mixture of both, consisting of reprimand followed by appeal and exhortation. Interesting though this kind of relationship is, it hardly merits discussion under a heading of formal industrial relationships. But between one extreme and the other are a whole range of variants in relationship patterns in which unions and collective bargaining may be tolerated but ineffective, or in which autocracy gives way to attempts at 'positive' management, with or without union support.

There remains the relationship made possible by the extension of collective bargaining beyond what are considered to be the traditional limits. We have already discussed the ideological recommendation for extending collective bargaining (concerned with industrial democracy) and the practical extension. Productivity bargaining represents the best example of the practical extension. Productivity bargaining, apart from requiring a scarcely precedented degree of preparation, analysis and planning on the part of management, also extends the boundaries of work-place bargaining. Personnel managers who have been engaged in productivity bargaining report that it becomes difficult to observe the formal distinctions between consultation and negotiation. Flanders stressed the importance of building and maintaining 'the habit of discussion'.[1] The Prices and Incomes Board makes the same point: 'We do not believe that it is possible to exaggerate the importance of full discussion and agree-

[1] *The Fawley Productivity Agreements, op. cit.*

ment at plant and workshop level. Methods of work and traditional practices cannot be changed by decision of an industry or a company, but only by the men who do the work. Where there is no formal machinery for plant or workshop negotiations, it should be created.'[1] Discussions of this sort, embracing as they must not only rates of pay but the reorganisation of work, management and supervision, changes in training and conditions, can hardly be demarcated as belonging to the negotiating process which deals with 'issues' or to the consultative process which deals with 'problems'. Productivity and plant bargaining are therefore contributing to the growing belief that the division between negotiation and consultation should be demolished.

Whatever the future of formal joint consultation no one would suggest that the process of informal consultation about work between managers, supervisors and workers, should be diminished. There has been a tendency to re-emphasise the importance of 'informal consultation' recently, particularly in the Electricity Generating Industry where considerable claims have been made for its effectiveness.[2] But it does not seem to be justified, however worthwhile these developments, to inflate a characteristic of everyday management-employee relationships, and a necessary and fundamental one at that, into a part of the structure of industrial relations.

There will probably always be a tendency for management to stress the integrative nature of business organisations, despite Fox's warnings of the dangers of a unitary frame of reference.[3] There will also be a tendency for sub-groups in the business organisation to pursue diverse and divisive interests. Management will stress the importance of integrative relationships because they are instrumental to the achievement of its objectives, not because they represent reality; integrative relationships are management's ideal of what things should be. But integrative relationships must depend, to some extent, on shared values, standards and attitudes. Etzioni,

[1] National Board for Prices and Incomes, Report no. 36, *Productivity Agreements*, H.M.S.O., 1967, p. 38.

[2] H. Sallis, 'Joint Consultation and Meetings of Primary Work Groups in Power Stations', *British Journal of Industrial Relations*, vol. III, no. 3.

[3] A. Fox, 'Industrial Sociology and Industrial Relations', *Royal Commission Research Papers*, 3, 1966.

in analysing the sources of power and compliance in various types of organisation, distinguishes between coercive, remunerative and normative power and the respective kinds of 'congruent involvement', alienative, calculative and moral. Organisations, he concludes, can accordingly be classified as coercive, utilitarian or normative. Business organisations are utilitarian, the source of power is remunerative and the kind of involvement they encourage is calculative. But Etzioni points out two other characteristics: when two kinds of power are exercised over the same group they tend to cancel each other, and 'in most organisations the higher the rank, the more normative the control exerted on it'.[1] This analysis helps to explain the continued stress by management on integrative relationships. They are applying power based on a source which they share and which is perfectly appropriate to the upper reaches of management, but they are applying it to subordinates who are normally controlled by remunerative (or, worse still, coercive) means. In these circumstances, 'integration' and remuneration may well neutralise each other.

Whether integrative relationships are effective or not may depend in the ultimate not on the intentions or good wishes of the members of the organisation, but on the nature of the organisation and its business. It is a truism by now that 'Theory Y' techniques are most appropriate to the management of managers.[2] Whisler and Harper have pointed out that employee appraisal, as an integrative technique has progressively shifted in the U.S.A. from application to the shop floor to application to managerial personnel.[3] Integrative relationships may be perfectly appropriate to a business organisation where the employees are upward mobile, are presented with open-ended career opportunities, share basic attitudes with higher

[1] A. Etzioni, *A Comparative Analysis of Complex Organisations*, Free Press of Glencoe, 1961, p. 202.

[2] D. McGregor, in *The Human Side of Enterprise*, McGraw-Hill, 1960, distinguished traditional, authoritative styles of management as 'Theory X' and modern, integrative management as 'Theory Y'. McGregor admitted that it might be 'decades' before Theory Y could be applied to motor-car manufacturing, for example.

[3] Whisler and Harper, *Performance, Appraisal Research and Practice*, Holt Rinehart & Winston, 1962, p. 429.

management and are egoist rather than fraternalist in their response to relative deprivation.[1]

So management begins with a built-in tendency to regard integrative relationships as an ideal pattern. If management is sufficiently perceptive, it may see that they are inappropriate to the kind of tasks that have to be performed and to the composition of the work force which performs them. Management may then decide, rather than abandoning integrative relationships, to change the character, tasks and social composition of the work force in order to make the application of integrative techniques more appropriate and feasible. It is this kind of process which seems to best explain some aspects of job-enlargement and of the gradual extension of staff status to manual employees. Management is thus engaged, whether it knows it or not, in a considerable exercise in deliberate social experimentation and change. This may be a perfectly appropriate means to the achievement of managerial ends, it may even achieve social good as a by-product, but it is important that we should remember that, in this respect, social change *is* being pursued as a means to managerial ends and that managers, in the politest possible sense, are irresponsible agents of social change on this scale.

Integration may, in practice, mean victory, a victory so complete that negotiation need never take place. Nothing can better illustrate to managers the 'irresponsibility' of integration achieved as the result of one party getting its own way than when integration is brought about by the union rather than by management. This situation, in which the union exercises absolute effective control over the work of its members, is not uncommon. It manifests itself in the union or the work-group deciding questions of manning and individual allocation to work, the time allowed for work, the distribution of good and bad jobs, the construction of shift and holiday rotas. It can result from the union officials or stewards controlling the distribution of resources so large as to make them more powerful than management; they control rewards and therefore they control work. Management and supervisors often acknowledge this situation and have to 'work through the stewards'; they do this because it is the only thing they can do, the stewards have become the

[1] The terms are taken from and are explained in W. G. Runciman, *Relative Deprivation and Social Justice*, Routledge & Kegan Paul, 1966.

effective supervision, the official supervisor retains only some job expediting and administrative functions. If foremen have disciplinary problems to deal with (and this may happen only when control procedures or senior management make the need to attempt to exercise discipline inescapable), they ask the stewards to deal with them on their behalf. The situation feeds upon itself because the supervisors' problems are likely to become painful only when exposed to senior management, so that it comes to be in the supervisors' interest to keep the state of affairs away from management by seeking peaceful accommodation with the steward.

The situation grows out of a number of characteristic features. The work performed is usually of a skilled and an essential nature. The workers are often organised by a union with an apparatus of demarcation and restrictive rules to apply and with a tradition of independence from other workers in the plant. The work is often carried out within a very complex managerial structure; the place of work may be small but it is isolated and at some distance from the managerial main stream. On the other hand, the work may take place in a very large, complex plant (like a motor-car factory), but the evolution of such a 'self-governing organisation' within the plant often takes place in a work section subsidiary to the main process.[1] In either case management relies heavily on decisions taken by foremen and supervisors who are isolated from support and assistance. And frequently these men are quite unsuitable for exposure to such considerable pressure. One characteristic of this kind of situation is that the men's leaders are often more capable and more intelligent than their opposite numbers. Work rotas and holiday schedules may be worked out by stewards, not only because they have an interest in the results, but because managers find the work too time-consuming or difficult. Supervisors may also be temperamentally unsuited to engaging in the kind of conflict which resistance to submission requires; where salary differentials and other material benefits of a foreman's job have been whittled away (as they often

---

[1] McCarthy suggests that the extent of centralised decision making is important but he adds that 'there are also variations in the level at which decisions are taken in individual firms and plants which affect the bargaining opportunities of stewards'—*Royal Commission Research Papers*, 1, p. 62.

are in this kind of situation), the only conceivable advantage in holding a supervisory post is security—security-seekers may become trouble-avoiders.

Whatever the reasons for its development, when the workers in a process effectively exercise control over the process they may well have come as near as possible to achieving practical industrial democracy; they have surmounted all the theoretical objections to workers' control. Unpalatable though the results may be for management, they represent a real example of a type of non-bargaining relationship; they also represent a kind of integration. Management may feel that they have been integrated in the same way that a rabbit has been integrated by a stoat, but the result is often a kind of peace.

The peace is broken sometimes by management trying to re-establish control or, at least, to re-establish negotiation. Peace may also end as the result of the very success which the workers have won. The resources and power which are at the disposal of workers' leaders may be so large as to provoke internal dissention, and there is always the possibility of some kind of internal corruption. Workers' control by their leaders depends upon strong internal discipline, and this tends to be threatened as wage differentials widen with other workers outside the group. This means that there is not only a growing temptation to employ rate-cutters and blackleggers, but that resistance to the temptation weakens as sympathy with their more affluent victims declines.

These may be extreme circumstances but they illustrate the point that where non-bargaining relationships have taken the place of collective-bargaining relationships, the change is the result of the triumph of one side. To the extent that it is safe to talk about a normal or desirable pattern of relationships it seems probable that non-bargaining relationships should be an accompaniment to, rather than a replacement of, bargaining. Where non-bargaining relationships have superseded bargaining the result is the hegemony of one side. When that one side is management the hegemony may be authoritarian or benevolent. In either case management is likely to claim that the relationship is in the best interest of the worker; it is necessary for management to make this claim (and to try to demonstrate its truth), if only to prevent the hegemony being broken. The dangers of this position are more obvious, at least to management, when dominance has been achieved by the other side.

But collective-bargaining relationships are never the whole of the formal relationships between employers and employed. Non-bargaining relationships include the communication, decision-making and control systems which are operated in order to get work done. The structure of those systems depends upon, among other variables, the ideology of management and the nature of the tasks performed. Important though these structures and influences are, they are not really the subject matter of the study of industrial relations, although they greatly influence the structure of industrial relations.

9 Interaction between Industrial Relations and the Personnel Specialist

Industrial relations involves more than a set of procedures in which the personnel specialist may be involved. Even where the personnel specialist has no direct responsibility for industrial relations, the relationship between employer, workers and trade unions sets him difficult problems. The trade unions are organisations representative of workers but the personnel specialist often regards himself as possessing an important worker representative role. Students may still opt for a career in personnel management because it appears to offer the chance of escape from commitment to a management ideology (while offering the opportunity of a managerial salary); some say that they see the personnel specialist as 'in the middle' between workers and management; more extreme still, that they wish to enter personnel work because it offers the opportunity of helping the workers. This kind of attitude, like all forms of benevolence, sounds helpful but is likely to be fatal to the patient.

It appears at first sight to be a paradox that the benevolent intentions of some personnel specialists accompanies a marked reaction against the welfare aspects of personnel work. The decline in welfare is in part a reaction against the personnel managers' early history. Personnel managers see themselves as having become more 'professional' as they grew further away from their welfare origins; an interest in employee welfare is no longer identified with the way to posts of high influence, status and salary. Welfare, the original *raison d'être* for British personnel management, has fallen victim to the ambitions of the personnel manager. Where welfare continues to be a major preoccupation of the personnel department it often forms its only responsibility so that the image of welfare as the poor relation is further strengthened. In large organisations welfare seems often to be regarded as of no great consequence because investment in it seems difficult to justify from the standpoint of the company's interest. If this is so the personnel specialist finds it difficult to excuse his dabbling in essentially altruistic activity because he has for so long sought to establish himself as a peer among managers. But, whether an altruistic role would be justified for him or not, no-one has made a serious attempt to establish either the value or the need for employee welfare provision by the employers. We have become used to hearing coincidental arguments, over communication, safety, training, that what is profitable for the employer is invariably good for the employee. Welfare seems to represent a salutary example of an activity which, because it seems unprofitable, cannot rely on appeals to goodness alone for its support. The welfare content of substantive agreements has been comparatively neglected in Britain both by unions and by management. There is some evidence that the T.U.C. is seeking to remind unions of the leeway that remains to be made up. Non-direct payments may become a more important element in substantive agreements; it is possible that continued efforts at income control in a competitive labour market may encourage this development because, at last, we shall be able to convince ourselves once again that what is right is happily also what is profitable.

This ambivalence of attitude and the conflict between the personnel specialist's history and his aspirations, complicates many of his problems in the area of industrial relations. It explains, in part, the complex relationship between the personnel specialist and the trade unions which regard him sometimes as friend, sometimes as enemy and sometimes as competitor. One relatively simple explanation for this confusion of relationships derives from the alternative set of judgments which are available about the nature of workers' interests and the manner in which those interests are best represented.

This unitary frame of reference suggests that there are no necessary and deep divisions of interest between sections of the industrial community. This view is characterised by expressions which by now have come to be seen as naïve, expressions like 'there are no longer two sides to industry, we are all dependent upon each other's efforts for our mutual well-being'. This is a view which originates from early human relations teaching and research, notably Elton Mayo's work in the Hawthorne Experiments in Chicago, 1927–32. The view is accompanied by explanations of industrial conflict as representing functional breakdowns which can usually be corrected by improved communications. This relatively simple view of industrial conflict has given way (among those by whom it is not completely rejected) to a more sophisticated account in which the aim continues to be the avoidance of conflict but where it is accepted that conflict can be 'functional' to the organisation in which it takes place. A whole series of techniques are recommended for ensuring that the conflict continues to be acceptable in terms of pursuit of the organisation's goals and does not become disruptive. These techniques include the avoidance of authoritarian styles of management,[1] the pursuance of 'collective goal-determination[2] and the evolution of staff-appraisal programmes as integrative rather than control mechanisms.[3] All these approaches are open to interpretation as involving the apparent dismantling of the apparatus of authoritarian bureaucracy in order to ensure the more effectively that the organisation's goals will not be hindered by the sort of conflict and resistance to which *apparent* authority gives rise. But the control of the situation which management exerts is likely to be more total if it has the appearance of being milder; the objective therefore is more control, not less. A feature of many firms in which management techniques of this sort have been employed is that management either does not permit or does not negotiate with trade unions. And the defence of this situation, if defence is believed to be necessary, is that trade-union organisation is really not necessary because (a) terms and conditions of employment are better than in any comparable plant, (b) separate representation of employee interests is unnecessary because management adequately represents the employee's interests, both out of goodwill and out of self-interest.

[1] The pursuit of Theory Y as opposed to Theory X in McGregor's terminology, see *op. cit.*

[2] A. P. Raia, 'Goal Setting and Self Control', *Journal of Management Studies*, February 1965.

[3] For a forthright attack on such devices see Odiorne, *Personnel Policy: Issues and Practice*, Merrill, 1963.

Many of these techniques are 'personnel' techniques and their use represents at one extreme the personnel specialists' competition with trade unions in a workers' representative role. Less extreme and more typical is the personnel specialist who out of amiable but disorganised goodwill has his 'office door always open' and maintains such effective relations with shopfloor workers and union representatives that he has effectively eliminated the unions as an independent force (a general indicator of this state of affairs is management's general and warm appreciation of the helpfulness, maturity and good sense of a particular convenor or shop steward).

The alternative to this unitary frame of reference is that divergencies of interest are a real and inescapable accompaniment of organised work processes, that it is essential for disparate interests to be independently represented and that the most effective instrument of representation so far devised is the trade union. This is the view of the T.U.C.: '. . . the essential characteristic of free trade unions is that they are responsible to the workpeople themselves who comprise their membership and cannot be directed by any outside agency. . . . Neither a benevolent state nor a benevolent employer can provide this means whereby the great variety of circumstances and individual preferences represented in a trade union can be reflected in a collective choice.'[1] But to accept that this degree of independence is good for the membership and good for the political and social health of society at large is one thing, to accept that it is good from the point of view of the ownership and management of a particular industrial enterprise is another. The point is well made by Sherman Krupp: '. . . the needs of organisation cannot provide imperatives for policies in society. Conflict viewed pathologically in organisation may, in a pluralistic society, preserve the distinctive and necessary differences in values. . . . Conflict may be, in its larger setting, not merely the pathological expression of unresolved differences but an imperative in a democratic society where the concentration of authority, of power, is itself a pathology.'[2] The difference in the origin of these two judgments explains why managers in general and perhaps personnel managers in particular will con-

[1] 'Trades Unionism', *op. cit.*, p. 29.
[2] *Pattern in Organisation Analysis, a Critical Examination*, Holt, Rinehart & Winston, 1964, pp. 183–4.

tinue to claim for themselves a representative function which is not justified within the wider context; they seek to represent, not because it is better for the represented, nor because it is better for society, but because it is better for the firm. Managers can be expected, therefore, to engage in role trespass because their representation of employees is a necessary posture for them to strike in their conflict with unions. There are other reasons for competitiveness between unions and personnel specialists. Antagonists, even when their relationships are hostile and bitter, develop a technical mastery of each other's methods and a respect for each other's skills. Personnel specialists are often paid for their 'expert' knowledge of union methods and attitudes; this expertise may encourage a feeling that they represent those for whom they are required to develop a sympathetic understanding; they are no more entitled to represent them than is an ambassador the citizens and officials of a foreign capital.

If there are general problems of representation as between personnel specialists and the trade unions, these problems concern the conflict between the authority of the employer and the challenge to that authority exercised by the unions. There are more specific problems which arise when the personnel specialist exercises functional responsibility in the industrial relations field. In Chapter 4 we outlined some of the factors taken into account by management in determining a wage and salary policy. In the broadest terms these factors could be grouped as economic, technical (in a literal, production-engineering sense), social and tactical (pertaining to the employment relationship itself). The personnel specialists are not equipped, by training, experience or aptitude, to be equally influential in each of these areas. It is indeed particularly dangerous in this context to generalise about the personnel specialist because it seems that those who have developed expertise in some directions have done so at the expense of others. We distinguish later (Chapter 15) between five levels of personnel specialist performance: consultancy; employment forecasting; maintenance; operational; clerical, and we discuss the kinds of training which may be appropriate at each particular level. Industrial relations experts, as the evidence of the C.B.I. suggested,[1] are selected often because of their experience in the commercial and technical aspects of the affairs of the enterprise,

[1] Quoted on p. 37.

and they are employed at the level of maintaining existing employment machinery with the least disturbance to production, subject to the control of costs. It is difficult to avoid the impression that many industrial relations specialists are masters of a range of complex financial, procedural, statistical and technical skills welded together by considerable personal judgment and intelligence, but they often do not see themselves as personnel specialists because they regard personnel management as the concern either of moralists or of would-be social scientists.[1] Mastery of some of the factors which we suggested as being influential not only does not lead necessarily to mastery of the others; they may be even incompatible. The industrial relations specialist who sees himself as commanding a tough, difficult and very complicated job may share the engineer's disrespect for expertise in the social-science field where he sees no quantification, no noticeable skills and a great deal of common sense and goodwill.

It would be dangerous to react by labelling the skills of the industrial relations experts as inadequate and the experts as reactionary. There is so much that is wrong with managerial performance in industrial relations in some British industries that more competence at a maintenance level, the simple introduction of the kind of expertise possessed by industrial relations specialists, would be sufficient to raise performance without seeking more sophisticated solutions. Whether this kind of skill will be sufficient will depend in part on the industry and the firm's situation and of the relative weight and importance of the respective factors we have discussed. There might well be dangers, however, in concluding that the planning of substantive employment policies everywhere required the application of expertise focussed mainly on non-technical and non-commercial factors. Quite apart from Petrie's warnings about the unbusinesslike concentration of personnel professionalism, considerable improvements could be brought about by a management which planned its employment policies as a cohesive, inter-related strategy. But there are two important qualifications. The first is that

[1] This judgment is subjective but there is some evidence to support it. The Collins survey demonstrated that some occupational areas rich in industrial relations specialists had very low membership of the I.P.M. (Crichton and Collins, *op. cit.*)

the expert, whatever his expertise, must win influence over the direction of his enterprise. The second is that expertise in the situation that exists is likely to be inadequate if the current situation is made up of ill-conceived procedures and systems or if the situation is subject to rapid and comprehensive change. It is these last two circumstances which prevent absolute reliance on the industrial relations expert operating at the maintenance level.

The collective bargaining structure set out in Part 2 was described in terms of a polarity between the extremes of the two bargaining organisations, and we suggested that the point of engagement of the personnel specialist between the two poles would influence his behaviour and the kind of expertise he would contribute. To put it more simply, the employing organisation pays its money and takes its choice as to the kind of personnel expertise it gets. One kind of specialist may be a long-term strategist, concerned with business plans and forecasts, and the adjustment of employment policies to meet distant objectives. At this point he is concerned to influence and to change the system rather than to acquire a technical mastery of its complexities; he is more of an innovator than an operator. But others have to run the system and this requires a different expertise. These are the organisation's frontier guards, they are expert tacticians and their skills include an understanding of complex procedures and of the behaviour of their opponents. Their mastery of these skills will limit their ability to innovate or to see the need for innovation. Their own expectations are to some extent limited by the expectations of their opponents, and they may develop an understanding of their opponents which is greater than their understanding of the policy formulators within their own organisations. We suggested that a balance has to be struck, or an internal agreement has to be 'negotiated' between the influence of aspirational optimism and the influence of aspirational rigidity. We shall now look more closely at these specialists.

10 The Development of Personnel Management as a Specialist Activity

The development of personnel management practice has been uneven. It tends to be quite different from one organisation to another although certain general trends can be distinguished. These differences can, to a large extent, be explained by a combination of variables in the particular history of any organisation. We shall go on to examine the general trends in the development of the personnel specialisation later in this section, but first it may be useful to attempt to recapitulate what the variables are which seem to determine differences in practice.

Ideological differences affect the attitudes of managements and unions. Etzioni suggests three main categories of organisation: normative, utilitarian and compulsive.[1] *Normative* organisations are those in which the service ideal prevails, such as in hospitals or social-service agencies and where 'the lower participants', whether clients or low-status staff, are carried along by the committed professional élite. *Utilitarian* organisations such as manufacturing or commercial undertakings expect to get employee cooperation in working towards the objectives of the organisation through financial inducements. In order to increase commitment, employers may also make ideological appeals to their staffs, but some companies are unsuccessful in getting positive cooperation whilst others have built

[1] A. Etzioni, *A Comparative Analysis of Complex Organisations*, Free Press of Glencoe, 1961.

up strong commitment on the part of their labour force. In *compulsive* organisations, such as the army, prisons or other closed communities, the staff know that their orders can be backed up by the imposition of sanctions upon the recalcitrant.

There are few personnel specialists employed in normative or compulsive organisations. Most are found in utilitarian settings. There, managements may take up a number of different positions in dealing with the workpeople in the employment of their companies—these have been listed as traditional–autocratic, benevolent–paternalistic, bureaucratic and participant. The union challenge to management control has been concerned with the increase in participative management. Yet many managers are reluctant to relinquish rights or prerogatives to employees whilst retaining legal responsibility towards the shareholders only. The most extreme position is taken by those companies which refuse to recognise the existence of unions in their plants or, by encouraging staff associations, seek to prevent their employees from joining the ranks of organised labour as a strong force. At the other end of the spectrum is the company which is completely dominated by the restrictions imposed by organised workpeople and which seems to have contracted out of man management by turning over the arrangement of shift and overtime rota planning to the convenor, by accepting for engagement only those union members submitted by the local branch officials, and other activities normally regarded as important management decisions.

In both these instances managements are endeavouring to avoid conflict, yet the absence of conflict may be inappropriate. A certain level of tension is necessary for high productivity—too much or too little may result in confusion or apathy.

Conflict within an organisation may be constructive or destructive, depending on whether the basic assumptions of the opponents are understood and tolerated by both sides and whether there are suitable mechanisms for dealing with the conflict. Fox has argued that many managements fail to understand that the unions will have different basic assumptions from their own.[1] They take the attitude that workpeople's goals are the same as their own and all that is necessary is to weld the different members of the work force into

[1] *op. cit.*, 1967.

one team. Some managements proceed solely by guesswork, intuition and experience; others may endeavour to find an analytic framework for guiding their decision making—three successive orientations of this kind have been described as the 'scientific management', 'human relations' and 'socio-technical systems' schools of thought. In each case different values are brought into the situation and affect attitudes to personnel management.

The unions, too, bring along differing attitudes towards the employers. Political philosophies affect their strategies both in national affairs and in the struggles for participation in ownership and executive decision making in the organisation. They may have to deal with personal rivalries for leadership or apathetic members.

Personnel management practice is not only affected by managements and workpeople's ideologies but also, as Joan Woodward has pointed out, by technological differences.[1] The technology of some industries creates more tensions between management and employees than the technology of other industries and it is very often in the more stormy organisations that the management fails to consult personnel specialists in advance about the effect of changes in technical planning on the social system. In the calmer organisations there is more time to think, to develop preventive action, to discuss problems before they arise. Personnel management practice, then, will vary in different kinds of industry and services in accordance with technological developments. Leonard Sayles has suggested that union attitudes vary with their stage in technological development.[2] The old-established skilled trades display conservatism, the assembly-line workers erratic behaviour, the new technicians are strategists, and the labourers and jobbing workers are apathetic.

Personnel management practice will also vary with the size and complexity of the organisations. Many companies have branches or subsidiaries and there may be many different choices of what activities to decentralise and leave to local initiative and what to keep under close control at headquarters. The traditions developed in the original plant may be transported wholesale when a new branch works is being set up in an area where traditions have been quite

[1] 'Industrial Behaviour—Is there a Science?', *New Society*, 8 October 1964
[2] *Behaviour of Industrial Work Groups*, Wiley, 1958.

different, and sometimes these may be accepted by the local employees, and sometimes they may be resented acutely.

The make-up of the labour force will also affect personnel policies and practices—women and young persons are protected by restrictive legislation, irksome to many employers. Men would seem to constitute a more flexible group of employees, able to do shift work and overtime, whereas women have to be wooed by good working conditions. Yet men are more likely to be organised into unions which impose their own restrictions and which have to be consulted formally by management before changes are initiated. Increasing specialisation in the labour force creates many difficulties in communication, in status rivalry, and so on.

In addition to these differences in technology, size and complexity and the make-up of the labour force within the plant itself, there are differences in the setting. There are traditional differences in attitudes to work in different geographical areas which stem from the experiences of workpeople during the industrial revolution and from subsequent developments—Wales is well-known for its high absence rate, Lancashire for its highly organised working women—we could go on elaborating these area differences. Some of the new employers moving into development areas have inherited difficult problems of managing workpeople because of the resistance set up by the behaviour of their predecessors. There are also local differences in social structure which have to be considered and different attitudes to social class. Some companies are better at adapting to changes in social structure than are others.

The state has been concerned about the provision of *minimum standards* of working conditions for women and young persons for over a century, but the Factory Inspectors' mandate has been to try to encourage companies to provide more than the minimum, and the men have been carried along by this tide. The state, anxious not to intervene in the collective bargaining process if it could be avoided, nevertheless had to legislate for the 'sweated trades' to have minimum rates of pay. More recently, employers have been obliged to provide written contracts and to compensate redundant workers. *Normative standards* are established by collective bargaining processes. The state has, however, been concerned in recent years about the low level of the norms which are acceptable in bargaining. The

Carr Committee examined the problem of training for skills and suggested that both sides of industry should give consideration to the country's need for more skilled workers.[1] The collective bargaining mechanisms proved too slow and legislation was brought in to force the pace. *Optimum standards* are clearly different in different organisations, and attempts are being made to disseminate information about better methods of diagnosis and treatment of problems, and to provide examples of good practice. We shall go on to discuss the role of the personnel specialist in developing optimum standards.

It would be unwise to ignore the influence of outstanding personalities in the development of personnel management practice. These may be personnel specialists or they may be general managers working to bring about changes in their employing organisations, or they may be active in management professional associations or in academic posts. Some organizations are more concerned with personnel problems than others which are more interested in technical matters or marketing.

Having listed some of the variables affecting personnel management practice we can now go on to look at general trends in historical development.

DEVELOPMENTS UP TO THE SECOND WORLD WAR

Gradually, during the nineteenth century, employers began to discover that effective management of an enterprise required specialisation and delegation of responsibility. Although control of staff or management of personnel was delegated to subordinates, the functional specialisation, personnel management, was not separated out till the late nineteenth century.

The earliest kinds of personnel specialisation were, in fact, not intra-mural but carried on by people outside the organisation—on the one hand, officials of employers' associations become the authorities on collective bargaining and, on the other, self-conscious welfare work was first started in the communities around the factories with the families of employees, and it was only later on that

---

[1] Ministry of Labour and National Service, *Training for Skill*: Report by a sub-committee of the National Joint Advisory Council, H.M.S.O., 1958.

his activity was brought inside the plants themselves. These two spects of personnel work developed separately at first and it was ot until very much later that they began to be thought of as two elated aspects of maintaining the organisations.

Gradually, the larger companies had found that it was necessary o develop a department within the organisation which kept records f staff, information from which could be made readily available for eneral reference and in case of disputes. This personal records file night be linked to the wages office records files for rationalisation of lerical work or it might be kept separately in the employment office. Employment officers had begun to be appointed to help the super-isors with recruitment and sometimes with interviewing of new taff. The men's employment officers of the larger companies ustomarily kept the records of agreements and were able to advise nanagement about precedents where cases were straightforward. It vas only when shop-floor negotiations failed and precedents could tot be found, that the employers' association was called in to con-luct a works conference. Procedures were developed to try to ensure hat, where possible, settlements would take place on the shop floor. Gradually this records officer became consulted more and more bout the conduct of negotiations and in some companies he was sked to act as the agent of the company in bargaining. When new ppointments were made in smaller companies, union officials might e offered posts as personnel specialists because of their experience n negotiating.

At the same time there had grown up a number of welfare depart-nents in the companies which had a particular concern for their mployees. At the beginning no one was very clear about their func-ion, but there were two main reasons for appointing women welfare vorkers. During the last decade of the nineteenth century, the vomen Factory Inspectors urged yet again the importance of em-ploying a senior woman where there were women employees, be-ause since the mid-century they had seen the benefits of appointing vomen supervisors to watch over 'the health and morals' of women nd young persons. The Factory and Workshops Act, 1901, laid new mphasis on 'welfare', by which was meant improved physical tandards in the workshop—better facilities for making tea and ating food without contamination, proper sanitation, provision of

cloakrooms or coat-racks and standardisation of those other aspect
of working conditions which are today taken for granted by factor
workers (although they have only recently been made compulsor
for shops, offices and railway premises)—heating, lighting, cleaning
and fire precautions.

Welfare work and welfare facilities began to be brought into th
factory when it was realised that family welfare often began with
the bread-winner's relationships in work. As well, some employer
had for some time been providing community services such a
housing, meeting halls and recreation grounds. So, when industria
welfare workers were appointed they took on personal counsellin
and responsibility for organising employee services such as recreatio
clubs, canteens and benevolent funds.

The women welfare workers had considerable difficulty in align
ing their objectives with those of the rest of management in man
organisations. Niven has collected accounts of the early stages of th
work of some of these so-called 'pioneers'[1] (this very descriptiv
noun gives an indication of the way in which they saw their task,
Their training alongside intending social workers in universit
courses was not a well-integrated course of preparation. Fieldwor
emphasised the practical skills of personal counselling but theor
was not closely related. It was concerned with social economics an
social philosophy until, later on, courses in industrial psycholog
were introduced. It is perhaps no wonder, then, that welfare wor
and social reform were not clearly separated in their minds. I
consequence, the industrial welfare workers had great difficulty i
managing their roles. Some became too actively 'the conscience c
management', urging reforms which were not acceptable to thei
colleagues. Yet this was hardly surprising given the vague terms c
reference with which many began. Niven recounts one anecdot
which is very telling. A woman welfare worker was appointed to
tin box works. This was a new appointment and she was to repor
to one of the directors, who stressed the necessity for improvin
standards among the girls employed there. The symbol for this ne
era was to be white tablecloths in the canteen and these were dul
provided. The welfare worker could not understand why the cloth
became grubby round the edges but never on top, so she watche

[1] M. M. Niven, *Personnel Management: 1913–63*, I.P.M., 1967.

the girls and found that they brought so little to eat that they were
not prepared to unwrap it on the tables but preferred to keep it on
their laps. From then on she began to see that she had to be concerned with rates of pay and security of employment if she were to
make an effective contribution to raising the girls' standards. Yet
this had not been envisaged in deciding to appoint a welfare
worker.

The women welfare workers were, at first, recruited from the
middle classes. They were graduates or otherwise well-educated,
and interested in the world of work. They had a strong conviction
that they would improve the lot of industrial employees by inter-
ceding for them with their employers. Yet there were some doubts.
How could the women welfare workers really understand how women
on the shop floor thought and felt when they were so different in
social class and education? This led to one resolution at least that
more candidates from working-class backgrounds should be recruited into social studies courses.[1] There was little change in the
background of recruits, however, until the Second World War because of shortage of scholarships for working-class students.

The men, who had begun to assist in preparing cases for collective
bargaining in the plants for the employers' associations' representatives, had come up the hard way from the shop floor or from being
office boys. Their general approach was different from that of the
women welfare workers and they usually had the ear of different
levels in the management hierarchy—the women might be on home-
visiting terms with the managing director and might report to one
of the directors, whilst the men expected to work to the works
manager and with the foremen. It was not until after the Second
World War that men had suitable opportunities for taking personnel
management courses at universities. These differences in basic
education and social class made for a number of communication
difficulties which have taken years to work through in some companies
and in the 'professional' group which was started by the women. In
consequence, many of the more advanced firms had separate
specialisations within the personnel function marked off for men
and women.

[1] Joint University Council for Social Studies and Public Administration,
publication on training, 1921.

Gradually, as a group, the industrial welfare workers began to clarify their objects and their methods of attaining them. The limited effectiveness of the personal counsellor and organiser of employee services was quickly realised, so they struggled to find other jobs to do for management which would entitle them to a place in the management team, in order that they would be brought in on discussions of importance such as the determination of wage rates or the deployment of staff (which in times of depression often meant short-time working for many). They were not very successful in getting in on these discussions for all their efforts and despite their willingness to take on many other jobs. Perhaps they took on too many—a number of personnel departments today are burdened with responsibility for cleaners, security men, fire services, etc., which pin them down with routine tasks that are a hindrance to their need for time to think. The welfare workers set up first-aid services and claimed to have special expertise on legislation connected with health, safety and welfare; they developed skills in administering benevolent funds, canteens and recreation clubs; they recruited and selected women employees and helped the supervisors with disciplinary matters. They became interested in the education and training of young workers, for, since there was less opportunity for the well-motivated and intelligent boy or girl to get into secondary or further education before 1944 than there is now, they believed they must try to help them to develop their talents either within the organisation or by making use of such educational facilities as were available from the W.E.A. or extramural classes.

A number of men welfare workers were appointed during and immediately after the war. Niven says: 'It was as men came out of the forces back to their old firms, having been officers and accustomed to greater responsibility than their [old] jobs required of them, that many became apprentice supervisors or welfare superintendents. As the boys became skilled men the supervisor's influence extended, for he was now led into the life of the whole factory by virtue of knowing the men in it—so the nature of his work developed. . . . The work of the women could not develop in quite the same way since they had no-one to train for wider fields.'[1] Hyde

[1] M. M. Niven, private communication.

he founder of the Industrial Society (1919–), was particularly nterested in the welfare of young men in industry.

Women have rarely been involved in bargaining although many ave been active in promoting joint consultation. Where there have een only women personnel specialists, bargaining has usually been arried out by one of the senior line managers supported by experts rom the employers' association. This may, of course, happen also vhen there are men personnel specialists, for line managers often eem to be more readily prepared to delegate responsibilities in ther aspects of the personnel function than they are to let go of argaining. Despite the fact that they were normally excluded from argaining it is important to consider the contribution of the welfare vorkers, because they were very influential in determining the de-elopment of personnel management as a specialisation in terms of deology and in range and depth of work.

Despite the increase in the range of their activities during the irst 40 years of the twentieth century, and despite the favourable osition which many of the earlier welfare workers had, by virtue of heir appointment by a member of top management, nevertheless hey felt themselves to be peripheral 'outsiders'. The history of the ersonnel specialists as a group is the history of a struggle for status –to become full members of the management team—for only by so loing did it seem possible to align their goals with those of the rganisation. (Perhaps more truly for some of the pioneers this cceptance by the group would have enabled them to try to align he goals of the organisation with their goals.) Since they were sel-lom successful in getting in on the inside the alternative was to per-uade the top management to adopt a written personnel policy, to levelop a series of agreed personnel practices. By quoting from these greements or citing precedents they were able to work for con-istent standards. They claimed to be advisers only but in many ubtle ways they were able to exert control over their colleagues.

The first specialist personnel activities, bargaining and welfare vork, can hardly be regarded as central to personnel management s it is now perceived, but, as has been suggested, other work had egun to be added. In 1943 Moxon listed the functions of a person-el department under six headings: *employment, education and raining, wages, negotiation and consultation, health and safety*, and *employee services.*[1] The employment sector of the work was developed first, partly in order to assist other managers with recruitment, partly as part of the struggle by the personnel specialists to win a foothold. During the inter-war years advances in industrial psychology led to the development of selection techniques, but these were used in only a few firms—most companies could afford to make mistakes in picking employees during the depression. There are obvious advantages in centralising advertising and the making of contacts with employment agencies, but it did not seem to be very necessary to rationalise this activity until the pressures of full employment drove companies into doing so. Some companies found it necessary to provide fairly extensive training schemes for skilled workers, and by the beginning of the Second World War the need for supervisory training was starting to be recognised. It was given great impetus during the war by the importation of the T.W.I scheme from America on a lease-lend arrangement.

The claim to take responsibility for wages administration was perhaps the most excessive because the activities of the personnel specialists in this sector of work were limited. Rate fixing for piece workers or workers on incentive bonus schemes normally took place outside the personnel department in production planning or cost departments or was regarded as a function of the foreman. The introduction of time-study schemes linked piece-work or bonus payments even more closely to production, so that the personnel department might only negotiate basic rates, cost of living increment or other additions not closely linked to the daily job. The personnel specialist was expected to make external comparisons on pay and other benefits (which at that time were restricted mainly to salaried staff), whilst internal differences were settled by agreement in the works, usually without reference to the personnel department unless some point in dispute became a matter for extensive collective bargaining. Although personnel specialists tried to urge their special knowledge about incentives, financial and non-financial, they were not consulted about these in most companies. Nor did they have a say in the matter of earnings rather than rates, for overtime was also at the departmental managers' discretion, as was the

[1] G. R. Moxon, *Functions of a Personnel Department*, Institute of Personnel Management, 1943.

allocation of 'good jobs' and 'bad jobs'. They became, perhaps, experts in disincentives rather than incentives, as they were expected to deal with disturbances to smooth working—evidences of discontent such as alleged victimisation, work stoppages or go-slows, strikes and lockouts, labour turnover, absences and lateness.

STAFF MANAGEMENT

So far the discussion has been about *labour management* in British industry. Personnel work began with a concern for manual workers whether as individuals or when grouped together to bargain collectively. It was not until the inter-war period that this concern was extended to 'staff'. At this time 'staff' were not often organised in trade unions. They had many more privileges than workpeople and much greater security. However, they did require more careful selection and training for these reasons. By 1934 there were enough specialists in *staff management* to want to form their own association. These staff managers were employed mainly in London and mainly in department stores and offices servicing the very large manufacturing companies. There are, of course, large numbers of staff employees in the Civil Service, local government and other service organisations, such as hospitals and prisons. The development of personnel management practice in these organisations has been quite different from that of industry, partly because the majority of employees are staff—manual workers are in the minority—partly because they are public services and the controlling government behind them has had great influence on the adoption of certain different ideologies. These are a few examples: the concept of the administrator as a man who should not be an expert in anything but the art of administration has led to the almost complete absence of long-term functional specialist appointments; the concept of setting an example in personnel management led to the establishment of Whitley Councils after the report of the Whitley Committee in 1918, and to tough restrictions on increments in wages and salaries in times of economic stress; the concept of decentralisation has led to the leaving of as much discretion as possible to many local units to make their own arrangements about staffing, whilst at the same time the concept of centralisation is applied to recruitment into the Civil Service and to salary policies for all the services directly controlled by government departments.

In consequence, it becomes difficult to discuss the concept of a personnel specialist in the public services. In the centralised Civil Service, in theory at any rate, such office holders can be promoted after a short period. Their orientation is not towards a career in personnel management but a career in administration. In practice, many stay for long periods in personnel specialists' posts as bargainers, training officers, welfare officers, establishment officers. In the decentralised local authorities there are some appointments of establishment officers who are responsible for recruitment and selection of clerical staff, but most administrative, professional and technical appointments are made either by the elected representatives themselves or by their senior professional officers.

THE WAR PERIOD, 1939–45, AND SUBSEQUENT DEVELOPMENTS

Like the First World War, when there was an extraordinary growth in the number of personnel specialists and in the range of work they were asked to do, the period 1939–45 can be taken as a watershed in the history of personnel management. The Second World War brought considerable changes in the ideology of our society; the levelling experience of the bombs, rationing, conscription and service overseas or in munitions factories and mines changed attitudes to industrial welfare work. It came to be felt, in the new egalitarian climate, that any remnants of a middle-class philanthropic approach to personnel work were no longer appropriate. Workpeople themselves should be quite capable of running their own welfare programmes, possibly with some administrative help, and the Welfare State providing 'equality of opportunity' in education, a comprehensive health service and, above all, full employment, should remove the necessity to make interventions on behalf of individual employees with social needs, for more education should make people more articulate and better informed about services available to them.

During the war the terms *labour management* and *staff management* which had come to be accepted in the late 1920s and 1930s had been dropped in favour of *personnel management* to indicate a new concern for both industrial and staff employees. Since the war there has been a move towards reducing the difference between industrial and staff status. It was thought to be unreasonable, by some influential pace-setting employers, that a skilled man with many years' service should have less entitlement to holidays, sick pay, pension and other fringe benefits than the young office staff, and some schemes were introduced to grant staff status to long-service manual workers. A number of pre-war staff 'privileges' were incorporated into manual workers' contracts through collective bargaining, although the unions seem less enthusiastic about staff status than one would have expected, and more recently legislation has provided greater security for all grades of workers through the Contracts of Employment and Redundancy Payments Acts.

On the other hand, more white-collar workers are becoming organised in trade unions, so that employers have had to reconsider their personnel policies for clerical and executive staff and particularly their salary policies. The old methods of individual bargaining no longer seem appropriate or satisfying for many clerks, technicians or professional staff. Managements have been under pressure to give recognition to white-collar unions, whose techniques in bargaining have often been very different from the traditional manual workers' unions' techniques. Salary policies have also had to be reconsidered in the light of greatly increased earnings of manual workers.

It took a long time to get used to the idea of continuing full employment. Perhaps most affected by this were first-line supervisors and middle managers who found they needed to learn more subtle ways of managing staff than the old hire-and-fire methods. Personnel specialists were called in to train them in human relations skills—in how to select, train and counsel employees and, particularly, how to deal with discipline. In recent years, this simple wholesale approach to supervisory training has been criticised for not bearing a close enough relationship to supervisors' real needs, but it was an important step forward for personnel specialists to move from planning operative and apprentice training (which emphasise manual skills) into organising courses and quite often providing teaching themselves for supervisors.

Since the industrial revolution British workpeople have struggled for a share in the ownership of industry and a share in its management. A number of private-enterprise organisations developed co-partnership, share-distribution or profit-sharing schemes in order to meet criticisms about the shareholders being profiteers at the expense of employees. These schemes were normally developed by the company secretary and accountant working together. When employers and unions later switched their interest from such direct profit-sharing to other schemes, usually known as 'fringe benefits', which seemed more relevant to employees (because the expression was in their terms, not shareholders' terms), the same company specialists continued to work out the mechanism of the schemes. The personnel specialists were seldom asked for their considered advice and at meetings sponsored by bodies such as the Industrial Society the attendance was mainly by these other experts. On the other hand, when fringe benefits became a matter for detailed bargaining the personnel specialists were involved, but working within the limits set by the board and its financial advisers. These large payments necessitate high-level policy decisions. It would appear that these are often made without taking into consideration the opinions of personnel specialists.

In 1946 the first 'nationalisation' scheme was put into operation for coal and during the next few years other basic industries were taken over by the state. The unions' challenge to management control on ownership would seem to have moderated. There would now seem to be no clear policy about further nationalisation, co-partnership or co-determination emerging from national-level discussions, and the members themselves appear to be more satisfied with increasing wages and fringe benefits than by urging profit-sharing schemes.

The challenge on participation in running the business has also been put to the test when the mechanics of sharing in policy making and of executive control have had to be worked out. To what extent could the unions and non-union members be involved in policy making; how could policy decisions be communicated intelligibly to the man on the shop floor? Experience of wartime absentee committees had confirmed the unions in their intention not to become associated with management in day-to-day formal disciplining of workpeople. Their decision to remain 'the permanent opposition' has meant that there has had to be a reconsideration of the meaning of industrial democracy or government by consent.

Much of the running about employees' involvement in policy making was made in the nationalised industries. The Nationalisation Acts provided for joint consultation to be established in these industries, and the Ministry of Labour campaigned to encourage private-enterprise firms to set up joint consultation committees. In most organisations the machinery of joint consultation became the responsibility of the personnel specialist. But understanding how to establish the best kind of agenda content in order to develop the processes of consultation and communication has been very difficult. Research into the breadth and depth of joint consultation has not encouraged complacency about finding easy answers and, indeed, has raised the question about whether joint consultation is the right kind of answer to the problem of realising an industrial democracy.[1] Some companies which have tried to involve their workpeople's representatives in making major policy decisions have found that they have expected too much—the workpeople considered that management was paid to take such risks as making major investment decisions in new product lines. In other companies joint consultation led to considerable complaints about undermining executive responsibility when foremen or grievance procedures were bypassed.

'Human relations' research has suggested other ways of improving communications and increasing employee involvement: job-enlargement schemes, more supervisory training, development of a better understanding of organisational roles among managers may be alternatives to the more formal committee mechanisms. Formal committee discussions were found to be no substitute for good informal communication.

Clegg and others have argued that joint consultation alongside negotiation is unnecessary.[2] The real concerns of workpeople are expressed by their negotiators in bargaining. By excluding any discussion of terms and conditions of employment in joint consultation the remaining issues are bound to be peripheral in interest to work-

[1] National Institute of Industrial Psychology, *Joint Consultation in British Industry*, Staples Press, 1952; E. Jaques, *The Changing Culture of a Factory*, Tavistock, 1951.
[2] H. Clegg, *A New Approach to Industrial Democracy*, Blackwell, 1960.

people and are management's concerns rather than those of work-people. Yet it is also recognised that the structure of British unions does create a need for a committee to settle matters of concern to all employees in one plant, such as holiday dates, and also that the unions have not been successful in following through the Whitley recommendations that workpeople should be just as concerned as management with the future of the organisation over the long term. Joint consultative committees appear to fill certain gaps if they work well.

By the mid-1950s the range of personnel work had become well-recognised and, although it had been suggested that to the Moxon analysis of sub-specialisations there might be added communication and possibly organisation analysis, it came to be seen that these were embodied in the other six specialist sectors and that it was the depth rather than the range of work which was now being extended. By now, the inter-relationship of the various aspects of personnel work was beginning to be better understood but, despite this, a number of companies had developed only one or two limited specialist activities. There were reasons for this: partly it was a question of perceiving what needed to be done, partly often a matter of historical accident about delegation of work, so that different parts of the personnel management function were distributed among a number of widely separated departments. (In a recent research project Crichton, Hamblin and Lawson found that the so-called personnel manager of one company dealt with office staff and apprentices; the assistant personnel manager and safety officer dealt with works recruitment, safety and general advice to foremen, but more or less independently of the personnel manager as he had been there for many years; the accountant was responsible for welfare schemes, the works manager for bargaining.)[1]

THE 1960S

In 1964 Forman summarised the major developments and changes in the personnel function during the previous 10 years:

    (a)   *wider recognition of the function* as an integral part of manage-

[1] Anne Crichton, A. C. Hamblin, R. J. Lawson, unpublished study of 'The Occupational Role of the Personnel Officer' (1962–4).

ment with emphasis on achieving optimum results from the human resources of the business; wider scope accorded to the function; improvement in the status accorded to the Head of Department; greater concern with policy as distinct from routine and executive tasks; extension of responsibility to the field of planning as distinct from operational activity;

(b) *greater concern with labour policy* and less with detailed matters of labour management; greater delegation to line and departmental management for dealing with negotiations at shop-floor level and with relationships and disciplinary matters at this level accompanied by growing competence and interest of the new generation of professionally trained managers to implement a stated policy without frequent intervention and assistance by the personnel specialist in the course of day-to-day administration; new dimensions of the industrial relations field—National Incomes Policy and industrial legislation, the role of Trade Unions, of employers' organisations and of the Government (and Ministry of Labour in particular) in this context; positive bargaining closely geared to the primary objectives of the enterprise;

(c) *the shift of emphasis towards staff management*; the reasons for this including:
   (i) the growth in absolute numbers and in proportion of white-collar workers;
   (ii) the growth of staff unionisation;
   (iii) the diminution of difference in pay, conditions and status between staff and wage earners;
   (iv) in relation to senior staffs, the growing recognition of the vital importance of securing high standards of management and personnel and performance; the addition of new dimensions of the function, e.g. the analysis, description and evaluation of the great variety of work done by staff at all levels; salary structure and administration; the task of recruiting, training and developing managers;

(d) *planning* management succession and manpower deployment as a basis for management development, retraining programmes and budgeting;

(e) *increasing involvement of the personnel function with organisation structure and communication*, both of which concern people in every function of management and at all levels and, in so far as responsibility for these matters falls to any of the specialist functions, it rests with personnel; furthermore:

(i)   organisation sets the basic pattern of relationships and if it is not soundly conceived it will set a limit on the extent of attainable co-operation and effectiveness;

(ii) communication and media are themselves important to the operation of the Personnel Department, of other departments and units and the enterprise as a whole; but concern with communication goes far beyond media and involves acceptance of the need to communicate; the root of this is motivation—of individuals and groups, which calls for study and understanding and the Personnel Department should be equipped (if necessary with outside help) to undertake such study and to achieve the necessary understanding for action; all this relates closely to elements of management and other training, as well as to the basis of personnel policy itself.[1]

Since this was written we have, perhaps, become more aware of the implications of the new legislation or new government activity in the 1960s. Since the war there has been acknowledgment of the need to stimulate British industry in a competitive world. Advice and admonition have proved to be too slow to achieve the improvements in the standards of management necessary for an advanced industrial country and both political parties have begun to bring in legislation in order to back advice with sanctions.

In the '60s new legislation to raise minimum standards has been brought in, the Contracts of Employment Act, 1963; the Redundancy Payments Act, 1966; the Offices, Shops and Railway Premises Act, 1963; and revisions to social security schemes to improve sick pay and unemployment insurance benefits. These Acts, whilst affording protection to individual employees, also increase the prospects for getting greater mobility of labour.

[1] M. B. Forman, first thoughts presented to the Publications, Information and Research Committee of the Institute of Personnel Management for revision of the Moxon pamphlet, to be entitled, *The Functions and Organisation of a Personnel Department*, current working papers mimeographed, I.P.M., 1964. Forman emphasises that this is one individual's interpretation rather than a collective view of the situation.

A national manpower planning programme has been begun in order that the labour force may be put to better use. This is linked to a revised educational programme which should increase the supply of technologists and technicians coming out of institutions of higher education. The Industrial Training Act, 1964, enforces industry's co-operation in this programme of increasing the supply of skills, through setting up Industrial Training Boards.

The Prices and Incomes Board, which was established to try to control certain aspects of inflation, has not only made recommendations in its report about how much an award should be, but it has also attempted to argue the case for better management in order to increase productivity, and has made suggestions about the methods which might be used to increase labour effectiveness in certain occupations.

Later we shall go on to discuss the impact of these new national boards upon the personnel specialist.

Development in Industrial Relations
and Development of the Personnel Specialist

1   Established Facts

The difficulty in defining a personnel specialist was explored in a survey addressed to employers in South Wales in 1963.[1] We have already reproduced the list of job titles which emerged from this survey on pages 12–13. In the seven counties of South-east Wales and Monmouthshire, Collins located 299 organisations employing 200 or more workpeople.[2] 254 (85 per cent) responded listing 2,274 specialists. Collins divided these into two groups of 585 and 1,689 respectively. Group A (585) he called the *technologists* and Group B (1,689), the *technicians*. The technicians were employed on a narrow and very specific range of duties; the technologists were those who might be considered to be 'building and maintaining the organisation'. (Since the *technicians* were not employed in collective bargaining activities we shall confine the rest of this discussion to the *technologists*.)

Collins suggests that when allowances are made for differences in the distribution of industry in Wales and the rest of the United Kingdom it can be argued that there are approximately 13,500 Group A type personnel specialists in the United Kingdom as a whole. This can be compared with 2,600 full-time trade union officials and between 120,000 and 200,000 shop stewards.

[1] Anne Crichton and R. G. Collins, *op. cit.*
[2] Collins also had the problem of preparing a full list of employing organisations in South Wales—he had to resort to directories of public-service organisations to supplement the Ministry of Labour's list of industrial and commercial employers.

The responses to the questionnaire indicate that most personne officers are employed on general duties and are not considered to specialists within the function. In Group A there were 365: 62·4 p cent in general personnel work; 57: 9·8 per cent in industri relations; 37: 6·3 per cent welfare officers; and 126: 21·5 per ce training technologists. (The survey was conducted before the impl mentation of the Industrial Training Act which may have shifte the balance since then.)

57 per cent of these people were working in organisations en ploying more than 2,000 staff (which made up 17 per cent of tl respondents); 12 per cent were employed in organisations employi less than 500 employees (46 per cent of respondents); 101 organis tions did not employ Group A type specialists but 70 of these ha less than 500 employees.[1]

The degree of specialisation within personnel work was highe in mining and metal manufacturing. Public administration and d fence, engineering and electrical, chemicals and textiles had a hi ratio of general personnel officers. These were often working alon side specialist training officers. The specialist industrial relatio officers were most frequently found in metal manufacturing a mining. Collins argued that the tradition of the engineering indust was that bargaining was done by line managers and, therefore, the was not the same pressure for industrial relations specialists emerge.

There were 47 single-handed personnel officers; seven of these organisations employing more than 1,000. They were numerica most significant in food, drink and tobacco, construction and 'othe industries, although they were also to be found in metal manufa turing, engineering and metal goods.

A number of difficulties emerged during the preparation of tl questionnaire and in sorting out the responses:

(a)   Instructions to respondents mentioned: employment; neg tiation and consultation; health, safety and welfare; employ services and training, as personnel functions. Wages admini tration, personnel research, organisational analysis and con munications were not specially mentioned.

[1] Collins points out that many of these were small engineering works department stores (often co-operative shops).

It was decided, arbitrarily, to give instructions to include safety officers and medical staff but to exclude security and catering staffs unless these had any other personnel duties.

Secretarial and clerical staff were to be excluded. This posed a difficult problem of demarcation—when does a secretary count as a personnel specialist? There are many women employees in personnel departments who carry out responsible activities such as engagement of clerical and manual women workers, maintain custody of records and initiate reviews of senior staff salaries, organise recreational facilities, and also type letters and keep minutes of meetings. Junior personnel executives may have more restricted access to confidential information and less opportunity to exert influence.

)) The public services did not consider that the questionnaire fitted their situation. It was argued that the job titles were unsuitable, that they did not employ personnel specialists but only general administrators or executive officers who might have a specialist personnel management role for some part of their career. (13 out of 77 organisations employing over 1,000 staff said they did not have specialists and most of these were in public administration or defence.)

c)) Large numbers of staff employed in personnel work were not included, e.g. nurse tutors, because no-one thought of them as personnel specialists at the time. Other organisations included line or functional managers with very part-time responsibilities for personnel activities. It is thought that many of these difficulties of perception occurred in the public services.

The survey raised a number of general questions to which the answers are not known:

1)) What might be the most efficient combination of general and specialist personnel work?

b)) The emergence of large numbers of training officers was changing the balance of personnel departments. How best could the status rivalry between these new training officers and other personnel specialists be managed? Should training specialists be trained first as general personnel specialists or as training specialists only?

(c)   Little was known about career patterns of personnel specialists
At what stages in life did they do personnel work? Did man
stay in this work as a long-term career or was it mainly
transitional job? It was difficult to answer questions about th
right kind of training without knowing more about this.

(d)   Titles gave no real clue to authority and responsibility—wha
in fact was the job content, range and depth of work?

A survey carried out in South Wales may be dismissed by many a
being atypical, but this is not thought to be so. Although any non
metropolitan survey tends to miss the head offices of the large
companies, and, as well, there are bound to be traditional are
differences—in Wales an extra emphasis on mining and met
manufacturing and an absence of small businesses—yet there ar
advantages in looking at a development area such as South Wale
because most of the larger employing organisations established sinc
the mid-1930s are branches or subsidiaries of nationally well-know
companies.

THE OCCUPATIONAL ROLE OF THE PERSONNEL OFFICER

A study in depth carried out at the same time as the Collins surve
by Crichton, Hamblin and Lawson, examined the personnel depart
ments of 15 manufacturing plants in South-east Wales and Mon
mouthshire.[1] It had been hoped to see 20, i.e. one-third of the 6
companies employing 500 or more employees (chosen on a stratifie
sample), but the researchers were unable to complete this numbe
It was found that only one of the 15 companies had its head office i
Monmouthshire (with subsidiaries elsewhere); the other 14 wer
branches of companies with headquarters in London, Birmingha
and Manchester.[2] This would seem to indicate a certain reliabilit
about the findings of the study in breadth reported above so far a
manufacturing companies and public administration and th
nationalised industries are concerned.

This second survey which was carried out by means of case studi

[1] Crichton, Hamblin, Lawson, *op. cit.*

[2] The other five companies which we were unable to visit seemed in no wa
very different. They too were branches of nationally known companies.

as not yet been written up except in respect of the training special-sation.[1] Hamblin has shown that the general personnel officers who were not specialists in training but who were responsible for it did not spend much time in thinking about training problems or initiate much action. They were involved in the detail of day-to-day living, meeting needs as they seemed to emerge, dealing with local crises or pressures from headquarters.

The daily activities, for many, centred round the employment function—recruitment and selection, follow-up of absentees and bad time-keepers, resignations and, occasionally, redundancies. There were also recurrent regular activities (which some resented fiercely) such as preparation of statistics for the Ministry of Labour or the Central Personnel Department, or the organisation of meetings of joint consultative, suggestions or safety committees. Some spent a good deal of time on the shop floor with foremen and with the con-venor or they visited colleagues in the management team in their offices for general discussion. It was easier for them to have casual conversation with the foremen than with other managers shut away in offices, so they were better able to cope with this method of work-ing at first-line-management and higher-management levels rather than with middle managers whose time was more tightly scheduled and whose paper work kept them at their desks. Many seemed to prefer a pairing relationship to joining in a group discussion, for example on production problems.

In at least five of the 15 plants, the company had prided itself on an 'advanced' personnel policy during the war period. At that time the management had gone to great lengths to establish 'good' ad-ministrative procedures to implement the board's policy.[2] The personnel departments were stuck with these procedures 20 years later, frozen in time, for what had been 'advanced' then was no longer so. How, then, could change be brought about? Much de-pended on the amount of centralised control and the initiative coming from the head office, or the discretion allowed to the local personnel specialists to develop their own plans for change. This was often linked to tight or loose control over bargaining. There

---

[1] A. C. Hamblin, Training Supplement: *Personnel Management*, March 1966.
[2] The importance of establishing policies and procedures in order to establish the personnel specialists' 'legitimate' power will be discussed in the next section.

were plenty of tensions between headquarters and the plants, particularly when someone else at headquarters had become alarmed at the conservative nature of personnel work and had decided to stir things up by setting up a Central Training Department alongside the Central Personnel Department, in order to develop movement in one sector of personnel work. Where there was an inactive or non-existent central personnel department, or where the local managers were strong enough to resist intervention from central servicing departments, the local management found its own level. This could be very far back or very far ahead in the history of developments in the personnel management function. In one company the local manager had just decided that he would need to appoint one of the company's management trainees as personnel specialist to set up a department, because the introduction of the Contracts of Employment Act, 1963, required more careful record keeping. This company (food-processing industry) was unionised but the manager had, until then, been able to control the 500 staff himself. In another process plant the personnel specialist was appointed in the mid-1950s from the police force to deal with security matters. He had taken over all personnel functions and true to his initial training he saw his job as one of peace-keeping. The company was unionised but the pressures from the unions were inconsiderable, the market was expanding and there was little or no pressure of competition. The elaborate training scheme for young employees concentrated on citizenship courses, the welfare schemes were lavish, the frame of reference was benevolent paternalism.

It might have been thought that the newly established companies would have a better chance to get away from tradition and start afresh, but, of course, this is impossible. The workpeople bring with them their attitudes to work, the managers carry over their values from their previous experiences in life. In South-east Wales and Monmouthshire workpeople are not unduly militant but they are knowledgeable about their rights and have developed practices to protect themselves which managements must accept or negotiate to change. We studied two companies about two years after their establishment on greenfield site when they had just moved into the productive stage. In the one case the general manager and his personnel specialists had tried to develop personnel policies in line with a new technology and enlightened democratic values. In the other the general manager was determined to be tough. His second personnel manager had only recently arrived when we were there; the first who had taken a personnel management course was unable to provide the service thought to be necessary, the second had no training but long experience of bargaining, and a complicated triangular relationship between general manager, central personnel department and local personnel specialist had begun to be worked out. The second personnel man has now moved on too.

We have seen both general managers brushed aside by later events as the companies moved more into the middle, for the one was ahead of his times (and shareholders put on pressure), the other behind (and the central personnel department stepped in here). The experience of these two plants shows the difficulty there is in competitive and highly unionised companies to find enough time to work out personnel policies and practices in isolation at plant level. Today organisations are not closed social systems (if they ever were) but are subjected to many pressures, not the least being time.

The personnel specialists themselves could be divided into four groups: those who had qualified through experience; graduates; graduates in the social sciences; and those with personnel management training. It did not seem to us that courses in personnel management had been very helpful to those who had taken them but, of course, some had taken them quite a long time ago, before the behavioural sciences had developed to the extent that they have today. Those who had been introduced to the behavioural sciences were impatient (and most appeared unintegrated into their employing organisations), since they could not see how best they could use their knowledge. Others had not really understood what were the implications of the courses they took for personnel work. South Wales did not seem to have attracted its fair share of the more intelligent and acceptable personnel management diploma holders, for Wales has always exported men with initiative.

Education in the social sciences was clearly considered by employers to be much less important than personal acceptability. Some senior personnel men regarded people who had been on courses with great suspicion because they had no business tool-kit when they emerged and they had a student's approach to work—too casual-seeming and with different standards about a full day's work. The emergent students, then, had to fit in with the organisation's expectations of them, to accept the structure of the personnel department which they joined or be written off as 'too academic'.[1]

Did the well-staffed departments do more analysing? Use more theory? Get better results? These questions are difficult to answer but we can cite an example. In one well-staffed personnel department, decentralisation had enabled the personnel specialists to provide a service which responded quickly to local expression of needs. The central personnel department was small and was mainly concerned with presenting data to the board and obtaining financial resources for the plant personnel departments. The department which was studied had endeavoured to keep up with the times since its inception in 1946, and it was clear that where it had failed (and here an injudicious decision to establish a merit-rating scheme fashionable about 1949, a high absentee rate, and a lack of foresight about management development were quoted to us as examples), this was largely due to lack of perception about what the personnel function could have done to analyse and deal with the problems—to some extent for lack of suitable guidance from theory. There was, perhaps, too much decentralisation, so that major problems were not considered at a high enough level. The personnel director in London and his next-in-line at the plant (like the personnel man who had begun in the police force) were given wide scope because their personal judgment was trusted by the top management group. They did try to analyse problems, time was set aside for the reading of theory, but there were considerable crises in the personnel function every now and again as a result of market changes.

In $3\frac{1}{2}$ companies (one plant was divided between textiles and sewing and the personnel specialist had different functions in each half), the personnel specialists had no connection with bargaining

[1] Compare the Liverpool University course in industrial sociology, which provided opportunities for entry into personnel management or research but did not have many successful candidates who chose to stay in the former after experience of supervised practical work. The criticism was not personal but general. Their analytical training seemed to misfit them for the lower rungs of the personnel management ladder.

(which was considered to be a line management function), in seven their activities were severely limited by the central personnel department, in $1\frac{1}{2}$ there was not much activity, and in three they had great discretion. In the 10 companies where the personnel specialists were involved, bargaining took up a lot of energy; thus, much depended on the staffing of the personnel department to allow time for other activities to be developed, and for the company to take the initiative rather than the defensive position. The central personnel department was much more important than the local federation in establishing attitudes, although departments might have to work with both. In seven companies, central personnel department representatives expected blow-by-blow reports of negotiations and would come down to the plant to negotiate themselves if, at the first stage, settlement was not reached. Three of the companies were active in their local federations. One had no central personnel department, in one the central personnel department was local, and the third was the decentralised company described above. In this company a decision had been taken to give up time to federation work, in order to promote less defensive thinking and a more positive policy among the local employers in the industry.

Few of the local personnel specialists had much influence on wages structures or the level of earnings. Work-study departments fixed incentive rates by agreement in the workshop, departmental managers arranged overtime or short-time working, basic rates were fixed in national bargaining. They came in only when there were disputes, as firefighters, and we have described how their discretion was frequently very limited here. Fringe benefits such as pension schemes and sick pay schemes were usually settled at head office. The local personnel specialists were seldom consulted and we are not sure whether the central personnel departments had much say. Was this to exclude the local union members from interference or was the high finance regarded as too complex for personnel specialists to understand?

These findings have not yet been published. The case studies have been written up but we have not yet analysed the findings across the 15 companies, so that this account must be taken as impressions by the research staff who compiled the data.

The implications are gloomy if one measures this non-influential role against Lupton's vision of the personnel consultant.[1] Yet, if one remembers the absence of any concern about good personnel management found by the Production Efficiency Board of M.A.P. during the war or by the early Personnel Management Advisors of the Ministry of Labour in the post-war years, there is development of the function.

What lessons can we draw from these findings? They demonstrate that the decision to appoint a personnel specialist, where the need to make such an appointment is seen as following specific government recommendations or pieces of legislation, has in the past been likely to produce a jobbing personnel officer operating at routine levels and quite uninfluential and the extent to which new protective legislation stimulates development of concern about personnel management is questionable. It might stimulate personnel department activities in quite insignificant directions (such as improved personal record keeping).

Findings about the once-upon-a-time leaders in the field who have been left behind illustrate the danger of personnel specialists relying on technique rather than developing an analytical approach —the technique is often short-term in its application, is questioned by subsequent research and is made inappropriate by change. *Personnel administration* which uses techniques uncritically and fails to evaluate their suitability from time to time is bound to fall behind. Skills in analysis are less easily marketable than administrative skills but they are likely to persist as an asset. Ends should dictate the means, not means the ends.

The difficulties of the young social-science-trained specialist may illustrate the fallacy of looking for a ready-made product at the end of a university course. Vocational education needs to be supplemented with professional training. The student may leave the university equipped with knowledge of research methods and behavioural-science theories, but ability to analyse organisational problems and prescribe remedies presupposes an integration of this knowledge with some understanding of business planning. It takes a long time for the student to make an adjustment because his new employer does not always provide the necessary next stage in experience but may expect him to fit in at the bottom of the personnel

[1] Tom Lupton, *Industrial Behaviour and Personnel Management*, I.P.M., 1965.

department, taking his share of routine administration and learning peripheral personnel techniques.

Whatever the expertise brought in, it will not be employed in a significant way as far as the firm is concerned, unless the general management sees the need for employment forecasting (and the implications of this for industrial relations) and the consequent need to appoint suitable specialists to work at it and to enable them to relate to the management of the organisation in an analytic and predictive fashion. If personnel management is stuck on as an adjunct, it will necessarily be involved in peripheral activities or in developing expertise in ephemeral techniques which will fossilise along with the personnel department.

The problems of centralisation and decentralisation of personnel work have seldom been discussed.[1] It seems clear that this is an issue central to the problem of personnel management training. Should the trainee personnel specialist aiming for employment in central personnel departments have a different kind of training from the men looking for employment in local plants? Should there be men trained to set up new personnel departments who could also move on to review personnel services in a plant going through a stage of rapid change? Should there be bargainers who can concentrate on bargaining and not need to try to combine it with too many other jobs? It would appear that functional specialism within the six sectors of work of the personnel department is only one kind of specialism and that these other kinds need also to be considered.

SURVEYS OF MEMBERS OF THE INSTITUTE OF PERSONNEL MANAGEMENT

We do not know of any other general surveys of personnel specialists which have been made in Great Britain.

Collins has argued that we might expect to find some 13,500 per-

---

[1] Though K. D. M. Dauncey of the Steel Company of Wales in 'Dynamic Aspects of the Personnel Manager's Role', *Personnel Management*, September 1958, did discuss the possibility of centralising bargaining in a large personnel department at one period in the firm's growth, then decentralising it down to the production departments at another stage if thought to be more appropriate for maintaining the line managers' interests and bargaining skills, and possibly recentralising again later.

sonnel specialists (technologists) in the United Kingdom. These are the people who would be eligible to join the Institute of Personnel Management if they were interested in 'professional' association. In fact, the I.P.M. has a membership of 8,000, of whom more than 1,000 are overseas, 1,000 are students, and many others are retired or no longer in personnel management posts.[1] We can assume, then, that there are about 6,000 practising personnel specialists interested in associating. What of the other 7,500?

Collins compared his general survey of personnel specialists in South Wales with the local membership of I.P.M. Of the 139 members and 16 subscribers, 59 were not in personnel work (40 per cent). The 96 practising members were only some 14·6 per cent of the Group A personnel specialists in the general survey. (Group B were considered to be ineligible for membership.) Collins says: 'Two major [industrial] groups, metal manufacturing and engineering and electrical goods, are over-represented in branch membership. Mining and quarrying is considerably under-represented. Public administration and transport and communications are also under-represented. . . . Branch membership represents about 20 per cent of specialists in general personnel work; 8 per cent of training technologists. Less than 3 per cent of all persons engaged in industrial training work in South Wales are I.P.M. members.'[2]

Crichton examined the distribution of a 20-per-cent sample of I.P.M. members in 1950 and 1960.[3] Like Collins she found that the engineering industry was well-represented: 21·5 per cent of members in 1950, 25·5 per cent in 1960 (engineering, aircraft and vehicles). There were no other large numbers except in chemicals, 11 per cent; and service trades, 12 per cent, in each distribution. Those employed in textiles and clothing had diminished from 15

[1] In a survey made in 1960 Crichton found 29 per cent were not in personnel work—Anne Crichton, 'The I.P.M. in 1950 and 1960', *Personnel Management*, December 1961.

[2] R. G. Collins, 'A Survey of the Employment of Personnel Specialists in South Wales 1964', mimeographed.

[3] Anne Crichton, 'Changes in the Status of the Personnel Officer since 1939', *Personnel Management*, December 1952; Anne Crichton, *op. cit.* These were studies of a 20-per-cent sample of I.P.M. members—details taken from record cards. The accuracy of the records has been questioned—members fail to send in details of job changes.

per cent in 1950 to nine per cent in 1960. Coal and steel had increased from four to 7·5 per cent. Collins suggested that the industrial relations specialists in these two industries do not perceive themselves as personnel specialists and feel they have little in common with the 'general personnel officers' found in engineering. Equally, he believes, training specialists found the I.P.M. services too general and not specific enough to their interests.

The I.P.M. has been disappointed with its recruitment of staff specialists. There has been little change in the composition of the Staff Management Association since its formation—personnel specialists in commercial organisations such as insurance companies, wholesale businesses and in public service organisations have not been attracted into membership. They may have been deterred by what they consider to be an industrial bias in I.P.M.

There may be many good reasons for this failure to enrol the 7,500 potential members. Clearly some are geographically distant from branch activities or are 'non-joiners' by temperament. There are many rival bodies also looking for members: the British Institute of Management, the Industrial Society and the Employers' Federations are associations of employers and may be rated more highly by the personnel specialists' employing organisation as deserving of support—both for financial support and for the giving up of time to their affairs. The I.P.M. seems to attract the career man rather than the organisational man—the one who identifies with his occupational group rather than with managers in general. In 1960 approximately 40 per cent of members had had more than personnel management jobs. This would seem to indicate that the career administrators in the public services and the career managers in the larger companies are unlikely to be focussed on similar problems. Nor are the functional specialists such as training officers (in Collins' survey 301 out of the Group A personnel officers).[1] It could, therefore be argued that the I.P.M. in recruiting between 30 and 40 per cent of potential members is providing a particular service for *general personnel officers*.

In 1961 Crichton argued that 'membership of the I.P.M. gives no

---

[1] The I.P.M. has been endeavouring to meet the needs of functional specialists in training in recent years by changing the examination scheme and putting on meetings for their specific interests.

guarantee of professional competence (though it gives some indication of educational attainment and interest in personnel problems)'. She queried why members joined—use of the Appointments Service, perhaps? Getting a start with employers who were maybe more prepared to short-list members? Possibly because it guaranteed a certain seriousness of purpose to employers? For the opportunity to attend meetings at which they could join in discussion with others sharing their interests? Or for a chance to keep up to date in refresher courses?

The I.P.M. has been faced with difficult decisions about its composition. If we can accept that there were 1,800 personnel specialists before the war, rising to 5,000 in 1945 and 13,500 today (estimates which may be far out, of course, but which indicate something of the growth rate), then it can be seen that the problems of membership and training have been great.[1] The pre-war I.P.M. was a small compact group mainly made up of trained women and men from the larger 'more advanced' manufacturing companies. (Sharp estimated that 75 per cent of pre-war members were women; by 1950 Crichton found this had been reduced to 47·7 per cent, and by 1960 to 30·5 per cent.) During the war period the dilemma became acute—whether to continue to insist on high standards of training before entry for the few or to bring the many new recruits to the occupation into membership to try to raise their standards to the norms already established. Certain compromises about training were reached: the I.P.M.'s senior members were seconded to the top personnel posts in the Ministry of Supply factories (and they trained many subordinates) or as Personnel Management Advisers with the Ministry of Aircraft Production (and they mothered many newly appointed personnel specialists); emergency short courses were laid on by the universities; the I.P.M. branches co-operated with the Ministry of Labour in providing 'refresher' courses for newly appointed personnel specialists in their localities. For the I.P.M. had really no choice—it was necessary to integrate the newcomers or perish. In any case, how relevant was a pre-war training? The emphasis on social work was over—the

[1] 1,800–5,000 was estimated as growth during the Second World War by G. R. Moxon in *The Growth of Personnel Management in Great Britain during the War*, I.P.M., 1946.

ndustrial welfare worker was peripheral to the real job of personnel management. And what should be the new training—training for general management within a plant, or training in the social sciences?

The issue for the I.P.M. has been how to balance admission through experience in industry with admission from training courses into membership, and long arguments went on for years as compromises were worked out. It was clear that almost all of the most senior posts were being filled by men whose preparation for the work had not been through a 'recognised' training. On the other hand, many of the students selected for full-time training courses were unlikely to go far up the hierarchy for reasons of limited acceptability or for failure to develop expertise. This was not entirely their fault, since the courses did not give them immediately applicable techniques to use in their first jobs, nor had they had time to develop a thorough enough depth of knowledge of how to use the behavioural sciences. The courses provided part of a general education with a vocational bias and what students made of their opportunities depended very much on individual ability to find the right niche later in order to go on developing.

The following table shows the numbers in membership of I.P.M. and the numbers taking and completing training in the last 10 years.

	In membership	Taking 'recognised' courses	Part-time courses and private study	Completing	Admitted to graduate membership
1956	4040	151	52	86	127
1961	5217	234	320	135	419
1966	7939	318	1077	277	1101

We were unable to get out figures for those entering through the 'experience' clauses of the constitution (because some were admitted directly to corporate membership and were not clearly distinguished in the records from those who were upgraded), but a certain discrepancy can be seen in columns 4 and 5 which indicate the difference in some degree, since column 5 includes 'trained' and 'experienced' candidates for admission to the lowest practising grade.

In 1950, 40 per cent of I.P.M. members had been to university.

By 1960 this had increased to 48 per cent. It is not certain how many of the 1950 group were graduates, but in 1960 of 146 graduates in the 20-per-cent sample only 14 were graduates in the social sciences.[1] Of course, others had taken social-science diplomas or one-year courses in personnel management, but these can hardly be regarded as thorough groundings in the behavioural sciences. Assuming there were 70 social-science graduates in this 'professional' group (i.e. 14×5), these were still very few and far between as expert influences on British management.

SALARIES SURVEYS

Comparative Salaries

What is the price of a personnel specialist? Surveys carried out by the British Institute of Management, Associated Industrial Consultants and McKinsey and Company show that he is fairly low in the hierarchy of managers. Graham compared the three findings in an enquiry into professional incomes.[2] 'The British Institute of Management found from their survey that "managers engaged in the marketing side of the business seem to earn consistently higher rewards than any other function, followed by those in accounting, administration and personnel functions. Production and maintenance managers appear at the end of the remuneration range by function." These results have been largely borne out by McKinsey and Company. . . .' In their 1963 Survey of Top Management Remuneration in the United Kingdom they found that 'the relationship between the earnings of the top executives (i.e. the managing director and those executives reporting to him) of a company tend to change with the size of the company, here measured in terms of turnover. . . . As a company becomes larger so does the relative importance of the head of personnel: in a company with a turnover of £1 million, the personnel manager's

---

[1] A social-science graduate is not necessarily a behavioural-science graduate. He may have a degree in economics. It was in 1963–5 that most British chairs in Sociology were established.

[2] John Graham, 'Incomes: How Much do Professional People Earn?', article reprinted by the *Scotsman*, 1966.

salary would be about one half that of the head of marketing, but at the £100 million level the proportion may be as high as three quarters.' Graham goes on to show, however, that the head of personnel was at the foot of the list of key executives, getting only some 30 per cent of managing directors' total remuneration.

A report of the 1966 survey of executive salaries by Associated Industrial Consultants states that: 'Personnel managers have also improved their position with continuing demand. The whole range of their salaries has risen by approximately 10 per cent. As the effect of the Industrial Training Act becomes more widespread, the position is likely to increase further in importance and remuneration.'[1] A table shows that the personnel man is paid less than the average executive but he is certainly not at the bottom of the league table.

A.I.C. SALARIES SURVEY, 1966

	Upper quartile	Median	Lower quartile
All jobs	£3,600	£2,700	£2,000
Personnel	£3,250	£2,400	£1,675

Personnel Specialists' Salaries Analysed

The Institute of Personnel Management has carried out three salary surveys among members in 1956, 1961 and 1965.[2] The first was addressed to employers and was related to their concern about the advertising of vacancies through the appointments service at too low a level to be suitable for 'professional' people. The I.P.M. decided to take a stand at that time on minimum salaries for women.

In the 1961 survey there was a 43-per-cent response rate thought to be unbiased when submitted to checks. The 1222 respondents were divided into 10 categories as follows:

[1] 'Trends in Executive Salaries', *I.P.M. Digest*, February 1967.
[2] *Personnel Management Salaries*, Feb./March 1961, I.P.M., 1961. 'Personnel Management Salaries: Results of the 1965 Survey', *I.P.M. Digest*, 1 Oct. 1965, 11 Feb. 1966.

I.P.M. SALARIES SURVEY 1961
SALARIES ACCORDING TO POSITIONS HELD[1]

	Personnel Officers		Average Salary £s	
	Men	Women	Men	Women
Personnel assistant	41	25	1070	736
Personnel officer	300	185	1344	947
Personnel manager	151	18	1779	1443
Staff manager	29	20	2176	1209
Deputy/assistant chief personnel officer	68	11	1647	1114
Chief personnel officer	111	22	2156	1308
Head of specialist department	80	14	1633	1404
Regional/group personnel manager	33	4	2407	*
Personnel director	15	—	4169	
Personnel director, member of board	10	—	3189	

* too easily identifiable to be quoted

These other points were made in the report:

(a) Salary increased with age up to 55 +.
(b) There was a direct relationship between salary and length of service.
(c) There was a direct relationship between number of employees and salary paid.
(d) Personnel officers controlling others tended to receive a much higher salary than those who had no such control or were single-handed.
(e) Those responsible to directors earned considerably more than those responsible to the works manager.
(f) There were considerable differences between industries—high-paying were agriculture and forestry, mining and quarrying, retail and wholesale distribution; low-paying were textiles, leather, clothing and footwear.
(g) 55 per cent of men and 42 per cent of women dealt with recruitment, training and management development; 52 per cent of men and 18 per cent of women dealt with industrial relations and trade unions; 40 per cent of men and 26 per cent of women advised the board of management on personnel policy.

[1] 1961 Survey, Simplified Table 2.

(h) 18 per cent of firms employing 1,000–1,900, six per cent of firms employing 2,000–4,999 and three per cent of firms employing over 5,000 have only one personnel specialist, but some 213 companies had more than 10 personnel specialists although only three of these employed less than 5,000.

In the 1965 survey it was found that salaries had increased by one-third. The median salary for men was £2,018 and for women £1,273. Chemicals paid highest, textiles lowest. Women could earn highest salaries in professional occupations such as banks and public service. In carrying out this survey an unsuccessful attempt was made to try to discover the levels of work of the respondents. They were asked to estimate what they did under three headings: operational, advisory and creative. The final report said:

Establishing levels in a field such as personnel management is difficult. The personnel function differs quite markedly from company to company depending on a number of factors, of which previous history is of considerable importance. Other factors which may be mentioned are the size of the work-force; the proportions of what used to be termed 'staff' and 'labour'; the nature of the enterprise and its products; the degree of unionisation; the management structure and so forth. Companies exhibit a great range of attitudes towards a personnel policy from the very advanced with a clearly defined and communicated policy to those having little or none. The level of sophistication of personnel management not unnaturally follows these attitudes from company to company. Furthermore, the replies to the questionnaire showed that personnel management is tending towards specialisation. There were indications that certain parts of the general function such as training, remuneration or industrial relations tended to be dealt with by specialists in those fields rather than the 'general' personnel manager or personnel officer. This pattern is well established in many large companies and is extending to the more sophisticated medium-sized companies. Nevertheless, four broad levels are distinguishable.

Senior personnel manager: in charge of the personnel function at the level of determining company policy; unlikely to be found in a small company where the policy making function is more probably held by a director with broader responsibilities, e.g. a financial or administrative director. The senior personnel manager may well be operating in a general management sphere at director level. He may not undertake the complete range of personnel activities but may, in some cases, concentrate on industrial relations or on management development, etc. (165 respondents.)

Personnel manager: in charge of a personnel department with an operational role; carries out a range of functions, possibly with limitations. Many industries in this category make some contribution to policy development but do not have final responsibility for company policy. The size of personnel departments covered clearly varies substantially. (450 respondents.)

Senior personnel officer: has an operational role but with supervisory responsibility over one or more operational personnel officers; exists only in medium and large organisations. (172 respondents.)

Operational personnel officer: has an operational role and carries out a range of personnel functions, possibly with limitations; for example may exclude training or remuneration; alternatively may concentrate on either staff or labour; may supervise staff below personnel officer level. (780 respondents.)

Specialists: those dealing with education and training, management development, remuneration, industrial relations and consultancy. (233 respondents.)

The survey excluded the lower age groups because it was limited to certain membership grades. It must also be remembered that the respondents were giving a subjective picture of themselves.

12 Objectives of Personnel Specialists: their Roles and Relationships

There is no standard British textbook on personnel management approved for use in qualifying examinations.[1] If there were it might be possible to build up a picture of what was expected of the normal practitioner (using normal here in a technical sense to mean average in, or central to, the group). The last influential full-scale account of British personnel management was published in 1945.[2] Much has happened since then.

Yet there has been much discussion of the developments in the range and depth of work in pamphlets and journals in this period. Personnel specialists are encouraged by academics to be introspective about their work, and representative members of the 'professional' group have met from time to time to reconsider the contribution which personnel officers could make. One study, published in 1957 by such a study group, examined a number of the traditional difficulties of the personnel specialist.[3] It was particularly concerned with the problem of the roles and relationships of the personnel officer to the rest of management and to the employees who might wish to seek his counsel. How could he manage to be seen as unbiased by these employees whilst at other times acting as management's agent and representing their viewpoint? And how could he be identified with the management group whilst reminding them of the workers' views? Should he seek concessions

[1] We understand that several are in preparation at the time of writing.
[2] C. H. Northcott, *Personnel Management*, Pitman, 1945.
[3] Guy Hunter, *The Role of the Personnel Officer*, I.P.M., 1957.

on employees' behalf? The study group argued that his role was that of 'remembrancer' so that workpeople's views would be taken into consideration in making policies (but not their representative).

Although the study group recognised that several roles are held concurrently by personnel specialists in their occupation (and this is quite apart from other roles such as citizen, member of family, householder, etc.), they did not really clarify the issues sufficiently. Personnel specialists are likely to be *managers of part of the organisation*, *part managers of the whole organisation* and, in some of their activities, *public relations officers* for the organisation or *liaison officers between disparate parts* within it. It may be useful to spell this out in more detail because the liaison officer role is one which has been misunderstood in the past, as we have already discussed in considering relationships with the unions, and the other two have not been carefully examined.

As *managers of part of the organisation* they may have to take line-management responsibility for the work of the personnel department or one of its subsections, such as training or wages research, or they may have functional responsibility for advising about personnel policies and practices in a product group, a plant or a department. The *managers of part of the organisation* roles have been fairly well explored in the past. A good deal is known about the organisation of the different sections of personnel departments, and the functional specialist relationship to line managers has been explored over the years. Here, perhaps what are not so well-known are the choices of priorities which are made within this role. Are these a function of personality, or organisation structure, or of other influences such as training or 'professional' contact? The rivalries which have developed between collective bargainers and training officers for senior status may also be due to all of these and there has been no real study of personnel specialists working as a team.

As *part managers of the whole organisation*, they are expected to see their responsibility for managing their part in context—to recognise the relative importance of any demand for resources or to assess the general implications of any course of action which may be proposed, to look at priorities in the light of information available to them.

Simon develops the argument that functional specialists generally tend to fail in role-taking as managers of the whole organisation[1]. They find it difficult to identify with the whole (because they are so greatly identified with their own part). They are not very good at balancing costs against values in making administrative decisions. They tend to measure the degree to which goals have been reached (adequacy) rather than the degree to which goals have been reached relative to the available resources (efficiency).

Drucker suggests that for *managers of the whole* it is necessary first to clarify organisational objectives.[2] 'Once the goals are clear it can always be determined whether they are being attained or not.' He discusses eight objectives of management, three of which are the particular concern of the personnel specialist: manager performance and development, worker performance and attitude, and public responsibility. He says: '... performance and results in these areas cannot be fully measured quantitatively. All three deal with human beings. And as each human being is unique we cannot simply add them together or subtract them from one another. What we need are qualitative standards, judgment rather than data, appraisal rather than measurements. ....' The other five areas in which objectives have to be set are: market standing, innovation, productivity, physical and financial resources, profitability. These are the particular concern of other functional specialists but of general concern to all managers, including the personnel specialist. The personnel specialist is a follower and not among the managerial élite in any of the organisations categorised by Etzioni, since building and maintaining the organisation must always be a secondary objective.[3] In this position he must, of necessity, be prepared to accept the primary objectives of the dominant élite and to fit his goals and his values to theirs.

'Efficiency' and 'justice' are two words which occur frequently in statements by personnel specialists about their intended contribution, but what is meant by them is not always very clear. Since these are relative and not absolute concepts, individuals and groups can formulate their own norms about both. As *part manager of the*

---

[1] H. A. Simon, *Administrative Behaviour*, Macmillan, 1945.
[2] P. F. Drucker, *The Practice of Management*, Harper & Row, 1945.
[3] A. Etzioni, *op. cit.*

whole organisation the personnel manager may feel himself to be at some disadvantage. He is liable to feel that he has to defend 'justice' (or adequacy) rather than 'efficiency' for he has to make out a case for investment in the qualitative areas described above, to convince other managers about the less tangible values. He may feel at a disadvantage about his technical language because other managers use the language of figures. He may not be regarded as having sufficient expertise unless he can show great familiarity with costs. Yet as Simon also argues, personnel management decisions 'cannot always be evaluated in monetary terms because the monetary effect of a particular personnel policy cannot be directly determined'.

Many managers are not aware of the value element in their decision making. They seek to weigh one set of facts against another but as Drucker and Simon both point out, selected facts are value-laden, and management evaluation measures are rudimentary—variables not well understood. Simon says: '... somewhere, sometime in the administrative process weights actually are assigned to values. If this is not done consciously and deliberately, then it is achieved by implication in the decisions which are actually reached ... [And] defining objectives does not exhaust the value element in an administrative decision. It is necessary to determine, in addition, the degree to which the objective is to be attained.'

The history of the personnel specialists, like the history of many other occupational groups, shows an obsession with status levels. These are, of course, vital to the contribution which it is possible to make to the management of the whole organisation. The personnel specialist who becomes a director naturally has a very different frame of reference from the personnel specialist who reports to the works manager. How, then, is it possible to *earn the right to status* so that one may be asked to make a useful high-level contribution to the determination of company policy? For the higher up the organisation one goes, the more likely are other managers to understand the time-spans which are the concern of the personnel specialist—building and maintaining an organisation are long-term activities.

This raises the question of the training of the personnel specialist for his *part manager of the whole* role. Petrie has described the problem clearly.[1] The more specialist expertise is built up in a personnel department role (i.e. as manager of a part), the less likely is the man going to be able to fit into this other role. This raises the questions: whether should there be a general training for all managers who would move through different functions (rather like the Civil Service administrative grade), or functional specialist training first and, later, additional training for those who move into general management? Or should there be tiering of training with different courses of preparation for different levels? Should companies recruiting management trainees rotate them through the whole range of management activities including the personnel specialisation and then allocate those who seem best-fitted to work in that sector? Today the perception of the organisation as a sociotechnical system poses the same problems, with different emphases, from those of the Urwick Committee of 1947 which enquired into this.[2]

In their *public relations* or *liaison officer roles* personnel specialists have membership of two groups at once and are expected to inform the one about the other when appropriate. Since each group has a different frame of reference, this may not be a comfortable position to be in. If the personnel specialist can be perceived as an expert somewhat detached from both the groups this may make these roles more tolerable, but such independence has certain disadvantages too, for most of us like to be liked and brought into the centre of things as well as to be respected which may mean staying on the edge. The main difficulty of the personnel specialist in these roles is related to his perception of group membership. Where does he belong?

The *public relations* or *liaison officer* roles can so easily lead to the feeling of being an outsider with no real place in the organisation that the personnel specialists have had mixed feelings about them from the start. The *public relations activities*, such as attending a Ministry of Labour Rehabilitation Committee, or making representations to the local housing authority or sitting as a co-opted member on the Education Committee, are perceived by the other managers as so peripheral to the company's interests as to be almost irrelevant.

[1] D. J. Petrie, 'The Personnel "Professionals", Who Needs Them?', *Personnel Management*, September 1965.
[2] *Education for Management*, H.M.S.O., 1947.

In a recent research project the production managers said that, in their opinion, the personnel specialists should preferably be available to share the burden of entertaining visitors to the plant whether they were retailers or foreign competitors or visiting firemen.[1] This duty, of course, seemed burdensome and marginal to the personnel specialist.

As *liaison officer* between management and workpeople, the role has certain attractions and certain difficulties. The role, by itself, was rejected by the early personnel specialists who demanded a place in the management team. They were happy to go on using their special skills as counsellors to individual employees or as confidants to union representatives, provided that the role could be held in combination with a managerial role, whether as personnel department specialist or part manager of the whole. For although the counsellor or confidant or conciliator role has its attractions, they were not enough to outweigh the loneliness associated with the neutrality and detachment of a consultant whilst still being a full-time employee. The study group of the Institute of Personnel Management which examined the role in 1957 concluded that it could be carried alongside the bargainer's role (which was evidently regarded as most identified with management), since the unions would be well able to perceive when one or other hat was being worn.[2] Many personnel specialists have made difficulties for themselves in the past by failing to see the distinction between the role of intermediary or interpreter or go-between and the roles of 'buffer' or representative of a special interest group—a distinction which would help them to manage this seemingly paradoxical situation. They represent management, not the unions nor any other interest group, but they may be able to help these other interest groups to formalise their claims against management without either being associated with the claims or standing in judgment upon them. They can be expected to understand the viewpoint of others, without necessarily having to identify or disassociate themselves.

The advantages and disadvantages of carrying so many concurrent roles, of having membership in so many different groups is obvious. Peripheral membership of many groups conflicts with having a

[1] Crichton, Hamblin and Lawson, *op. cit.*
[2] Hunter, *op. cit.*

central position in one or a few groups for reasons of time alone. It seems to be particularly difficult for personnel specialists to become committed to full membership of any group but that of their own department. Whilst all group members have to wrestle with the problems of aligning their values with those of the groups to which they wish to belong or of trying to shift the groups' values nearer to theirs, personnel specialists seem to have greater problems in becoming accepted into full membership or of accepting other members without reservations.

All groups establish norms of behaviour which they expect their members to observe, and deviance from the norm is punished in various subtle ways. The norms will be a series of shared values, an agreed frame of reference, certain ways of behaving. Personnel specialists have to decide which of the numerous groups to which they belong should be given priority. As we have already shown, the groups to which they belong in their *public relations* or *liaison officer* role do not seem to be so central as those in the *manager of part* or *part manager of the whole organisation* roles. However, there seems to have been the most satisfaction and the least difficulty in establishing the department or functional manager role and the greatest struggle to get into the whole management team. Here, there is likely to be considerable ambivalence about accepting and identifying with this group's norms as Simon's arguments about difficulties in role-taking suggest—for the personnel specialist is likely to have a pluralistic frame of reference which may make him seem too complicated a person if other managers are single-minded.[1] His job in personnel management means that he must be as much concerned about *justice* as efficiency, so he tends to feel that he must keep reminding the group about values they would prefer to ignore at times.

In the case studies in South Wales we discovered that many personnel specialists preferred to do their work in pair situations rather than in group meetings. This seemed to be a more profitable use of time than being present when a lot of 'irrelevant' business was being discussed. It may also be an indication of the way in which personnel specialists find it most comfortable to work. They may choose

[1] Fox, *op. cit.*

the job because they prefer to relate to individuals rather than groups.

The personnel specialists have great anxieties about power, as we can judge from the many discussions there have been about the *advisory* nature of the relationship of personnel specialists to other managers.

As we have pointed out, organisational objectives differ. In some organisations, management sees it to be necessary to maintain control by stressing managerial rights and prerogatives. In others, management virtually hands over social control to the union branch. Some companies plan their personnel policies with great care, others meet crises when they arise. In consequence the patterns of work of the personnel specialists are very different.

Nevertheless, we can identify certain levels of company activity in personnel management. The board of directors and senior executives decide on substantive amounts to be distributed to employees whether as wages, salaries or fringe benefits. Personnel directors must be involved in these discussions if they are board members, but there are few personnel directors. The evidence of attendance at the Industrial Society's meetings to discuss pension schemes would seem to indicate that accountants and company secretaries are more likely to be involved in strategies than personnel managers or other personnel-department specialists. Thus the strategies not only of how much but also the methods of distribution are unlikely to be decided by the personnel specialist, although we cannot know how much they influence the decisions. It seems likely that they do have some influence in presenting comparative data about other companies' schemes, as for example on 'staff status', and they can make strong representations about the effects of a redundancy on local goodwill.

The personnel specialist is likely to be given the role of negotiator. Perhaps we can begin to understand his role better if we consider the table on page 122, which endeavours to set out the complexities of intra-organisational collective bargaining relationships. In Chapter 7 we have tried to show how strategies and tactics are related. The board of directors, responsible for strategies, is likely to be at some distance from the manager who undertakes the bargaining—

he tactician—for the reasons discussed in that chapter. Indeed, in many smaller companies, the bargaining is done by the employers' association official on their behalf.

We have tried to demonstrate the advantages of this division of function. The professional bargainer, whether employed by the company or the association, is less emotionally involved in the substantive amount to be distributed, more in the subtleties of the playing out of the ritual.

It has been suggested that one of the difficulties in British industry in moving towards better adaptation to technological change has been the aspirational rigidity of the collective bargainers. Flanders welcomed the Fawley productivity bargaining because it involved line managers more thoroughly in the process of negotiation.[1] Indeed, he has argued the necessity to move away from the pattern of appointing functional specialists to negotiate on behalf of the company.[2]

Flanders' plan to strengthen line management would bring strategies and tactics closer together by cutting out the professional or semi-professional negotiator, the personnel specialist, using him only as adviser.

This is a plan to decentralise strategic decision-making as far down as possible. It depends upon well-trained, strong and competent line managers supported by well-informed personnel specialist advisers who are able to carry out productivity bargaining at plant level. The line managers would become the strategist tacticians; the personnel specialists would be expected to help them to develop strategies.

It is clear that computerisation is likely to increase the tendency towards centralised personnel management, towards standardisation of records and more long-term manpower planning and long-term training programmes. It should follow that the personnel specialists concerned with terms and conditions of employment will also be brought into this complex—to become more concerned with aspirational optimism.

Yet what will happen then to the bargaining ritual? Will it

[1] Flanders, *op. cit.*
[2] Flanders, 'The Future of Personnel Management', *Personnel Management*, December 1965.

change? Or will the line manager manage to cope with the branch official? How should he be trained by the personnel specialists who are to be the advisers?

Dauncey's experience of decentralising bargaining at s.c.o.w. did not last very long because of the unevenness in the ability of the departmental managers to withstand pressure from the unions and the consequent inconsistencies in agreements which ensued.[1] Nerve and timing in the bargaining ritual are all important. It seems likely, however, that Flanders sees the plant as the basic unit for decentralisation, not the department, but even so there could be difficulties.

As the job of negotiator has been the high-status specialism in personnel management until recently, it seems likely that it will not easily be relinquished except for something which offers better prospects and more satisfying relationships. At least in bargaining the skills or lack of them are obvious and the results immediate; other specialised activities in personnel management are likely to offer less tangible rewards. It seems likely that many will wish to perpetuate the present pattern of industrial relations.

[1] Dauncey, *op. cit.*

13 The Development of Expertise: Professionalisation

What is a competent personnel specialist? This is a difficult question to answer since there is no recognised standard of minimal competence as there is in such professional occupations as medicine, accountancy or teaching. In the case studies of personnel departments in South Wales we found it difficult to decide where to draw the line between personnel clerks and junior personnel officers. Their present responsibilities were often similar though their aspirations were different. There was a good deal of what is normally recognised as personnel work being done by clerks and a considerable amount of routine work being done by personnel officers.

We have suggested that legislation determines *minimum* standards of personnel management; collective bargaining *operating* standards; example, published work, conferences and training courses may help to raise the sights of personnel specialists to develop *optimum* standards for their organisations. In tracing the historical development of personnel work we have tried to show how the perception of the range and depth of work has changed over the years. The response of companies to this enlarged perception has been uneven and we have suggested some of the variables determining different outlooks of managements. Management is choice and many managerial choices are dilemmas—whether to increase communication and slow down decision making in order to enable more people to participate in discussions, or to restrict it for the sake of faster action, whether to invest heavily in training for the future or by using the money for other development work to attract already trained people only when they are needed. These examples are intended to show that standards in personnel management are related to the needs or perceptions of needs in a particular organisation. They are not absolute but relative to the situation and there are no satisfactory objective measurements of success although certain indicators are used for measuring performance such as labour turnover, time lost, etc.

Even in legislating for minimum standards the state has been concerned with relatives rather than absolutes so far as organisations have been concerned. From the beginning, the Factory Inspectorate recognised the difficulties of standardising working conditions and took the opposite view, that employers surpassing the minimum laid down in regulations should be encouraged and upheld as examples to the laggards. In the Factory and Workshops Act, 1901, the principle of self-inspection was brought in—employers or their representatives were expected to record data in the absence of the Inspectors for their own information and control rather than being controlled by the Inspectorate. The legislation enacted before the 1960s was not concerned with the development of employing organisations as such. It was concerned with the protection of the unorganised individual employee and the institutions of collective bargaining or location of industry policies. Now it has been recognised that the community's plans for economic growth are dependent on the effectiveness of the *employing organisations* which are important institutions in the community. Failure of any one industrial or commercial organisation to invest in training, to make full use of labour, to abide by the prices and incomes policy is seen to have repercussions for the economy as a whole and to jeopardise national development. Yet though this is given general recognition as a national programme, its application at plant level is still to be achieved.

Marshall has pointed out that there is a difference between what he calls quantitative and qualitative social services.[1] It is easy enough to legislate for every citizen to have rights to monetary payments (provided he satisfies certain conditions) and to ensure that every

[1] T. H. Marshall, *Citizenship and Social Class*, Cambridge, 1950.

citizen is treated alike, but when the right is extended to provision of schooling or medical attention differences creep in. What is important in shifting the emphasis from quantity to quality is the staffing of the service. The clerk can administer monetary payments from the rule book, but only the trained doctor or teacher can ensure the qualitative standards of a professional service to patients or pupils. There would appear to be an analogy here. The personnel clerk can keep records of individuals' overtime or accidents for the Factory Inspector or make out Contracts of Employment, the wages clerk can keep records of payment for the Wages Inspectorate or calculate National Insurance deductions or redundancy pay due, but to become a satisfactory *personnel manager* of an on-going and developing *organisation* is a different level of activity altogether.

The questions then arise: is there a clear distinction between routine work and a professional approach? If so what is the appropriate training for each? Is personnel management an identifiable professional occupation?

CHARACTERISTICS OF A PROFESSION

Millerson defines a *profession* as a 'type of higher grade, non-manual occupation, with both subjectively and objectively recognised occupational status, possessing a well defined area of study or concern and providing a definite service, after advanced training and education'.[1] *Professionalisation*, he says, 'is the process by which an occupation undergoes transformation to become a profession'. This process of institutionalisation often results in the formation of an association which tries to induce conformity to group norms. Aspiring professions tend to model themselves on those already well-established, and so they emphasise standards of competence and integrity. After building up solidarity in the early stages such an occupational group will try to become exclusive. Applicants for membership will have to be sponsored by existing members who will guarantee their acceptability. Education, training and experience judged suitable for the occupation will be prescribed. Once admitted to membership the individual will be expected to conform to a code

[1] G. Millerson, *The Qualifying Associations*, Routledge & Kegan Paul, 1964.

of behaviour. His membership may be displayed by letters showing his status in the organisation.

Learning, ethics, association, subjective and objective recognition —these are the characteristics of a profession which we will now try to examine in relation to personnel specialists.

WHAT SHOULD BE LEARNT?

We have traced the development of thinking about the range and depth of personnel work in the historical chapter and the chapter on roles and relationships, but it may be useful to summarise this again here:

(a)   Aspects of personnel management are: employment; education and training; wages and salaries; negotiation and consultation; health, safety and welfare; employee services.

(b)   Personnel work may consist of repetitive routine or semi-clerical activities or may be analytic, trying to diagnose the organization's needs using behavioural science theory. Probably most activity falls between these two extremes. Writings suggest that personnel specialists react to pragmatic problems by using 'fashionable' techniques or that they are guided by experience rather than theory.

(c)   Personnel work is concerned with feelings as well as objective reality. Personnel specialists vary between those who are in touch with others' feelings and those who are out of touch. Some communicate well, have good timing, are insightful; others are less effective. This is another kind of analysis which may be learnt or can be entirely intuitive.

Work on task and process levels (b) and (c) is carried on simultaneously but not necessarily in congruence – the diagnostician may be out of touch with feeling; the routine clerk insightful.

(d)   Concurrent roles: 'part manager' of the whole, manager of part of the whole, public relations officer, liaison officer within the organisation.

WHAT ETHICS?

Differing professions have different ethical problems to solve. The main purposes in setting up an ethical code are to preserve the independence of judgment of the professional, and to safeguard his clients where they are liable to exploitation (as they might be in seeking medical treatment or financial advice). In addition, professional ethics assist in building and maintaining the professional group as an association of practitioners. Thus, Millerson argues, the need for a code is strong where the practice is non-institutional and fiduciary, and weak where the practice is institutional and bureaucratic; it is strong where the technique involved is a complex intellectual or practical technique and where this technique is not understood by the client; and it is strong where the contact with the client is direct and personal and individualised. For the doctor or solicitor the need for a code is strong; for the professional employed in a bureaucratic organisation, with a well-comprehended technique and an indirect and impersonal relationship with clients, it is weak.

In outlining the history of the development of personnel work we have tried to indicate the confusions of the early personnel specialists about ethics. They were uncertain about the basis of their practice. Were they bureaucratic employees owing total loyalty to the organisation, or independent 'buffers'? Was the nature of their practice fiduciary or were they expected to feed in information about individuals to the organisation in order that corrective action might be taken in developing new policies? Was their technique just 'common sense' or something more? Who were their clients—management or workpeople? For many years it was not clear who their clients were—were they the individual employees whose interests must be guarded against an exploitative management? Or were they the rest of the management team who must be guided and controlled so that conflict with workpeople would be kept to the minimum? And what of the community's interest? The personnel specialists made their choice that their clientele should be the rest of the management team but have shown a certain reluctance to abandon their representation of the other two groups.[1]

[1] Guy Hunter, *The Role of the Personnel Officer*, I.P.M., 1957; the I.P.M. in its evidence to the Royal Commission in 1967 found it necessary to refer to the idea of a 'third force'—an independent mediator.

What, then, should be the personnel specialists' code of conduct? They were hardly in a position to lay down *their* terms to the rest of management when begging for a place in management, and all they could hope to do was to try to discover how well their values, their frames of reference, their behaviour patterns would fit in with those of potential employers so that there would not be a great conflict of interest and they could live together in harmony. In contrast, the stereotype of the professional man is essentially a man who is given great discretion, who has internalised independent values—an expert, detached, controlled and controlling. As we have seen, the personnel specialist may not have great expertise to offer; he has not usually wished to remain detached, his occupational group has not given him enough clear guidance on standards of competence or what are professional norms of behaviour for him to be self-controlled (in a professional sense), although he has had strong feelings about controlling.

If, then, the personnel specialist does not have a clear code of conduct to guide him, can he be regarded as professional? Blau and Scott in their study of formal organisations distinguish between professional and bureaucratic behaviour.[1] Professionals are guided by internalised norms and by standards set by their colleagues in the professional group. Bureaucrats are geared to organisational objectives and look to the formal hierarchy for guidance. The early welfare workers (who were, perhaps, more professionally orientated than the personnel specialists of today who are more bureaucratic) found that the conflicts between their objectives and organisational objectives were difficult to manage because a business is a business and is not a social service run for the benefit of employees. By emphasising employees' social needs they were thought to be unrealistic and inefficient. In consequence, the more 'realistic' personnel specialists, their successors, have sought membership of the management team rather than 'professional' isolation and impotence.

ASSOCIATION

Yet there is an ambivalence which is demonstrated by the data as we

[1] P. M. Blau and R. W. Scott, *Formal Organisations*, Routledge & Kegan Paul, 1963.

have seen. Personnel specialists may wish to become part of management but do they wish to become 'organisation men'? Some do, it is clear. Many others find support and help in 'professional association'. We have pointed out that arguments about the most suitable training for management continue, whether to train generalists or to expect those who start as specialists to go on to general management later on.

Because personnel management training was linked to social work training in the early days, it has long had a place in the universities, which other management training courses have not until recently. This has been a very important factor in professionalisation, for it has meant that there has been a readily identifiable nucleus of reasonably well-educated entrants to the 'professional group', the I.P.M. At the same time, as we have pointed out, there has been the problem of integrating the practitioners who had not been through courses and who were objectively recognised to be doing an equal or better job compared with those who have been trained.

Wilensky describes professionalisation as a soul-searching process, and the I.P.M. has done its share of this.[1] The history of the group has been one of a struggle between providing better services to existing members or propaganda to the unenlightened, on marginal resources. From the beginning the group had been selective about its invitations into membership. During the Second World War, however, the need for helping the nation to improve its personnel management practice was so great that non-members were invited to branch meetings and experienced men and women without training were welcomed into membership. (This policy of admitting senior practising personnel specialists (men) had been begun earlier in an attempt to improve the balance between men and women members.) Yet there has always been a problem of how far to take this policy. On the one hand it was argued that training was of vital importance, on the other that training was no criterion of acceptability or effectiveness. The Training and Membership Committees worked on their separate problems for years, the former endeavouring to raise standards, the latter to improve recruitment campaigns. In the mid-1950s they were brought together and their real conflicts

[1] H. L. Wilensky, 'The Professionalisation of Everyone?', *American Journal of Sociology*, October 1946.

began to be clarified and compromises sought. What were the admission requirements which could be made compulsory in order to discipline the young and to leave loopholes for those transferred into personnel work later in life?

Millerson distinguishes *qualifying associations* from *professions*. He argues that members of a professional association, to become truly professional, must not only be self-conscious about professionalism but recognised by others as professional.

It seems appropriate to consider the association of personnel specialists in their search for professionalisation as having the characteristics of a qualifying association rather than satisfying all the criteria of a profession. All the management professional associations have the same problems. And it is beginning to be recognised by the old-established professions that traditional methods of training do not prepare their students for working in organisations as members of a team or as managers. Professionals and managers both have their difficulties today in reorientating their traditional approaches. The process of management has been described as 'identification, evaluation, co-ordination and control'. This might equally be applied to the professional process, but the emphases have been different—the manager having been more interested in the past in co-ordination and control, the professional in identification and evaluation. So each group is moving in the opposite direction and towards the other to some extent. The emphasis both in management and in professional training today is on fact finding— research, planning, decision making, execution, evaluation.

Yet, this being said, professional people think that they are different from managers or bureaucrats. They perceive themselves to be more ethical, concerned not only with the individual patient or client, but with the principles of seeing each client as an individual with special needs of his own, unwilling to categorise and depersonalise him. There is something of this in the personnel specialist's approach. His value system is weighted towards certain selected objectives which to him are more meaningful than the other objectives of management. Yet, the personnel specialist, looking to his 'professional' association for guidance on values, will get little except in very general terms, since the i.p.m. is well aware that its members do not wish to be alienated from their organisations, that they are ambivalent. From time to time ideological pronouncements are made, such as the Jubilee Statement of the I.P.M. in 1963, which may have assisted personnel specialists in a small way in trying to sell their ideas about personnel policy making. Yet it is possible that their colleagues in management will take notice of other bodies which seem to have less of an axe to grind, such as the Industrial Society (an association of employers), the British Institute of Management, or research consultancy institutes like the National Institute of Industrial Psychology. Professional associations are notoriously self-interested groups.

'A WELL-DEFINED AREA OF STUDY OR CONCERN'?

The I.P.M. gives recognition to a number of examinations set by educational bodies for admission qualifications. We must, however, consider the external examination set by the I.P.M. itself to be the 'professional' entry test. In its evidence to the Royal Commission the I.P.M. said:

> The standard of the examination is set at pass degree level. The basic qualification for entry is either G.C.E. in five subjects of which two are at 'A' level, or experience of work in a personnel department. Equivalent requirements apply to Scotland and Northern Ireland. There are exemptions from certain subjects of the examination for holders of appropriate university degrees and professional qualifications.
> The present examination consists of four papers:
>> Business Economics and Business Administration,
>> Industrial Relations including legal aspects,
>> Personnel Management (two papers).
> Candidates may take subjects singly or together and may retake any subject in which they fail on two subsequent occasions.
> At present the examination scheme is being revised and the Institute hopes to introduce an optional paper in education and training.[1]

The I.P.M.'s evidence to the Royal Commission would seem to indicate some dissatisfaction with the present levels of training: '. . . There will be a recognised need for a sustained policy over long

[1] I.P.M. evidence to the Royal Commission, paras. 97, 98, 100.

periods to permit the creation of conditions and attitudes without which successful industrial relations policies cannot emerge. Long-term organisation planning, including manpower forecasting and a deeper insight into motivation and human behaviour, needs to be developed and brought to bear on personnel policy. Personnel departments staffed with specialists *trained in the job*, will have a significant part to play in such developments. *It is the continuing responsibility of the Institute to assist its members through adequate training and experience to fulfil that role.*'[1]

It was in 1954 that Drucker asked: 'Is personnel management bankrupt?'[2] He argued that it had made many promises but had failed to fulfil them. Yet there was hope that one day it might be more successful in doing so. He suggested that there was too much reliance on techniques of personnel administration; theory had been too little developed. There always would be difficulty in measuring the attainment of personnel management objectives, but it was clear that many companies could not see the wood for the trees nor could their personnel specialists help them to see the wood any more clearly for they were bogged down with day-to-day routines.

It may be useful to consider what is this theory which, one day, may be able to help managements with their personnel problems. It will be recalled that the industrial welfare workers went to classes in social economics and social philosophy and, whilst their studies did provide a useful basis for understanding why workpeople might wish to challenge the employers' view of efficiency and justice, they did not provide an effective framework for analysis of day-to-day problems within the organisation.

During the First World War, however, industrial psychologists began to show how reference to theory could be used to improve understanding of problems of fatigue or to decide on the optimum number of hours to be worked in a week. In the inter-war period industrial psychology began to provide data about: individual differences; learning curves; motivation to work; interviewing procedures in selection, vocational guidance and employee counselling; ergonomics; optimum hours of work, fatigue, stress, absence.

At this time such theory as was known was applied mainly to try

[1] I.P.M. evidence to the Royal Commission, para. 84 (our italics).
[2] P. F. Drucker, *op. cit.*

to maximise the contribution of individual employees to the organisation—vocational tests and structured interviews were found to be helpful in selection; an understanding of learning processes was useful in setting up training programmes; job analysis became a basic tool for examining work flows, for the deployment of staff, for evaluating jobs and for merit rating as well as for recruitment purposes; a theory of motivation provided a basis for reconsideration of incentives in the transition to a full-employment situation where fear of the sack was no longer important. Yet there were only a few companies which used this data to any real extent.

Industrial psychology being concerned mainly with individuals, there was need also for a theory about organisations. 'Scientific management', which began to be developed round about the turn of the century, seemed to provide the link between theory and practice because it was concerned with attempts to explain organisation structures, with time and motion study (later known as work study or organisation and methods study) and with improved recording as a basis for prediction and control. But it was less successful in providing a sound theoretical basis than industrial psychology. Concepts which were developed about organisation structures had more exceptions to them than seemed proper—they often seemed to state dilemmas rather than to offer guidance to management, as in the propositions about keeping spans of control small and restricting the numbers of levels in a hierarchy to improve communication possibly at the expense of co-ordination and control. Time study often seemed to create greater difficulties than it resolved, and prediction of human behaviour was perceived to be less easy than prediction of costs or sales from company records. These too-simple approaches of the 'scientific' or 'classical' management theorists have been shown up by Woodward's study of organisation structures in s.w. Essex in 1957.[1] This study demonstrated that different structures seemed to be appropriate for different technologies and that where managements had tried to fit the structure to the classical descriptions in inappropriate technical situations the tensions between management and workpeople were acute. Equally, the too-simple premises of the early time-study men have been attacked by a number of researchers who have shown that where these

[1] J. Woodward, *Industrial Organisation: Theory and Practice*, Oxford, 1965.

techniques are applied by managements without considering the context—the total culture of the group being studied—they are unlikely to succeed.[1]

The 'human relations movement' developed out of the findings of the Hawthorne experiments of the late 1920s, in which the importance of small groups both for their members and as a component part of organisation became clear.[2] It was an American movement but it had considerable influence in Britain too, but not until much later on (1947 onwards). In the early stages, 'human relations' had great appeal to certain managements who thought it could offer help in developing skills for avoiding conflict between workpeople and management, and for diminishing resistance to change. Large-scale programmes of supervisory training were linked to the idea of learning better human-relations techniques, but these programmes were superficial and concerned mainly to teach good manners and not to promote thorough analysis of difficulties in personnel management. During the last 20 years, however, much more research into small-group behaviour has been promoted and the findings suggest that personnel specialists could use this learning to advantage. It bridges the difference in approach to organisations made by psychologists and sociologists and explains how the individual fits into the whole. In addition this learning emphasises the interaction between task and process—or between intellectual and feeling levels of behaviour. It is concerned with analysing the interaction between formal and informal groups, leadership, dependency, authority, the ability to contribute to discussions, trust and mistrust.

In Britain the students of small groups quickly moved over into the sociological study of organisation. The two most influential research groups in the 1950s were the Tavistock Institute teams with their psycho-analytic orientation and the industrial sociologists at Liverpool University. The Tavistock team developed separate preoccupations as time passed: Jaques at the Glacier Metal Co. moved from an investigation of joint consultation and working groups to the study of equitable payment and effective organisa-

[1] R. Cooper, 'The Psychology of Organisations', *New Society*, April 1965.
[2] F. J. Roethlisberger and W. D. Dixon, *Management and the Workers*, Harvard, 1939.

tional roles; Rice has been interested in inter-group relations and has worked with Bion on the formulation of theoretical concepts about small group behaviour; Trist became aware of the basic importance of technological factors in relation to the organisation of social systems at work. The Liverpool researchers also became interested in the effects of technical change and participation by workpeople in democratic management, and, more recently, in the effects of computerisation. Lupton in Manchester demonstrated the different frames of reference which were used by workers and by management in the same situation.

THEORY AND PRACTICE

Meanwhile personnel management practice had been developing to meet the demands of employing organisations. Some of these developments became fashionable and were adopted by other companies. The first personnel records were kept, not for prediction but for control. The collective bargainers kept records about behaviour for disciplinary purposes, the wages departments kept records of individuals' payment and deductions. Timekeepers kept details of absence and lateness. In addition to these personal records there were other official records which had to be maintained for the Factory Inspectors, Wages Inspectors or other government departments. The early collective bargainers minuted agreements about procedural rules and built up records of precedents.

It is probably true to say that most personnel records are still personal records. Attempts were made during the Second World War to get personnel specialists to work out statistics from these records (which were sometimes co-ordinated but often duplicated) and to take appropriate corrective action on absenteeism, accidents, labour turnover. Yet again the emphasis was on disciplinary control rather than thorough analysis. Since then statistical methods have improved and computerisation of records offers greatly increased prospects of analysing data. However, there is little evidence that personnel specialists are interested in making comparison with other companies yet.

During the first half of the twentieth century a number of useful personnel techniques were developed. To take a few examples: procedures were developed for the efficient recruitment and selection of new employees; methods of communication were greatly improved whether by developing more effective noticeboards or house journals or joint consultative agenda. Some of these techniques were able to be used universally with profit, others were applied injudiciously to organisations where they were inappropriate.

During the Second World War, there were confusions arising out of the use of the term, personnel management, to describe the two activities of managing personnel and being a specialist on personnel management matters. It was suggested by some that it might be useful to adopt the American practice of describing the specialist activity as *personnel administration*, but this did not 'catch on' in Britain, probably because personnel specialists were still very obsessed with their status level, which seemed to hold the key to their opportunity to make a better contribution in the management team. Yet though the term was not adopted the ideas of personnel administration were. Since the war, American textbooks have been used in personnel management courses because there have been no British textbooks as useful as these guides to personnel practice. Such pamphlets and books as have been published in post-war Britain have usually dealt with one sector of the work only (such as selection or training) and it has been valuable to have a more comprehensive survey of the whole series of activities of the personnel department and a discussion in which they are related to one another.[1] However, the limitations of using books written about behaviour for another culture pattern are obvious.

Not only were there cross-cultural differences. It began to be realised that the assumption that techniques appropriate to one organisation would necessarily meet the needs of another was unfounded. Even more difficult to cope with were techniques appropriate to one stage of organisational development which were no longer appropriate at a later period, and here it came to be seen that the personnel specialist might not have been facilitating but building in resistance to change, fossilising parts of the organisation by get-

---

[1] C. H. Northcott, *Personnel Management*, Macmillan, 1945, was so full of 'weighted value judgments' that it did not seem to provide a useful basis for teaching although it was the only well-known British textbook.

ting more inflexible written rules or agreed procedures or consistent practices.

The dangers of 'consistent' personnel administration are only now being recognised in many companies—the too rigid use of job descriptions, of organisation charts, of training manuals may be as great a disadvantage as were the advantages of introducing such techniques at an earlier stage when there was need for clearer definition of responsibility and authority in the work to be done.

Administrative procedures were usually introduced for reasons of consistency and fairness or because they were fashionable. Personnel specialists did not have adequate tools or adequate training to act as analysts of behaviour whether of individuals, groups or organisations.

We have already discussed the early formalised training of the industrial welfare workers with its emphasis on practical counselling skills and an understanding of social economics and social philosophy. It took a long time to realise that practical training in personal counselling was not the most suitable preparation for personnel work, but what should replace it? The full-time personnel management students began to be separated off from the social-work students in universities after the Second World War and to take different courses and have different fieldwork placements.[1] The content of these courses varied. In those universities which were orientated towards the humanities there was one orientation, in the technological universities another. These orientations may perhaps be described as 'an introductory course in the social sciences with special applications in personnel management' and 'a general management studies course with special emphasis on the personnel function'. It can be appreciated that in the former the emphasis was on the applied behavioural sciences and it was hoped that students would be able to relate these to practice through additional specific applied courses and in fieldwork; in the latter the emphasis was on applied courses which seemed to provide a meaningful basis for starting to make a useful contribution at the lower levels of the managerial hierarchy where students could expect to begin. There was, of course, a certain amount of agreement about what should be

[1] Full-time courses only are discussed here since they are normally expected to establish the optimum standards of education and training.

included—personnel management and industrial relations usually being 'core subjects'. The applied courses differ from one institution to another (and apart from personnel management and industrial relations) they include: managerial economics, financial and cost accounting, industrial law, statistical sources and methods and other aspects of social-science research methodology, operational research or work study or management decision-making and measurement and control systems. Experiments in learning about small-group behaviour have also been tried.

There has been considerable discussion about the theoretical content of courses, but little about the application. Fogarty and Lupton have both argued the necessity for longer full-time courses for those intending to become professional personnel specialists.[1] They visualise such a man as an organisation analyst, diagnosing the causes of malaise and suggesting remedial actions which can be taken, or possibly preventing the symptoms of malaise from appearing at all.

It has been suggested that one of the problems of the behavioural scientists is their inability to communicate easily with their public. During the 1950s there was considerable resistance to social-science research and many articles were published in professional journals to establish that it had limits beyond which it would fail to provide answers in the ethical areas. Isobel Menzies has drawn attention to the shortage of skilled researchers who are capable of working through their findings with the organisations which provided them with research facilities.[2] All the more is it difficult to find enough people skilled in interpreting and applying research done in other circumstances for other organisations, appropriate to the needs of their employing body.

Thus Lupton's argument that more courses in the behavioural sciences should be provided in universities in order to increase the number of skilled personnel specialists does not seem to go far enough unless these courses can develop skills at the process level as well as skills of intellectual analysis. In the previous section we

[1] M. P. Fogarty, 'An Independent Comment', *Personnel Management*, March 1963; Tom Lupton, *op. cit.*

[2] In a contribution to the S.S.R.C. conference on research, University of Kent, Canterbury, July 1966.

have attempted to examine the difficulties of the personnel specialist who is still an 'outsider' and not integrated into the organisation because he cannot communicate adequately with other managers.

Lupton has also argued that too much stress in the past has been laid on ideologies and that it is now time to concentrate on improvement of efficiency, which could be attained through better analysis. This argument, too, would seem to ignore the necessity to operate at the process as well as the task level. It is necessary to be aware of the values of the groups in which one seeks to have membership. Lupton, of course, was reacting to the inability of the early writers on personnel management to distinguish factual data from weighted value judgments.[1]

How then can the skills of the personnel specialist in managing (as well as analysing) group and organisational processes be improved? Understanding his own contribution might be one way to start. Personnel specialists might be better able to cope if they were more aware of the dynamics of groups and organisations, of the reasons for conflict, the mechanisms of defence, patterns of decision making and authority struggles. It would appear that an intellectual understanding of role theory might be useful in helping to clarify role ambiguities and role conflicts which lead to organisational stress. Sociology provides explanations of the process of developing and modifying values by clarifying role-taking and the function of reference groups for individuals. Others have described the external and internal structures of groups, or formal and informal organisation structures. These explanations make it necessary to accept a 'pluralistic' frame of reference. The concept of a 'pluralistic' frame of reference enables ideological conflicts to be seen in realistic terms. Yet these may be understood at an intellectual level but cannot be managed at a feeling level.

Homans has described the subtle variations in behaviour from one group to another, normative behaviour patterns, which are characteristic and distinctive.[2] Conformity to these patterns is expected of members and the tolerance of the group for deviants will have well recognised limits. There are struggles for power and resources in all groups, and Burns has shown how important it is

[1] e.g. Northcott, *op. cit.*
[2] G. Homans, *The Human Group*, Harcourt Brace, 1954.

that the different functional specialists should be able to communicate about their common problems if the organisation is to be able to adapt and innovate.[1] It has begun to be seen that conflict is not necessarily bad provided it is realistic and constructive. The difficulties of the personnel specialist in meeting the behavioural norms of the groups to which he belongs have already been explored. Frequently he has problems of coming from a different educational background, he lacks financial knowledge, he has limited technical knowledge, he is suspected of having a different ideology. He has authority problems.

The studies by Woodward and others demonstrate that the personnel specialist is often appointed late in the history of a new plant, or he is consulted at a late stage when the technology of change is already planned.[2] In consequence he comes into the groups at a considerable disadvantage, he does not know their norms nor their myths, and there is usually hostility in an established group to the introduction of a new member.

At present learning about feelings is usually left to chance. Yet need this be? Professional training of social workers concentrates on the management of feelings, as does much of teacher training. Professional training of personnel specialists may have to move this way. At first it will probably be necessary for courses to be provided in social-science laboratories since there will not be enough analysis of experience to be passed on by present practitioners of personnel management.

In spite of the Institute's emphasis on 'specialists trained in the job' and 'the continuing responsibility of the Institute to assist its members through adequate training and experience to fulfil [their] role', there has been a steady withdrawal from the responsibility for supervising professional education and training.

From its inception in 1913, the Welfare Workers' Association had developed close associations with university social-studies departments and played an active part in discussions about the development of curricula for social-work students (including industrial

---

[1] T. Burns and G. F. Stalker, *The Management of Innovation*, Tavistock, 1961.

[2] Woodward, *op. cit.*

welfare workers).[1] These close associations have continued ever since, although the proportion of students being taught in university social-studies departments is probably much lower today than it was then, now that there are several other methods of preparing for personnel work. Up until the early 1950s the I.P.M. had close contacts with the universities and technical colleges where there were students on approved courses. Representatives went around the country to attend student selection boards and to discuss syllabuses with tutors. During the '50s, however, the development of part-time courses in technical colleges and the decision to have an external examination for those already in employment who wished to qualify for admission to membership at an early stage in their careers made it impossible to keep up such close contacts with all the teaching bodies. Later still it was argued that the I.P.M. was not in any way concerned with the courses as courses but only with their products. The onus of learning enough theory and getting sufficient practical experience to pass the examinations was on the student, not on the Institute. There were to be no more reports on practical work or viva examinations—practical competence would be tested to some extent by the examination questions.

The examination questions do try to test the application of industrial psychology and industrial sociology in one of the personnel management papers, but the test of competence can hardly be considered to be stringent either in terms of finding out about ability to identify and evaluate problems of organisational stress, or to provide a specialist service to management in personnel administration, or to give a good general background in management studies generally. But this superficiality is the fault of all the full-time and part-time courses, too, apart from the new degree schemes which have been started in certain universities, e.g. Strathclyde, but how far can they be considered as 'professional training'? They are, rather, vocational education.

[1] The I.P.M. was founded in 1913, and was first known as the Welfare Workers' Association. After various minor changes of name to indicate amalgamations of local groups and of men's and women's groups after the First World War, it became the Institute of Labour Management in 1931, and added the name of the Staff Management Association to its headed paper in 1934. In 1946 it changed to the Institute of Personnel Management.

Professionalism in the traditional sense provides a preparation not only at the intellectual level (professional education) but also at the level of making day-to-day relationships with clients (professional training). The medical student walks the wards in order to become a competent clinician. During this time he learns how to diagnose and treat cases under supervision. Theory and practice are integrated. At present this does not apply in personnel management education.

THE CHANGING SCOPE OF THE JOB

It would appear that, since the war, opportunities for personnel specialists have been growing—some are still engaged on low-level routine administrative activities over the whole range, whilst others have moved into the top management team as behavioural science consultants or have become involved in long-term forward planning, others still are specialising in one of the six functions—employment, training, wages, negotiation and consultation, health and safety and employee services in greater or less depth. Nowadays, the personnel specialist must usually choose between giving general advice on personnel policies and practices to a department or small works or becoming a specialist in some aspect of the larger personnel department's work. Petrie has discussed the dilemma which is created by this more intensive view of the functional specialist jobs to be done.[1] By increasing specific competence in one area of the work, the personnel specialist is likely to lose sight of the whole. His 'manager of a part' role is emphasised at the expense of the 'part manager of the whole'. In consequence, the more he becomes an expert within the personnel function, the less is he likely to be seen as a potential general manager. Yet the only way to be recognised as competent usually seems to him to be to get better at his specialist job.

This vicious circle can be broken by the outstanding personality who becomes recognised for his exceptional qualities over and above the occupational role, or possibly by moving from one company to another when the next stage of development seems to have been reached.

[1] D. J. Petrie, 'The Personnel "Professionals", Who Needs Them?', *Personnel Management*, September 1965.

The development of the personnel specialisation is left to individual or company initiative rather than to organised professional activity. There are good reasons for this as we have seen. A profession must be objectively and subjectively identified. The I.P.M. as a qualifying association has many problems. None of the management professions (save the company secretaries' and accountants') is given clear objective recognition. The I.P.M. has, in addition, to contend with the ambivalences of personnel specialists themselves about their professional identity. The rate of development of the behavioural sciences poses great problems, so that the question of 'what should be learnt?' appears to be constantly changing. The rate of growth of job opportunities poses the problem of educating and training people on the job. How can the older personnel specialists be brought up-to-date? How can the young ones be given a thorough enough training and then integrated into present-day management structures? The present refresher courses are not thorough enough to repair deficiencies in theoretical knowledge by themselves alone. They are more concerned with tactics than strategies. Where should the learning be done?

The I.P.M. has provided many short 'refresher' courses on different aspects of personnel work and has tried to indicate to the potential students what kind of shared experience they should begin from when enrolling by designating certain courses 'introductory' or 'advanced' or by circulating to a limited group of members. Courses are also offered by the Ministry of Labour in association with the I.P.M. from time to time and by the other management associations such as the British Institute of Management, the Industrial Society and by the research consultancy institutes: the National Institute of Industrial Psychology and the Tavistock Institute.

It can be argued that these courses are inadequate, that what is required is a crash programme provided by the Ministry of Labour or some other government-appointed body—not so much a programme of courses (though this might be useful) but individual advice and help to companies on a consultancy basis.

EVIDENCE FROM OTHER SOURCES ABOUT COMPETENCE

Personnel specialists are not at the bottom of the league tables of management salaries. This would seem to indicate that they are perceived to be making a necessary contribution to the organisation in which they are employed (though salaries within the occupational group do not seem to be a particularly good indicator of relative worth).

The number of personnel specialists is increasing and continues to increase particularly since the Industrial Training Boards have been set up.

Attempts to quantify different levels of working have not been very successful (as we saw in the discussion on the I.P.M. Salaries Survey of 1966), since 'the personnel function differs quite markedly from company to company depending on a number of factors. . . . Companies exhibit a great range of attitudes towards a personnel policy from the very advanced with a clearly defined and communicated policy to those having little or none. The level of sophistication of personnel management not unnaturally follows these attitudes from company to company.'

Does greater competence lie in greater specialisation? Hamblin's report on the general personnel officers in the South Wales study would indicate that lack of specialisation at least may end up in inadequacy.[1] Too many current crises in the personnel department drove out long-term thinking about training. Yet Petrie has argued that greater specialisation tends to limit the personnel specialists' prospects of advancement into top management.[2]

So the question arises, 'competent for what?' We suggest that the I.P.M. study group which came out against tiering of training in 1957 was mistaken. There are different levels of competence whether they can easily be identified and graded or not.

There is some evidence in published work about the way in which personnel specialists do their jobs. The literature can perhaps best be divided into:

(a)   Applied social science—studies which relate the problems of personnel specialists to theory, which help them to see how to

[1] Hamblin, *op. cit.*
[2] Petrie, *op. cit.*

use theory in their day-to-day work, e.g. the effect of social structure on manpower planning, the social, psychological and physical consequences of shift work.[1]

(b) Case studies or surveys which begin from practice but develop theories to explain the findings, e.g. the Glacier studies or Woodward's study of industrial organisation.[2]

(c) Case studies which recount experiences of personnel management which might be regarded as providing an example of 'good' practice, e.g. Fox's study of the handling of a redundancy, the Fawley studies.[3]

(d) Brief summaries of 'good' practice published by the Ministry of Labour, Department of Scientific and Industrial Research, the I.P.M. and other bodies concerned with raising general standards.[4] (D.S.I.R. publications stress the importance of seeing each situation as a different situation with its own particular difficulties.)

(e) 'How to do it' books on interviewing, performance appraisal, salary administration, etc., etc.[5]

It would seem that there are still many gaps at the analytical level, particularly in relation to the planning of change. This is not very surprising when the newness of the development of the behavioural sciences is considered.

Surveys of personnel activities can perhaps best be divided into

[1] e.g. V. Klein, *Britain's Married Women Workers*, Routledge & Kegan Paul, 1965; P. E. Mott *et al.*, *Shift Work*, University of Michigan Press, 1965.

[2] W. Brown, *Exploration in Management*, Heinemann, 1960; E. Jaques, *The Changing Culture of a Factory*, Tavistock, 1951; J. Woodward, *Industrial Organisation: Theory and Practice*, Oxford, 1965.

[3] A. Fox, *The Milton Plan*, I.P.M., 1965; A. Flanders, *The Fawley Productivity Agreements*, Faber, 1964.

[4] H.M.S.O., *Security and Change*, Ministry of Labour, 1961; R. Stewart, *Managers for Tomorrow*, D.S.I.R., 1957; D. H. Gray, *Manpower Planning*, I.P.M., 1966; R. B. Buzzard and J. L. Radforth, *Statistical Records about People at Work*, National Institute of Industrial Psychology; British Institute of Management, *Job Evaluation*, 1961; Industrial Welfare Society, *Suggestion Schemes*, 1950.

[5] e.g. E. Sidney and M. Brown, *The Skills of Interviewing*, Tavistock, 1961; J. Munro Fraser, *Handbook of Employment Interviewing*, 1st ed. 1950; G. McBeath and D. N. Rands, *Salary Administration*, Business Pubs.

those where the researchers' orientation is scientific and analytical and those where the interest is ideological—the emphasis in the former being upon efficiency, the latter on justice or democracy or some other value. Even the 'more advanced' companies who are prepared to let researchers in to examine their activities and then write up and publish them do not come out too well in these surveys. Mumford's study of computer installation indicates a blindness to the human relations aspects of technical change.[1] Kahn's study of the motor industry provides depressing evidence of failure to alleviate the effects of market changes.[2] Smith's study of the National Coal Board's transfer scheme for redundant workers and Cook's study of the railway redundancy suggest that some personnel specialists are quite good at coping with organisational change once marketing and technical decisions have been taken, but that they are not brought in at a preventive stage (though possibly there can be no complete or long-term prevention in a contracting industry).[3] It would appear that few managers are able to anticipate the human relations implications of technical and marketing change and can only deal with its effects. Personnel specialists are no better than others.

Other studies of joint consultation or of discipline show wide variations in practice. The N.I.I.P. study showed that, whilst some companies had tried hard to develop joint consultation and to make it work, others were not convinced that it was worth the effort of trying to develop it.[4] We know, too, that some companies at one time anxious to develop 'industrial democracy' by this means have become disillusioned about the value of this approach—they now lay more stress on developing managers' efficiency in their organisational roles, and question whether 'industrial democracy' can ever be achieved if negotiation is separated from consultation.

Two recent studies of disciplinary practice would indicate that employers (and workpeople) are pragmatic in their approach to daily

[1] E. Mumford, *Living with a Computer*, I.P.M., 1964.

[2] H. Kahn, *Repercussions of Redundancy*, Allen & Unwin, 1964.

[3] C. Smith, *Planned Transfer of Labour, with special reference to the Coal Industry*, University of London Ph.D., 1961, unpublished thesis; L. Cook, *Railway Workshops, the Problem of Contraction*, British Railways, mimeographed, 1956.

[4] National Institute of Industrial Psychology, *op. cit.*

living in many companies. It is difficult to lay down rules to cover every disciplinary issue, particularly such intangibles as incompetence and insubordination. In consequence, rules must be general statements of policy but precedents could be built up to clarify the limits of tolerance for workers and for managers. Plumridge found that in the 64 'progressive' firms which he studied the 'need for treating every case on its merits' was stressed.[1] He argued: 'This pragmatic approach appears desirable so long as it takes account of precedent and makes some attempt to anticipate possible future cases; if it does neither, it is likely to lead either to inconsistency or to embarrassment on some future occasion.' This raises the whole question of the evaluation and testing of personnel practices. (We seldom read about such evaluations except very occasionally in relation to selection.) Anthony has examined disciplinary practice in six companies where the unions were non-existent or identified with company interests rather than employee interests.[2] He develops a hypothesis that, in such companies, since 'discipline is something that happens to the people to whom it is applied', in an organisation where the rules are deliberately kept unclear 'the freedom from constraint which management has won may be cancelled by the anomie which it has created, a state of affairs in which management can no longer communicate in any real sense with the employees it is seeking to manage'. General evidence would seem to suggest that many personnel specialists are pragmatists, that they do not analyse facts or think about the weighting of values, that they do not even collect simple data which would help them to assess and reconsider what they are doing. If we break down the management process into research, planning, decision-making, execution and evaluation, most appear to be carrying out executive activities.[3]

It might be thought that too many brief summaries of 'good' practice or 'how to do it' books are still being published in the light of the findings of the behavioural scientists so far, findings which

[1] M. D. Plumridge, 'Disciplinary Practice', *Personnel Management*, September 1966.

[2] P. D. Anthony, 'Industrial Codes of Discipline', *Personnel*, January 1968.

[3] Flanders, 'The Future of Personnel Management', *Personnel Management*, December 1965; S. M. Herman, 'Techniques and Trivia', *Personnel Management*, September 1963. Both argue that it is the responsibility of the specialists to get their managements to use them properly as organisational analysts.

indicate most clearly that it is necessary for organisations to work out their own answers to problems and that it is not wise to take over, wholesale, solutions discovered by other companies to suit their particular situation. Yet it could perhaps be argued that standards of practice are so low in many organisations that it is necessary to try to encourage management to consider other ways of tackling their problems by providing examples of successful practice.

We do not know whether personnel specialists in general are able to read, any more than other managers who complain about being too busy to do so. The Ministry of Labour Personnel Management Advisors have found out that 'well-known' studies are not well-known to the personnel specialist at plant level. In the Crichton, Hamblin and Lawson study there was only one company in 15 where personnel specialists were encouraged to read new books and discuss them in staff meetings. In other plants this was not acceptable, and personnel specialists had to be available to meet the pressing problems of day-to-day living all the time. People worked out their ideas in discussion with a few injections every now and again from a day conference or short refresher course. One other large company blamed the poor quality of work of its plant personnel officers on its own failure to develop a progressive personnel specialists' training programme. The personnel specialists were isolated in plants geographically remote from headquarters and visitors from the central personnel department tended to concentrate on implementing policies already decided at a higher level when they came to see the local man. Annual personnel specialists' meetings at headquarters did not allow enough time to get over the socialising stage to begin real learning about new issues.

EXPERTISE?

The picture is blurred. On the one hand, there would appear to be a number of people very concerned about the advancement of personnel management and they have visions of personnel specialists of great competence, both intellectual and social. On the other hand, there are many employing organisations which are ill-managed and confused about their direction of advance, where personnel specialists are of low calibre and low in aspiration. They will need to be brought along into the second half of the twentieth century.

The 'professional' association provides a forum for broad general discussion of aspirations towards optimal performance, yet at the same time it is attempting to cater for the others. In meeting these two needs it does not seem to be succeeding in providing enough interest for the specialists within the function who wish to exchange specific detailed information about their activities (e.g. training officers), nor does it attract the 'organisation' man who is passing through the personnel department. It is not general enough in its approach to management problems for him, yet it is often too general for the experts employed in a limited sphere of personnel work. It appears to have little direct effect upon performance but to act more as a forum for sharing values.

The industrial relations expert is most clearly identifiable in this blurred picture. He can offer to cope with immediate crises (for this is his forte) and he can show results for his efforts. Yet this is only one part of the whole job of the personnel specialist, a part which perhaps might not be so necessary were the preventive activities to be properly carried out.

The I.P.M. provides support for the general personnel officer who is partly engaged in industrial relations work and partly in the wider activities we have outlined. Yet because it has these wider aspirations it fails to provide much detailed or specific guidance on the way to tackle the job, which might fit the personnel specialist for his role as part manager of the whole organisation or as expert in the part of collective bargainer. In the next section we shall go on to look at these roles of the industrial relations specialist as well as his public relations and liaison officer roles.

14   The Industrial Relations Specialist

In describing the evolution of the personnel management function as a specialist activity, we began by discussing the work of the employers' associations. The officials of employers' associations were the first industrial relations specialists and precursors of personnel specialists employed by the firms themselves.

It is clear that today the officials of employers' associations are seldom recruited from the 'professional' group of personnel specialists, although it is not impossible that this may happen from time to time. Our limited evidence suggests two reasons for this: on the one hand, the employers responsible for making the appointments are looking for men whose orientation is that of general manager rather than functional specialist, who see the issues in terms of management's rights and prerogatives and whilst knowing about union attitudes are unlikely to be in any way identified with them; and on the other, the 'career' personnel specialist is not anxious to get out of the mainstream of experiencing life in a personnel department for such a specialist appointment and may not be entirely sympathetic to the rather defensive line about management rights taken by many of the associations.

The personnel specialists' jobs in the associations' member companies developed out of the early appointments of clerks acting as custodians of agreements and personal records. We have described how this narrow job evolved into a general personnel management post in many organisations as the personnel department took on responsibilities, first for employment and later for the whole range of personnel activities. In some of the very large organisations, or those in which there is great activity in collective bargaining, there are still appointed functional specialists in industrial relations with narrow terms of reference—to prepare briefs and conduct bargaining sessions or to develop joint consultative activities or to research on comparative wage rates. However, in the main, wage and salary administration, negotiation and consultation are only part of the work of the personnel department, though they may be seen as a very important part of the general personnel job. It will be recalled that Collins found only 9·8 per cent of industrial relations specialists in his South Wales study and suggested that in general these specialists did not perceive themselves as personnel specialists and thus were uninterested in joining the I.P.M. The Crichton and Anthony survey of I.P.M. members showed that there were only 21 industrial relations specialists among their 521 respondents[1], which would seem to indicate that industrial relations is seen as part of the work of some general managers (Collins) or is a part of the work of general personnel officers and there are few employed on it full-time. The Crichton/Anthony group were employed as follows:

It will be remembered that we discovered in the South Wales case studies that industrial relations activities took up a lot of energy of the plant personnel officers. Discussions with foremen and shop stewards, dealing with grievances, organising joint consultative committees and sub-committees, and investigating wages matters engaged the main attentions of the personnel department staff for they had to meet constant demands from the local managers and the central personnel department for briefing. In addition they might need to inform the federation and seek its help. The need to meet these regular demands for information and help in handling day-to-day industrial relations matters, together with the service expected of the employment function and the management of the accumulated employee services, tended to fill the time of the general personnel officers.

[1] Crichton and Anthony made a 20-per-cent survey of I.P.M. members in Jan.–Feb. 1967 to determine their interest in industrial relations as part of a report to the Royal Commission about personnel specialists.

INDUSTRIAL CLASSIFICATIONS

	General personnel work	Specialist personnel work (incl. I.R.)	Both
Agriculture, forestry, mining and quarrying	8	4	12
Bricks, pottery, glass and cement	8	4	12
Chemicals and allied industries	52	14	66
Construction	14	5	19
Food, drink and tobacco	33	7	40
Gas, electricity and water	12	3	15
Metals, engineering, electrical, vehicles and shipbuilding	114	37	151
Paper, printing and publishing	19	—	19
Professional, insurance, banking, and public administration	14	6	20
Retail or wholesale distribution	18	3	21
Textiles, leather, clothing, and footwear	25	1	26
Transport and communication	4	3	7
Total	**321**	**87**	**408**

THE OUTLOOK OF THE PERSONNEL SPECIALIST TOWARDS HIS INDUSTRIAL RELATIONS ACTIVITIES

Yet how was this time filled? We have suggested in our discussion of the collective bargaining processes that, because the men at the point of contact in bargaining have different frames of reference from the men standing further back in the system (see chart on page 122), they develop different outlooks. We would argue that their role in this system develops a certain kind of attitude and we have tried to show how the preoccupations of the top management team differ from those of the personnel specialist concerned with collective wage and salary determination and the procedures of collective bargaining, because of the different reference groups. If the industrial relations specialist takes on the colouring of the opposition, it is because in preparing the defence against their demands he may become identified with them or be seen to be identified with them. Thus, in the past, and quite often today, the policy in appointing specialists in the bargaining process to represent management was to look for recruits among trade-union officials—to set a thief to catch a thief. Indeed, the ex-unionist might seem to be more loyal to management's interests than a career personnel specialist, for he had had to declare his move over to 'the other side', whereas the career personnel specialist might be less openly committed to a management ideology, too anxious to appear neutral.

We have discussed Lupton's attitude to this problem of ideological commitment in the personnel specialist—his suggestion is that the professional personnel specialist should aim to become a neutral expert analysing factual data and keeping clear of ideology and its possible limitations on action. We would argue that this detachment is a tenable position only for the consultant who is not an employee of the company. The collective bargainer is perceived as having commitment whether he tries to be detached or not, and this is his difficulty because the commitment or lack of commitment is perceived differently by the different groups in which he has membership. Thus, in the groups which are concerned with management of the whole organisation, he is liable to be regarded as too anxious to be the conscience of management, the 'remembrancer' about the workpeople's point of view rather than a man committed to the defence of management's rights and prerogatives; in the public relations role he has to speak on behalf of management to the press and so by simplifying the issues may appear intransigent to the unions with whom he must negotiate; in his liaison officer role, he may be very muddled himself, as we have suggested, not knowing with whom to identify; or, if clear in his own identification with management, not knowing how far to make concessions before being regarded as disloyal; or if identified with a 'third force' (the professional group?) being isolated in his 'neutrality' and liable to be mistrusted by all the other interest groups.

Yet Lupton pinpoints for us a trend in the activities of the personnel specialists. They have tried to resolve some of these difficulties about their ideological stand (difficulties which we would regard as insoluble) by making parts of the industrial relations specialisation 'more objective'. Thus wages and salaries become evaluated and graded so that some of the bazaar element of striking

a bargain is removed and a more 'just' and 'efficient' basis of payment brought in, fringe benefits become calculated, discipline subject to rules.

DEVELOPMENT OF TECHNICAL CONTROL AND UNDER-
STANDING OF SOCIO-TECHNICAL SYSTEMS

This is in keeping with the rest of management's response to the
union challenge to management control in the full-employment era.
The emphasis in this challenge in the first half of the twentieth century was on the social control of workpeople. Through fear of the
sack and time-study techniques more pressure could be brought to
bear on them to increase output. The 'indulgency' area was
diminished, the controls tightened. Many writers have drawn attention to this area of 'silent bargaining' between management and
workers which is concerned with efforts and rewards above and
beyond the openly arrived-at collective bargain. This is the continuous bargaining between workpeople and their immediate supervisors, but the limits of manoeuvre are affected by the general
climate in the work place and the pressures exerted upon individuals
by the groups of which they are members.

Baldamus has shown that workpeople have their own responses to
attempts by management to screw down the limits too tightly.[1]
Gouldner, too, demonstrated that short-term gains in control could
result in employees' unrest and wildcat strikes.[2] Since 1939 management's prospects of bringing great pressure to bear through
social controls of this kind are much less, and the controls have become less acceptable with increased choice of employer. The
threat of unemployment now affects only the very few, and workpeople have developed many defences against exploitation (defences
which now tend to be designated absenteeism, labour mobility or
restrictive practices). In consequence, management generally is
anxious to develop technological controls over work which will be
more effective. Time study has become work study and is concerned

[1] T. H. Baldamus, *Efficiency and Effort*, Tavistock, 1961.
[2] A. Gouldner, *Patterns of Industrial Bureaucracy*, Free Press of Glencoe,
1954; *Wildcat Strike*, Antioch, 1954.

with work flows and the breakdown of highly skilled jobs into component parts which may be undertaken by less skilled workpeople.

In recounting the history of the development of personnel management we have pointed out how this effort bargaining was conducted away from the personnel department, which was seldom
brought into the picture except to relate the general limits of the
extra money bargaining to the basic rates and to watch over the
procedures of bargaining so that grievances might be fully aired.
There were some companies in which close links were forged between time study and personnel departments so that discussion on
incentives attempted to draw on theory, but in the main such links
were rare and the one department worked quite separately from the
other. In consequence, work-study departments (which inherited
the position of rate fixers or time-study men) have gone on to plan
the technology of work flows and to calculate manning figures
usually without consulting the personnel department.

Woodward's work with production engineers has refocussed attention on the problem of integrating the personnel specialist into
the management team.[1] She argues that it is important to bring the
personnel specialists into closer relationships with production planners, in order to avoid unnecessary conflict being built into the plant
when production lines are set up. A plant is a socio-technical system,
not just a technical system. So, the question arises: how frequently
are personnel specialists appointed at an early enough stage in the
development of a new enterprise or at what point are they consulted
when technical change is envisaged by senior management? There
are reasons to believe that they are often ignored until irrevocable
technical decisions have been taken, so that they cannot advise the
rest of management about their probable implications for personnel.
Enid Mumford's study of computer installation demonstrates that
this applies to all organisations, not only to industry.[2] Woodward
has shown that there are considerable technological differences between one industry and another which seem to create fewer or more
conflicts. Process industry at one end of the continuum, jobbing at
the other, are relatively peaceful, but mass production in the middle
is more liable to disturbances. There are difficulties in organising

[1] J. Woodward, *Industrial Organisation*, Oxford, 1965.
[2] *op. cit.*

the flow of materials, the jobs are often physically demanding but psychologically dissatisfying, the men are thrown closely together and can nurse their grievances more readily. The personnel specialists in these industries are so busy dealing with firefighting that they have no time for long-term thinking, and they are more needed in these situations to do such thinking. Whilst Flanders has been working on the improvement of bargaining procedures and cites Fawley as a model, Woodward goes one step further and argues that the inefficiencies of Fawley need not have arisen had there been more careful social planning at the time of developing the technology of the refinery.[1]

DEVELOPMENT OF THE WORK OF THE PERSONNEL SPECIALIST IN PLANNING A SOCIO-TECHNICAL SYSTEM

At what stage should personnel specialists be brought into planning discussions and how can they best be integrated into planning teams or teams (such as operational research groups) concerned with the planning of change?

Miller studied the development of a steelworks on a greenfield site from the management's viewpoint, and Jones and Wedderburn from the unions' to consider how established employer–employee attitudes might be adapted to the new technology by careful preparation before starting production.[2] In this plant the personnel specialists were appointed right from the start and were able to have a large say in advising management on the whole range of personnel activities, but this is unusual. It is customary, rather, to appoint an employment officer when the plant is nearly ready to begin production, in order to recruit the labour already planned for by the production engineers. The steelworks was anxious to introduce many new techniques and in consequence large problems of manning and training arose. These had to be negotiated with the men, and they took many months to reach agreements about changes in traditional practices. Other steelworks which have not gone through this pre-

[1] Flanders, *op. cit.*; J. Woodward, 'The Right Management', *New Society*, 22 September 1966.

[2] Jones and Wedderburn, 'British Steel's Labour Challenge', *Management Today*, October 1967.

production planning process are bogged down in the problems of negotiating changes piecemeal or endeavouring to do package deals with unions.

This kind of situation was studied by Flanders who was giving attention to the means of developing administrative practices to help personnel specialists to move from firefighting in collective bargaining over into a more positive role as advisers to management. Flanders' study of the Fawley productivity agreements has provided an example to other companies which are trying to deal with resistance to change in their wages structures through focussing on the mechanisms of collective bargaining.

Woodward's work and that of Burns and Stalker on *The Management of Innovation* have led to a questioning of the effectiveness of thinking about management along departmental lines. The researches of these and other industrial sociologists would indicate that the most effective management for a company faced with the need to deal with change is a series of project teams and not a series of hierarchical departments. This way of thinking about organisation as a problem-solving institution made up of task groups dealing with parts of the general problem area creates new perceptions of roles and relationships. The tasks are not different but the methods of dealing with them are.

If this perception of organisation structure were to become as well accepted as the present hierarchical line and staff structures, it would open up new possibilities of integrating personnel specialists, since they would not be seen as policemen or firefighters but as diagnosticians, planners and executives. Woodward's work on sociotechnical systems may prove a growth point in organisation theory and may help to show how best personnel specialists may be employed. Flanders has been particularly urgent in stressing the need for the management teams briefed by their personnel specialists to take the initiative in industrial relations.[1] This pre-planning before production starts seems to be the only thorough way. The industrial relations specialist may prevent unnecessary conflict by attention, at an early stage, to technological problems—pre-planning layouts, manning schedules, demarcation issues, displacements and redun-

[1] A. Flanders, *Industrial Relations: What is Wrong with the System?*, I.P.M., 1965.

dancies. He may be able to predict consequences of technological decisions, and feed back his predictive results to the technical, financial and organisational decision makers so that adjustments may be made as a result of his forecasting. He can also help to improve training of foremen in disciplinary activities. There is also a possibility of changing on-going situations by joining operational research teams.

INDUSTRIAL RELATIONS AND PERSONNEL MANAGEMENT

It may now be useful here to reconsider the aim of personnel management, which has been defined as being: 'to bring together and develop into an effective organisation the men and women who make up an enterprise. . . . [It] is concerned with the development and application of policies and practices governing: recruitment, selection placement and termination; training, education and promotion; terms of employment, methods and standards of remuneration; working conditions and employee services; formal and informal communication and consultation, both through the representatives of employers and employees and at all levels throughout the enterprise; negotiation and application of agreements on wages and working conditions; procedures for the avoidance and settlement of disputes. . . . [It] is also concerned with the human and social implications of change in internal organisation and methods of working, and of economic and social changes in the community.'[1]

The order in which these activities are listed suggests first a positive approach to building and maintaining the organisation, and only when these fail to deal with the avoidance and settlement of disputes. Workpeople's challenge to management control is much fiercer in some organisations than in others, and management's desire for control varies too.

What is an effective organisation? There are different baselines from which personnel specialists have to start in their pursuit of efficiency and justice and the consequent unevenness of personnel work. We have suggested that ideological differences between management and workers, certain kinds of technologies, the make-up of the labour force and local or industry traditions might be four

[1] I.P.M.'s definition of personnel management, 1958.

variables affecting the personnel management activities of an organisation.

The personnel specialist is deeply involved in this struggle for power, for he may be asked to bargain for management or to advise management on its case, and if he is not reasonably well-identified he will find his position difficult. We have discussed the problems of role perception both by the personnel specialist of his own role and the expectations which the rest of management have come to have of him. We present below a series of continua to illustrate managements' response to the union challenge to management control. This does not include the challenge on ownership but only the challenge for participation in management. For the sake of clarity we have separated individual and group bargaining although they are obviously closely related.

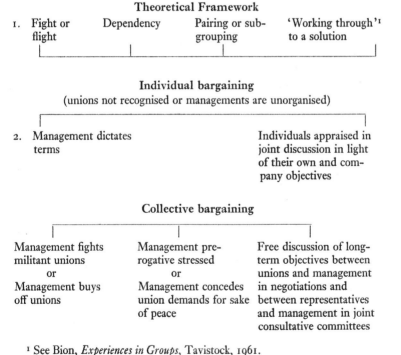

Theoretical Framework

1. Fight or   Dependency   Pairing or sub-   'Working through'[1]
    flight   grouping   to a solution

Individual bargaining
(unions not recognised or managements are unorganised)

2. Management dictates   Individuals appraised in
    terms   joint discussion in light
                                     of their own and company objectives

Collective bargaining

Management fights militant unions	Management prerogative stressed	Free discussion of long-term objectives between unions and management
or	or	in negotiations and
Management buys off unions	Management concedes union demands for sake of peace	between representatives and management in joint consultative committees

[1] See Bion, *Experiences in Groups*, Tavistock, 1961.

Firefighting in crises	Attempts at domination	Early discussion with appropriate	Prevents crises by planning
Flight from crises Denial of conflict or Apathy		officers of new possibilities in the situation	Manages to provide for constructive social conflict

The Whitley Committee, which reported in 1918, struggled with this problem of shifting the initiative from firefighting along the continuum. The solution proposed then was to broaden the base of subjects under discussion by unions and management beyond the immediate issues of bargaining, to look at common interests as well as conflicting ones. The Whitley proposals (i.e. Joint Industrial Councils) and much of joint consultation, good in theory, seem to have been ineffective in practice in raising the sights of the contending parties.

THE MANAGEMENT OF CONFLICT

Many personnel specialists would consider that they are making a more positive contribution to industrial relations by avoiding any confrontation in a collective bargaining ritual. This is the early 'human relations' approach, that there is no need for conflict; it can be prevented or managed. It may be useful here to consider what the industrial relations specialist needs to know about social conflict so that he may suggest a more analytical and planned approach for his management to adopt.

The necessity for organisations to change in order to keep up with the times produces internal conflict over power and resources as a new equilibrium is sought. How much conflict is constructive? And constructive for whom? The existence of many rival groups within an organisation makes these questions difficult to answer.

It is important, perhaps, to clarify the meaning of social conflict as we shall go on to use the term here. We take Coser's definition:

> ... a struggle over values and claims to scarce status, power and resources in which the aims of the opponents are to neutralise, injure or eliminate their rivals.... Far from being only a 'negative' factor

which 'tears apart', social conflict may fulfil a number of determinate functions in groups and other interpersonal relations; it may, for example, contribute to the maintenance of group boundaries and prevent the withdrawal of members from a group. Commitment to the view that social conflict is necessarily destructive of the relationship within which it occurs leads to highly deficient interpretations. To focus on the functional aspects of social conflict is not to deny that certain forms of conflict are indeed destructive of group unity or that they lead to disintegration of specific social structures. Such focusing serves, however, to correct a balance of analysis which has been tilted in the other direction.[1]

Coser defines social conflict as a struggle over values and claims to scarce status, power and resources. In industrial conflict it is difficult to separate the values from the claims because institutionalisation into the channels of collective bargaining has meant that differences in values have to be presented as claims, unless the formal system is by-passed in some way. Thus the various positions which may be taken up on the question of ownership have to be expressed either in political terms through other channels outside the organisation, or must become a claim for co-determination, employee shareholding, co-partnership or profit sharing, or for some kind of compensation for loss of ownership rights. This canalising of the expression of discontents and differences into the form of claims has been thought to be useful by some and unfortunate by others.

The Glacier experiment showed how much was concealed by the traditional procedures of bargaining, and the claim may present the symptoms rather than the cause of this struggle.[2] It is the policy of many companies and indeed of many experienced shop convenors to use the informal channels of communication to get more closely in touch with the realities in dispute rather than to go through formal procedures. Nevertheless, there still seem to be a number of companies in which there is insufficient trust for this kind of informal discussion, when the opposition is stigmatised as 'autocratic' or 'communist' and seen to have sinister motives about everything. It is in such a situation that it becomes difficult to distinguish the

[1] L. A. Coser, *The Functions of Social Conflict*, Routledge & Kegan Paul, 1956.
[2] A. K. Rice, 'The Use of Unrecognised Cultural Mechanisms in an Expanding Machine Shop', *Human Relations*, May 1951.

realities of claims from what is only a tension-releasing activity without real hope of bringing about change, when the possibility of working out satisfactory solutions to the revision of status, power and resources becomes almost impossible because the frames of reference of the two sides are so far apart.

The industrial relations specialists may be able to bring more realism into the bargaining situation. With more behavioural-science knowledge they should be able to see the claims for what they are and not what they may appear to be. They should be able to recognise real attempts to bring about change. Probably some do but others may not be as well able to analyse the situation.

Coser provides some guidance to the understanding of how success may be achieved. There is unlikely to be understanding and resolution of the real issues in a conflict where the ideological positions of the opponents are far apart and are strongly held. This leads to destructive conflict.

> Internal social conflicts which concern goals, values or interests that do not contradict the basic assumptions upon which the relationship is founded tend to be positively functional for the social structure. Such conflicts tend to make possible the re-adjustment of norms and power relations within groups in accordance with the felt needs of individual members or sub-groups.
>
> Internal conflicts in which the contending parties no longer share the basic values upon which the legitimacy of the social system rests threaten to disrupt the structure.
>
> One safeguard against conflict disrupting the consensual basis of the relationship, however, is contained in the social structure itself: it is provided by the institutionalisation and tolerance of conflict. . . .[1]

So the personnel relations specialist must work on two levels:

(a) to try to ensure that the basic assumptions of the opponents are understood and tolerated by both sides;
(b) to ensure that he preserves the institutions and the tolerance of conflict within his organisation.

The personnel specialist, then, may prefer to consider his role as one of understanding and interpreting conflict situations to those

[1] Coser, *op. cit.*

involved in them, for, as we suggested earlier, there needs to be a certain level of tension in an efficient organisation. Apathy or complete suppression of conflict may be as dysfunctional for productivity as too many disturbances. Status, power and resources can be held in so many different combinations that it is necessary for the industrial relations specialist to try to get more insights into the meaning of these concepts, both because he is involved personally (and we have seen how the personnel specialist has his own problems with all of these), and because he will be expected to determine the significance of conflict symptoms and suggest how it should be handled. The polarisation of hostile attitudes can be minimised in situations where the opposing groups as a whole, and not only their representatives, are enabled to perceive the different frame of reference of the other group and have the wish to make adjustments to it. It is for this reason that formal negotiating procedures must be supplemented by as many other channels of communication as can be devised. But Fox has also demonstrated that strongly held ideologies are important. There may not be the wish to make adjustments where the concept of management prerogative is thought to be vital or they will be made unwillingly and under protest.

Woodward has also argued that some line managers have a vested interest in conflict. It provides the only excuse for failure to meet tight production schedules.[1]

THE PERSONNEL MANAGEMENT TEAM

It seems possible that the kind of personnel specialist team which is appropriate to develop long-term personnel policies on a greenfield site in the early stages of a new plant is not necessarily appropriate to the stage when production begins.[2] Long-term policies require a different kind of thinking from day-to-day executive activity. Industrial relations specialists of both kinds are necessary. This kind of thinking ahead may require a very different kind of person from the skilled bargainer. It is not dramatic or exciting in the same way;

[1] Woodward, op. cit.
[2] Eric Miller, who studied the first two years of a new steelworks before production began, has commented on the different power position of the personnel department before and after the start of steelmaking.

different temperaments may be appropriate. As we have seen Stevens suggests that the industrial relations specialist is in a lose-lose position when it comes to bargaining.[1] He cannot win—all he can hope to do is to lose less and to lose it more skilfully. The bargaining situation is a game or ritual which has to be played out; hence he will try to defer decisions in order to gain time and, if it comes to bargaining, he must decide just how much to give way in order to retain faith in the procedures. This requires a very special temperament.

This kind of preventive specialist may be different from the day-to-day bargainer, but the day-to-day bargainer also needs to take the initiative rather than the defensive. To do this successfully he must understand the frames of reference of the workpeople, but not adopt them. Lupton and a number of Harvard researchers have shown that the man on the shop floor or in the office or store uses different 'logics' from his manager.[2] He is motivated by different desires which are seldom clearly expressed and frequently mis-understood. Management needs to try to understand these 'logics' if it is to appreciate the limits of financial incentives, for example, and the importance of group membership. The skilled bargainer is likely to be able to understand what lies behind so-called restrictive practices and to suggest how they can be reviewed, but he needs to develop special skills in communicating to management and to the unions so that his loyalties are unquestioned.

It would appear that there could be a new deal for personnel specialists if new ways of looking at organisation structures became common. Instead of being outsiders in an ambivalent position un-able to achieve clear uncluttered recognition of their roles, they would have an opportunity to make better identifications. As mem-bers of project teams they would be able to see themselves and be seen by others as part managers of the whole, thinking jointly about management's problems. As managers in specialist activities such as training or bargaining or researching into pay or fringe benefits, they would be managers of a part of the organisation's task activity. The ambiguities of the public relations role would disappear if

[1] Stevens, *op. cit.*

[2] T. Lupton, *On the Shop Floor*, Pergamon, 1962; G. Lombard, *Behaviour in a Selling Group*, Harvard, 1954.

public relations were handled by a project group, and internal liaison would also be the responsibility of a group (as demonstrated on the intra-organisation chart). The loyalties of the personnel specialist might well be strained, as no doubt he would still have to reconcile his personal and managerial values, but at least he would have to work them through in discussion with the groups in which he held membership and be seen more clearly for what he really is and not for what he is imagined and perceived to be. He would be less isolated and less driven to pair discussions.

There would still be inter-group rivalries, of course. What should be controlled by the central personnel department? How far should project teams take decisions and how far should functional specialists be advisory or reserve executive control? This is normal in any organisation. Group rivalries maintain interest.

FUTURE DEVELOPMENTS

If we take the management process to be made up of five elements—research, planning, decision making, execution and evaluation—the contribution of the industrial relations specialist seems to have been almost entirely in decision making and executive activities and not in the areas of research, planning, evaluation. The I.P.M. in its evidence to the Royal Commission (para. 75) has said: 'The study of human relations has made significant headway in the last few years, and diagnostic research into industrial relations would seem to be long overdue. Most of the work has been concerned with the formal structure and functions of trade unions and employers' organisations but there has been little or no rigorous analysis of the bargaining process itself or of the deeper causes of conflict evident in our industrial society.' We can only endorse these sentiments.

15 Raising the Level of Personnel Management Performance in Industrial Relations

The world does not owe personnel managers a living. They see themselves, inevitably, as central to the development of employment relationships and as having a considerable contribution to make to their improvement. But their view is not always shared by other managers or by the trade unions; indeed, personnel managers often complain of the problems of achieving influence and an understanding of their role. Before we discuss the improvement in the effectiveness of personnel managers, therefore, we must examine whether the effort is worthwhile, the influences which might affect them (one way or the other) and, finally, how improvement might be brought about.

The personnel manager has always been the subject of influence by government in his relations with managers and workers. One of the reasons for the growth in the numbers of personnel managers has been the development of employment legislation which required 'expert' administrators. He has also benefited from sporadic campaigns of government exhortation to improve some aspect of employee management (the introduction of T.W.I. and the post-war encouragement of joint consultation are examples). Legislation and government exhortation are two of many influences which have made the personnel manager live in an open system subject to influences outside those confined to the organisation. These influences have in the past tended to encourage the growth and development of personnel management, although the encouragement was accidental. We may now have reached the point at which government influence can become detrimental to personnel management although the effect is likely to be, once again, accidental.

The change came with the government's post-war attempts at income control. The point was reached in 1962, when the government announced the necessity of abrogating collective agreements which exceeded the guiding light of three per cent. The evolution of a third force, the government, in the collective bargaining process has continued with the current legislation on prices and incomes policy. The employer may perceive this development with mixed feelings; there may be circumstances in which he may actively welcome the shift of responsibility to the government's income control. But in those firms in which the personnel specialist has become the custodian of the procedures he is bound to see the authority and prestige which the negotiating role gives him as being threatened.

There are more specific examples. Public concern about industrial disputes in the motor industry occasioned the establishment of the Motor Industry Joint Labour Council in 1965. Its activities raise several questions concerning the role to which the personnel manager has been accustomed. In the first place the negotiating personnel manager is not only expected to respect the sanctity of procedural agreements, but he is expected to inculcate this respect among employees and their representatives. One of the principles of this respect is that there shall be no negotiation of unofficial disputes when procedures are broken so that employees will not be enabled to guarantee the urgent attention of management by striking in order to demand it. The Council apparently recognised the danger in its report: 'It was, however, necessary from the outset to avoid situations in which intervention by the Council might come to be regarded as an alternative to the full use of the normal procedure for the resolution of disputes.'

But one of the terms of reference of this Council was the investigation of unofficial disputes. If the Council were successful in avoiding this danger, the general question remains as to whether public concern about disputes is now so great as to deem this particular principle of negotiation worth sacrificing for the advantage of quick and urgent enquiry by an agent *outside* the parties to procedural agreement. It is not our purpose to discuss here the possible outcome or wisdom of this development but only its implications for the personnel manager. These seem to be twofold:

(a) The development of outside intervention seems likely to challenge some of the precepts by which his previous role as industrial relations specialist was defended.

(b) The necessity of outside intervention in order to solve the problems of industrial relations suggests either than the personnel manager was not fulfilling a role which might have been expected to be his or, if he was, that his performance in this role was inadequate.

The same implications attach to the many suggestions that the Ministry of Labour should assume a more 'positive' attitude to industrial relations problems. The Ministry's policy has always been to stand aside from a dispute until the existing machinery for its settlement has been exhausted. Public impatience with industrial disputes once again seems to demand that the Ministry should act with more urgency in bringing all its resources to bear before the full length of the procedural road has been travelled. Once again the personnel manager, where he is the custodian of the procedural agreements, must see that the dangers involved in premature intervention remain and are not lessened by public concern, which demands that anything is worthwhile in order to prevent or terminate disputes. Once again the personnel manager must see, in developments in this direction, not only a threat to his own position but a potential threat to order in the structure of industrial relations.

It may be of no great consequence, of course, if the personnel manager's position is threatened or even destroyed. The evidence suggests that in some instances, as far as the procedures and system of industrial relations are concerned, he is operating neither as a technologist nor as a technician, that he has no influence and responsibility at all. If this is so then to what extent are we justified in concerning ourselves about the possible impact of changes in government policy on the personnel manager?

Government policy may, as in the past, continue to have an accidental influence on personnel management, and it may deliberately and predictably set out to reduce its influence or it may encourage its development. In discussing which course should be pursued it will be preferable to discuss the *function* of personnel management rather than personnel specialists or personnel management; for historical reasons, personnel specialists are often inordinately concerned with problems of status which can easily bedevil and confuse discussions which ought to be more task and goal-centred. The three personnel management functions which are of central importance to the effective management of the organisation are: manpower planning (including management development and succession), education and training, and negotiation of the terms and conditions of employment. These are important because their effective performance necessarily involves elements of diagnosis and of forecasting the likely direction in which organisational change will take place; by involvement in manpower planning, training and negotiating (negotiating, that is, in anything but a narrow, agreement-minding sense), the organisation is making plans to meet the future correlate to its financial and technical plans. These three activities all seem to be necessary in order to facilitate the organisation's adjustment to change.

It seems difficult to deny that these are strategically important management functions. The question remains whether, by reason of their very importance, they ought not, therefore, to be the responsibility of line management rather than of functional specialists. It seems probable, though, that management is incapable of concerning itself with forecasting in employment matters unless forecasting is regarded as the responsibility of specialists. There may be several explanations for this state of affairs. It may be that general management is so concerned with the complex problems of technical and financial planning that these areas absorb all their personal resources. It may be that having emerged from a time in which labour was plentiful and relatively cheap to a period when it was scarce but in which its high price could be passed on to consumers, general management has not been conditioned to regard employment forecasting as important. It is important now. Its importance demands the activity of specialists with advisory responsibility for manpower planning, training and negotiating. Where they do not exist, or where their responsibility for forecasting has not been conceded, we see instances of technical innovation which have taken five or more years to plan being finally held up for unproductive months while the training, manning and negotiation problems are hurriedly and belatedly faced.

The question has been raised as to whether it matters whether personnel management is developed or diminished. The test would seem to be that it is important to encourage the growth and development of personnel management if, and only if, personnel management can become the instrument of forecasting, diagnosis and adjustment in these areas. If not, then its diminution, planned or accidental, by government policy becomes a matter of no great concern.

But if it is to be developed, what steps can the government take? If it is the forecasting elements of the personnel management function which we consider important (in terms of effective management), and if it is important that these elements are carried out by personnel specialists, then it is this diagnostic role which government activity should be directed at developing.

The development of a diagnostic role requires the pursuit of two objectives:

(a) The development of an awareness in the general management of business that employment forecasting (broadly defined here as manpower planning, training and the identification of long-term training needs and negotiation), is a necessary prerequisite to achieving efficiency and that it should be an inseparable accompaniment to the financial and technical elements of business planning. It is important to recognise that this objective cannot be achieved by directing attention to personnel specialists alone; the awareness of the importance of this relationship must be located throughout management in general in order to enable the specialists to pursue their tasks of diagnosis.

(b) The development of sufficient expertise among personnel specialists at work in organisations to undertake advisory responsibility for employment forecasting.

The discussion of the pursuit of these objectives falls into three parts relating to:

(a) The training and development of personnel specialists.

(b) The means by which managerial performance in terms of employment forecasting can be improved.

(c) The agencies which should carry responsibility for improving managerial performance.

TRAINING AND DEVELOPMENT OF PERSONNEL SPECIALISTS

Training for personnel management is carried out at a variety of full-time courses (often lasting one year) or equivalent part-time schemes in universities and polytechnics. The I.P.M. maintains standards by approving such courses and by setting its own examinations for which individuals may privately submit themselves. The I.P.M. and a number of educational institutions also provide 'short courses', usually in some specialist branch of personnel management and usually for people who are already practitioners.

There are also a large number of 'in company' courses in personnel management provided by employing organisations for their own personnel specialists, and personnel management or human relations usually feature in general courses provided for line managers. Courses such as these are often provided in staff colleges which are administered by organisations or industries.

It is not possible to generalise about training for personnel management without making an attempt to distinguish between the level of performance at which training is directed. The wide range of activities which personnel specialists undertake is reflected in the considerable range (£500 to £10,000) in the salaries which they are paid. Many classifications are possible, but it would seem reasonable to distinguish between the following categories in personnel work:

(a) Consultancy—in itself, of course, a complex range of activities but, in this context, an extensive and intensive study of organisational problems often resulting in planned change in employment and related activities. Consultancy is not undertaken only by specialist agencies on a fee-paying basis; industrial organisations have begun to undertake their own research and consultancy activities pursued by specialists.

(b) Employment planning—the area which has been discussed here, continuing diagnostic attention to ensure that the procedures and systems of employment policy 'fit' the technical, commercial and organisational changes which are being planned or which can be forecast as likely to occur. We are concerned to emphasise three areas of primary importance in this context: manpower planning, training and negotiation. The consequences of failure in these areas can include inappropriate recruitment programmes leading to unexpected shortages or redundancies, employees with inappropriate skills, and agreements which are incapable of facilitating change or containing conflict.

(c)   Maintenance—the area in which many personnel specialists are involved, the maintenance of the existing employment machinery with the minimum disturbance to production process subject to the control of cash. This is often called fire-fighting, but it should not be derided in terms of its complexity, difficulty or value. It is not, however, often concerned with planned changes or with making long-term and effective adjustment to change. In this area the tail tends to wag the dog in that the specialist's work programmes, objectives and attitudes may all be short-term and the time allowed in which to solve his problems, limited.

(d)   Operational—the area in which specialists are responsible for the operation of specific procedures or the pursuit of specific objectives concerned with operating acknowledged and familiar routines. This area would include the administration of canteens, safety programmes, employment interviewing, the consultative machinery. It must be emphasised that this activity is not delineated by the importance or otherwise of the work involved, but rather by the kind of activity in which the specialist engages in relation to it.

(e)   Clerical—this includes not only the clerical activities carried out in large personnel departments but the activities, not uncommon in small firms, of senior personal secretaries who have gradually evolved into, for example, staff officers to the works manager, with special responsibilities for some routine personnel activities like record-keeping, punctuality checking, welfare.

A great deal of confusion has been caused in the literature by the promotion of suggestions for training which are appropriate to one of these categories being discussed in terms of the others (the ambiguity in the terms often used has not helped either). The suggestion made by Lupton and Fogarty, for example, that training must be primarily directed at producing a social-science-based, research-orientated, personnel specialist operating at consultant level with access to the boardroom, has caused some dismay and uncertainty. While it cannot be denied that this kind of top-level activity should be encouraged (so that to speak against it carries the risk of being labelled stupid or reactionary), the hard-working personnel specialist sees some practical problems. In the first place he must believe that he is so ill-educated as to be fit only for redundancy ('trained' though he may have been); in the second place there are the difficulties of creating experts in sufficient numbers, confronted as we are with no noticeably large market for their services. It is the market situation which presents the biggest problem; who exactly is it who requires the services of the consultants who are to be trained? When all the other difficulties are overcome the consultant must in the end be recruited or engaged and he must then be permitted to operate. In the biggest and most advanced organisation, that this presents no difficulty is demonstrated by the fact that there are already specialists at work at this level, but for the rest, the work of bringing management and ownership to this point of perception may require not a revolutionary programme of training but a slow process of evolution through the levels of refinement in the work of the personnel specialists. It is for this, among other reasons, that we are emphasising the importance of developing the second category—employment planning; it represents a valuable and necessary advance on much current practice, it is not too remote from the development of existing resources and its achievement is a necessary preliminary to subsequent development to a consultancy level.

It is possible to suggest training objectives appropriate to the categories of personnel work which we have distinguished. The consultancy level requires academic disciplines which contribute to the analysis of complex socio-technical situations. It also requires personal and group relations skills to facilitate communication with senior management, but it does not necessarily require managerial skills which are normally applied in the co-ordination and control of subordinates and resources in the achievement of collective goals. The sort of academic framework would be met by extensive study in the social sciences, in research techniques, and in one or more of the numerate analytical disciplines—operational research, engineering or accountancy. The institutions most likely to undertake this training are the business schools at Manchester and London. Their work could also be supplemented by the higher-degree courses in managerial studies which are now being developed.

The second area of work, employment planning, requires a basis of understanding of the social sciences but not carried to the same expert length as it would be for the consultant. But the practitioner is now going to be taken by his work into managerial activities which require not only managerial skills but a basic understanding of managerial, commercial and technical environments and problems. Unlike the consultant, the personnel specialist in this second category must live with his problems and co-exist with other managers in their solution. Petrie has criticised the social-science emphasis in personnel training because, he says, it creates communication problems between the personnel specialist and the manager who sees himself as more business-orientated. There are real dangers to be overcome and they are particularly likely to affect the employment planner who is, in a sense, operating on the boundary between consultancy and the more obviously practically committed personnel workers. Training for this category of personnel work cannot be highly specialised because it must incorporate at least four elements: an introduction to behavioural science, an introduction to the business management environment, a critical examination of employment practice and the provision of some financial or statistical analytic techniques. This kind of training can be provided either by a business studies course which lasts for three years and which ends with a specialist degree course in personnel work, or it can be given in a short (six months) course for people in their 30s, already in personnel work, who may be sponsored by their employers before promoting them from a subordinate category of personnel specialist activity. The most appropriate place for this kind of training (either for the lengthier programme of preparatory training or for the much shorter, mid-career, conversion course) is the technological university. An essential ingredient of the longer preparatory course is that it should be realistically associated with periods of industrial field work. The existing university one-year courses provide a foundation which could be built on for this purpose.

Training for the other categories of personnel work requires the provision of techniques and skills which are appropriate to the tasks undertaken by the specialist in the industry in which he is employed. Training is, therefore, best undertaken on the basis of the industry or firm; general courses aimed at a wider market are liable to suffer from the same confused purposes as do many 'courses in foremanship' in which the course members are likely to be drawn from widely different task activities and to have consequently different requirements for training. Specialist personnel training at these levels is appropriately conducted by the employing organisations; its provision is, in fact, one of the results of the kind of situational analysis in which the higher-level personnel specialist (in the employment-planning category) engages. It is at the maintenance and operational level that day-release courses at technical colleges are important. They are particularly suited to establishing a relationship with the in-company activities of the students. There is some evidence that these courses might be revised so as to be related to the needs for training revealed by the job analysis (carried out by the college) of each student in his working environment; in this way the college course becomes closely related to the job requirements of the student and is an adjunct and encouragement to in-company training.[1] There is a separate need for technique and skill provision for lower-level personnel specialists in other, perhaps smaller, organisations in which the need for training is not perceived. It is in creating the awareness of need for in-company training that general courses of the kind provided by the I.P.M. and the Industrial Society will continue to be important. The development of an attitude which encourages training will also depend on the continued encouragement of the Ministry of Labour and the Employers' Associations.

There is one general consideration which is important. Training

[1] This suggestion was made by Mr Philip Marsh of Ealing Technical College at the Conference of Teachers of Personnel Management, held by the I.P.M., 1–3 January 1968.

for personnel management is not subject to the same financial support which has been applied to other areas of education and training. The graduate student who wishes to take a postgraduate diploma in personnel management must rely on the extension of the grant that has been made to him by his local education authority and the policy which is applied to him is not standard; from some authorities the student will receive no further support. If this is so there is no other source to which he can look for assistance. The Social Science Research Council refuses to accept a diploma course in personnel management for inclusion in its studentship scheme because it regards the course as vocational in nature. The older student may be at an advantage because he may be sponsored by the organisation employing him but, in this case too, a decision to take a full-time course may require the student to leave his employment and finance himself.

This state of affairs may or may not be desirable, but it demonstrates that training for personnel management is regarded as lying somewhere between education and industrial training so that it does not receive the advantage which the state has provided for either. It might be appropriate to consider means by which this gap could be filled.

There is a secondary problem in that training for personnel management must rely heavily on the provision of adequate fieldwork arrangements in employing organisations. An organisation which provides fieldwork experience during a student's course expends time and money, usually for no direct return. The provisions of the Industrial Training Act are largely aimed at encouraging and rewarding by grants, training on the basis of the industry concerned. Fieldwork training undertaken by an organisation contributes, in the long run, to the development of effective management in the industry (if not the firm), but the expenses of providing it cannot currently be included in the firm's return of expenditure incurred on training. A more liberal interpretation by the Industrial Training Boards of the importance of functional training which is necessarily carried out on a supra-industrial basis would be helpful.

There is one assumption about all this that needs to be questioned. In other fields of management training it is no longer acceptable to believe that improved managerial performance can be achieved by formal courses. The 'course/coarse' approach to training has been under constant attack. The Central Training Council and the Engineering Industry Training Board have stressed the importance, in supervisory training, of preceding training by analysis of the job to discover the areas in which training is needed. Others have gone further by stressing the importance of 'situational analysis', of examining the network of relationships in which the manager or supervisors operate. Williams describes the dangers of concentrating on a particular segment of the organisation and stresses that training is a process to which managers must be committed and in which they can only be assisted by the 'trainer-analyst'.[1]

The applications of all this to the personnel specialist are not often discussed. It may be, like the cobbler's shoes, that he is so concerned about the improvement of other people's performance that he never gets around to examine effectively his own organisational relationships and effectiveness, not in *training* terms at least; he talks about them often enough. But many of the constraints and role requirements which we have examined in the industrial relations field seem peculiarly suited to an examination of expectations and performance of managers and specialists within the organisation. It would be dangerous to conclude that whatever improvements need to be made can be achieved by the provision and improvement of courses. Other managers are involved. Neither they nor the personnel specialists will achieve a better understanding of industrial relations simply by providing them with pedagogic exercises.

[1] Derek Williams, 'The Analysis of Training Needs, Some Explanatory Steps', A.T.M. *Bulletin*, March 1967.

16 Improving Managerial Performance Generally

How can employing organisations be encouraged to diagnose their situation and to forecast the consequences of business and technical changes which are being planned so that they are more able to anticipate the need for adjustment in terms of training, recruitment, redeployment, re-negotiated wage structures and manning schedules? Government advice and exhortation has, in the past, been largely confined to techniques whereas the real need is for encouraging analysis within the organisation. Some form of consultancy service is necessary but the paradox has always been that consultancy services are likely to be used by those who need them least. If a consultancy service is to be established and if it is to achieve more practical results than can be achieved by exhortation, then it should be supported by the application of incentives or sanctions.

INCENTIVES

The Industrial Training Act provides a precedent for the financial reimbursement of firms where standards are sufficiently high to warrant it. It also provides a precedent for the more positive intervention by the state in industrial affairs. The government might also make grants to firms whose employment-forecasting activities were sufficiently advanced and who were judged to be planning their employment and industrial relations affairs in step with their other plans. It is, of course, difficult to suggest what would be the criteria on which these judgments might be based. Although the effects of forecasting would, it is hoped, include a reduction in the incidence of industrial disputes, it would be extremely dangerous to regard the number of disputes itself as being a reliable index (if only because 'bought off' disputes are not evidence of sound industrial relationships). If an index was believed to be necessary it might be possible to take into account the resources allocated by the firm to employment forecasting, but this too would not be an entirely satisfactory measure. Imprecision in this respect is not necessarily a grave weakness. The Industrial Training Act does no more to lay down the criteria by which judgments will be made than to leave judgments to the various Industrial Training Boards. Judgments about the effectiveness of the firm's personnel department in employment forecasting could similarly be left to the government's responsible agent.

SANCTIONS

The government could exercise influence by using its considerable power as a purchaser. There is some precedent for such influence but limited to the employment of disabled persons, and to the Fair Wages Resolution of 1891, 1909 and 1946. The government's importance as a consumer of goods and services produced in Britain is considerable.[1] If one of the factors taken into account in the allocation of contracts was the outcome of an appraisal of the effectiveness of the suppliers' personnel specialists in undertaking employment forecasting and of the suppliers' readiness to accept advice, this would be likely to have a powerful influence. The effect would be threefold:

(a) The carrying out of an examination by the consultancy service would in itself be influential.

(b) The recommendations and the manner in which they had been arrived at would underline the importance of this area of management activity to managements which might otherwise be sceptical.

---

[1] Public authorities' current expenditure in 1964 was £5,411 million, estimated to be 19 per cent of the gross domestic product; A. R. Prest, *The United Kingdom Economy, a Manual of Applied Economics*, Weidenfeld & Nicolson, 1966.

(c)   Any relationship between the acceptance of recommendations
      and the award of contracts would be a powerful influence
      which the government could use in improving managerial
      performance.

For the government to begin to exert this kind of influence would,
of course, represent a considerable departure from previous policy.
Influence and intervention of this kind would represent the government's taking a positive role in a sense different from that used in
the usual exhortations. The idea of government intervention which
is suggested here has been raised in at least one other quarter: 'The
frontiers of public intervention are, in fact, expanding all the time—
irrespective of which government is in power. Yet they have been
expanded in a curiously confused and haphazard way. . . . For in a
complex modern economy across-the-board intervention is often
clumsy and inadequate. To take an obvious example, one of the
major problems of British industry is the poor quality of much of its
management. In principle, government could use its purchasing
power deliberately to reward firms with dynamic and progressive
managements, and to punish those with slothful and unprogressive
work.'[1]

The assumption which we have accepted in making these suggestions about the objectives and nature of government intervention is
that the solutions which are likely to be the most effective are those
which industry is equipped and assisted to apply itself at the level of
the plant and the enterprise.

The kind of intervention which we have suggested is already taking
place and legislation has already begun to require organisations to
furnish information and to make forecasts. New government
machinery such as the Manpower Research Unit of the Ministry of
Labour and the Economic Development Council are encouraging
the preparation of accurate statistics, the maintenance of basic
records and the preparation of estimates of change. So far this
emphasis has been on using this material for national economic
purposes. Now that the process has started it requires a different
kind of lead from the government to encourage firms themselves to
anticipate change and its accompanying problems and to design

[1] David Marquand, M.P., *The Guardian*, 24 January 1967.

their employment policies and procedures to relate more appropriately to their commercial and technical situations.

THE AGENCIES RESPONSIBLE FOR IMPROVING MANAGERIAL PERFORMANCE

The Ministry of Labour

The Ministry of Labour presents itself as an obvious possibility as an agent for a consultancy service. Although the Ministry's Personnel Management Advisory Service has been discontinued as a distinct sub-department, the Ministry's staff continue to provide valuable advice on the practice and procedures of personnel management. Its conciliation officers also often find it difficult to distinguish between their work as mediators and their work as advisors, sometimes informally, on sound personnel management practice. Their continued and expert attention has also contributed not only to raising the level of managerial performance but, particularly in smaller firms, to improving the atmosphere of management–employee relations.

It does not follow, however, that the Ministry would be a suitable vehicle for conducting a consultancy service concerned with diagnosis, planning and adjustment. There are several reasons for doubt as to its suitability for this more strategic role:

(a) The Ministry's work in the field of conciliation is necessarily of a short-run nature, directed at reaching a solution to present and urgent problems. A consultancy service would require a deeper examination of situational problems and would be directed at objectives more distant in time.

(b) The tradition of 'neutrality' may be inseparable from the organisational character of the Ministry. Its staff of civil servants are directly responsible to a Minister who is answerable to Parliament. Professional staff were at one time recruited from industry to work in the Personnel Management Advisory Service but this experiment in recruitment was stopped, thus no doubt re-emphasising the administrative qualities of the staff. There is also the, at least potential, danger that members of the staff may be inhibited from providing forthright and positive advice because of the risks they believe themselves to run in provoking Parliamentary questions.

(c) The lack of managerial experience of the existing staff of career civil servants is probably of no great disadvantage in pursuit of the Ministry's present objectives. But a consultancy service which would aim at the integration of industrial relations policies and business decisions would require a blend of professional training and managerial experience which the Ministry's staff does not possess. For the reasons we have mentioned there may be real difficulties in employing both kinds of staff in the same service.

(d) The Ministry's tradition of neutrality may have to give way to the persistent demands which are being made that it should do more and do it quickly to 'solve' the problems of industrial disputes. Another threat to the tradition comes from the likelihood that the Ministry will become increasingly involved as an agent of the state in the application of incomes policy; to the extent that the state becomes a party to wage negotiations, the Ministry's neutral role will be under pressure. These are well-known problems with which the Ministry is no doubt familiar and is capable of surmounting but they raise the question, in this context, of the suitability of the Ministry for an enlarged consultancy role. Incomes policy and the state's interest in wage determination are likely to cause management and the unions to identify the Ministry's acceptability as an objective consultant as likely to be damaged.[1] Among the more obvious practical difficulties is the predictable fear that the consultant's investigations would reveal evidence of illegality which would have to be reported to the Minister. There are suggestions that

[1] There may appear to be a paradox in the argument presented here that the Ministry of Labour is, by its civil-service nature, too inclined to be neutral, while its changing role is likely to make it too committed as an agent of incomes policy to provide an effective consultancy service. The paradox is more apparent than real. Commitment as an agent of accepted government policy requires the sort of disinterested allegiance for which civil servants are trained; situational analysis and the energetic application of recommendations for change require a zealous initiative for which they are not.

the Ministry is already aware of the conflict between these two roles.[1]

It is therefore doubtful whether the Ministry of Labour would be a suitable agent for carrying out the kind of consultancy service which is required. This is not to say that its present work of advising at the level of personnel management procedures and practices is not invaluable and should not continue. This work is, in any case, inseparable from its conciliation activities and this work, of itself, contributes enormously to the bringing together of disputing parties in new and more positive relationships.

The Industrial Training Service

The Industrial Training Service, established in 1958 following recommendations of the Carr Committee, is a government agency which has established itself by virtue of the training consultancy service it provides. Although there is no evidence that the Industrial Training Act has diminished the demand for the service (the opposite is in fact true), there may come a time when the need for the service is reduced by the extent to which the Industrial Boards have become effective. There are other and more positive reasons for discussing the possibility of enlarging the scope of the I.T.S. to cover a wider range of personnel management functions than training.

[1] There are suggestions that the Ministry is embarrassed by the ambiguity of its present role and by uncertainty about the manner in which it may be continued after August 1967. On 30 January 1967 *The Times* reported the case of the Forrest Printing Ink Co. The Company had reported on 17 January to the Ministry of Labour that 51 employees were attempting to force the payment of a wage bonus, illegal under the Prices and Incomes Act. While the Ministry's investigations continued, notices of dismissal expired on 23 January and the factory closed. *The Times* reported employers' concern '. . . about the way in which the Government have apparently abandoned to its fate the first Company which looked to the progenitors of the Prices and Incomes Act for protection. . . . . . . it is hard to escape the conclusion that the Ministry are looking back nervously at the war and immediate postwar periods, when strikes were illegal and attempts by governments to prosecute strikers ended in fiasco and a change in the law. It is an open secret that the government hopes to get through until August, when the relevant part of the Act lapses, without being challenged to apply it.'

To separate attention to training from the other functions of personnel management is notoriously difficult and dangerous. Effective training must be concerned with more than the provision of resources to meet immediate demands for performance and skill; it necessarily concerns the analysis of what the organisation's requirements are and are likely to be. Effective training is, therefore, related to the diagnosis of weaknesses in the organisation, the appraisal of its employees, the analysis and forecasting of organisational and technical change and the evaluation of programmes. In other words, effective training is inseparably involved in the kind of employment management activity which we have suggested it should be the government's responsibility to encourage. Because of this association between training and the objectives of the kind of consultancy service we have been discussing it would seem to be quite reasonable to suggest that an enlarged Industrial Training Service, with widened terms of reference, could become a suitable vehicle for conducting this new consultancy service. The I.T.S. has considerable advantages. It is staffed by trained and experienced people, it has already acquired a considerable reputation in industry and it is sufficiently remote both from Parliamentary control and from any responsibility for other and more contentious aspects of government employment policy to be regarded as neutral without being seen to be innocuous.

A New Agency

The possibility remains for creating a new agency to carry responsibility for the consultancy service and for administering the apparatus of rewards and sanctions. Marsh has suggested the establishment of a body of procedural commissioners, 'to supervise the improvement and adaptation of dispute procedures. It would be an important part of their task not to weaken the authority of voluntarism, and they might be expected to work increasingly at the behest of the parties and with their co-operation. On the other hand the Minister of Labour would be free to make references to the commissioners, if he thought this would help him to improve procedural arrangements within a particular industry or firm. . . . The substance of their job would, in fact, be to ensure that in rapidly changing industrial situations, procedures were so altered and developed as to ensure the existence of the most effective voluntary arrangements possible.'[1]

The commissioners would certainly have difficulties to overcome. To begin with they would have no recourse to a widely recognised set of principles which could readily be incorporated in procedures because such principles are singularly hard to find. Marsh suggests two—that procedures should be 'acceptable' to the parties and that they should be 'appropriate' to the conditions of the industry—but even these criteria, broad as they are, are difficult to define and apply in every case. If flexibility and adaptability are important tests of procedure, why not leave the procedure to be determined by and within the industry itself? Because, says Marsh, the parties within an industry have shown themselves incapable of making adjustments so that 'change in procedures must be assisted by the mobilisation of some kind of external influence or pressure'. One possible criticism of this proposal is that procedures, important though they are, represent too narrow a range to be made the subject matter of such a body. This is a criticism which Marsh seems implicitly to recognise for he ends by suggesting that, in time, 'it should set out suitable criteria for firms involved in productivity bargaining, model procedures and so on. . . . It is conceivable, for example, that certain sorts of productivity agreements could be ruled out, e.g. those which were clearly likely to result in widespread up-bidding'.[2]

The more serious criticism of the proposal to set up a body of procedural commissioners is that it conflicts with one of the more valuable derivatives of voluntarism, that the relationship between the parties should be subject to their own influence and control. Marsh may regret the necessity but, he suggests, the opening to external influence is made inevitable by the incompetence of the internal experts. We have made the same point but have arrived at a different conclusion. We suggested in Chapter 7 that what Marsh has called 'procedural conservatism' and what we described more widely as 'aspirational rigidity' was the result not of incompetence on the part of those who operated the institutions of industrial relations but resulted rather from their failure to exercise control. The

---

[1] Marsh and McCarthy, 'Disputes Procedures in Britain', *Royal Commission Research Papers*, 2 (part 2), H.M.S.O., 1968, p. 91.

[2] *ibid.*, p. 95.

system, we suggested, is run by its operatives rather than its managers. If this is so, then what may be necessary is not an opening to external influence but an opening to internal management. If industrial top management became more aware of its responsibilities for industrial relations and more effective in their long-term management, perhaps we could more happily rely on the settlement of relational procedures by the parties concerned. Similarly, if the unions were more open to rank and file influence and to the pressure of shop-floor representatives, they too would be capable of more flexible and 'appropriate' adjustment.[1]

For these reasons the creation of a management consultancy service on a national scale would seem to be preferable to the creation of a procedural commission. The difference may appear to be a subtle one but it is important. A procedural commission would attempt to influence procedural relationships between the parties, relationships which most people accept are, ideally, determined by the parties themselves. A consultancy service would attempt to improve the performance of one of the parties, encouraging and equipping it to recognise and engage with problems which it has too often avoided. As far as the unions are concerned it is to be hoped that the necessary pressure will be exerted by the shift of power to the shop floor and by a more concerted union attack (itself a possible consequence of this transfer of power) on entrenched managerial obstacles to procedural reform, such as employer conciliation schemes and the notion of management rights.

[1] Marsh gives an excellent example of the apparent failure to make such adjustment to pressure: 'In 1966 rank and file dissatisfaction with the procedure in S.O.G.A.T. reached a point where a delegate meeting pressed the union to withdraw from the agreement altogether. In 1967 a similar motion to this effect was actually passed at the S.O.G.A.T. delegate conference. In the event it is not clear what action will be taken by the union leaders to give effect to this declaration of dissatisfaction, and at the moment of writing there is still no formal conflict between the Federation and the union on the subject'—*ibid.*, p. 37.

A wide variety of recommendations were made in evidence to the Royal Commission. Although it is assumed that opinion divides neatly between those who want to leave the voluntary system alone and those who would have more regulation and control, no such single dividing principle seems applicable to the opinion of those who gave evidence. No-one made out a case for no change at all. No-one, it seems, advocated a considerable withdrawal of existing regulatory mechanisms. Most of the expert and representative witnesses seemed, in fact, to want more control and regulation of industrial relations. They wanted of course, to control different things and they wanted control for different purposes, but they did not line up for or against voluntarism. Broadly speaking a great deal of the evidence fell into one of two groups: (a) that which advised more regulation of trade unions and of the relationships with their members; (b) that which advised a wider protection of employee rights and an extension of trade union privileges. Those who represented employers took the former course, those who represented employees or who sympathised with their aspirations, the latter (often, while advocating an extension of legal protective intervention, defending the unions against any further restriction by reference to the sacred voluntary principle).

The Engineering Employers' Federation, the Motor Industry Employers and many other representatives of employers recommended that legal sanctions should be applied to unofficial strikes and that trade-union rules should be open to inspection and approval by a more authoritative form of registration. The E.E.F. recommended that strikes and actions in breach of procedure should be subject to a fine for every day in which a worker takes part in them and that restrictive practices should be examined by a tribunal with powers to require those supporting them to desist. The C.B.I. changed its mind and, in a second visit to the Commission, added a recommendation that collective agreements should be given the force of law. The recommendations of the Inns of Court Conservative and Unionist Society have virtually become the industrial relations plank in the Conservative Party's political platform;[1] they included a new system of union registration, a comprehensive system of industrial courts, the legal enforcement of collective agreements 'if and only so far as this was the intention of the parties and it was expressly so specified in the agreement. The parties must be at liberty to continue to make "domestic arrangements" which are not legally binding if they so desire', a 60-day delay in strikes or lock-outs (only to be used in circumstances of national emergency), and a legal duty on employers to recognise and bargain with trade unions. The Institute of Personnel Management suggested a form of registration which would require that 'parties to substantive agreements must also conclude procedure agreements in a form acceptable to the Registrar', and that fines should be imposed on unions, employers' associations and members for acting in breach of agreed procedures (somehow or other the I.P.M. reconciled this suggestion with the statement that it was 'in favour of the principle of supporting the voluntary constitutional relationships between unions and employers by providing sanctions with legal backing to enforce voluntary procedure agreements').

So the employers, their sympathisers and their agents lined up in one corner. Their opponents took their places in the other, but also genuflecting to the voluntary principle, which both contestants were to regard with the respect shown by an all-in wrestler for the Queensberry Rules. The T.U.C. came nearest to asking for nothing (and was, according to Press reports of the day, roughly handled by

[1] With an important reservation: the Society's recommendations were hedged by the most careful qualifications (not always acknowledged in attacks from the left) which do not seem to appear in some of the statements of intention by the Party's leaders.

the Commission in its examination). The T.U.C. did not want labour courts, the legal enforcement of contracts or any legislation requiring union recognition or enforcement of bargaining rights. It thought there might be some merit in giving I.L.O. Conventions nos. 87 and 98 the force of law but suggested even here that a strong lead by the C.B.I. might alone be sufficient.[1] The T.U.C.'s one positive request for change in the structure of industrial relations was that arbitration at the request of one party should be reintroduced under the machinery dealt with by the Industrial Disputes Tribunal in 1951. The T.U.C.'s respect for voluntarism and the *status quo* was more complete than was shown by others. Professor Wedderburn, claiming that he favoured new laws which could be grafted on to the present voluntary system, went on to recommend a whole range of changes to include the legal 'encouragement' of recognition and collective bargaining by making it a condition of the legal privileges of limited liability under company law and a new 'legal floor of rights' for workers (including a right of appeal in summary dismissals, to an extended Industrial Tribunal). He recommended that collective agreements should not be made legal contracts and that legal sanctions to make unions discipline their members were inadvisable. He went on to propose a series of clarifications of current ambiguities in the law which, in general, support the situation of the employee and the unions. The Society of Labour Lawyers proposed a new form of trade-union recognition which would incorporate the circumstances under which a union might strike and the procedure to be followed before fines could be imposed on members. Among their other recommendations was a proposal that the legal protection of strikers and trade-union officials should be confined to 'properly authorised' strikes and should be extended to cover breach, inducement or threat of breach of contract.

In his evidence Professor Wedderburn said that the case for legal enforcement of collective bargaining was based on political views hostile to trade unions and that the 'law should not be based on political judgments over which no consensus exists'. It seems, however, that many of the positions taken before the Royal Commission

[1] The two Conventions provide freedom of association for workers, the right to determine their own policies and protection against discrimination against workers on the grounds of union membership.

were based on the political and social attitudes of the witnesses. There are those who would argue, in any case, that the law reflects a political ascendancy at a particular time, not a consensus. The problems of deliberately bringing about change in industrial relations are enormously complicated for we do not live in the comparatively innocent environment of 1891; we know enough to-day to realise the subtle inter-relationships of law, economics and sociology, and the difficulties of forecasting the consequences of deliberate adjustments. The current position of the parties in industrial relations reflects, in part, their respective power, and recommendations for change may reflect the wish to see the power relationship adjusted. In his own evidence to the Commission, Mr Cyril Grunfeld said, 'When in areas of full employment, the classic economic sanctions against labour are in abeyance, two alternative courses seem to present themselves: either to introduce legal sanctions in place of the economic—fines, damages, injunctions based on the threat of imprisonment or imprisonment itself—or to stimulate a higher standard of competence in industrial relations . . . there is, in Britain, no legislative short cut to industrial bliss.'[1]

But the law cannot be ignored; it is, at the least, part of the environment within which competence in industrial relations will be encouraged or will decline. The responses open to the state might be classified as follows:

(a) Direct restrictive and preventive legislation designed to coerce and constrain the activities of one of the agents in the industrial relations system. Legislation of this kind exists and its extension has been recommended for the further control of both unions and employers. It has general disadvantages. Its introduction may reflect a particular political balance and particular economic circumstances at a given time but it may have unplanned effects when times change. Its effects are also difficult to foresee. For this reason such legislation might be reserved to prevent or mitigate circumstances which are a threat to human safety, material well-being, freedom or dignity. There will rarely be consensus about the means to be adopted but

[1] Royal Commission, Minutes of Evidence, 12, Witness: Cyril Grunfeld, 420, H.M.S.O., 1966.

perhaps a fair test for the necessity of such legislation is that there should be consensus about the existence of circumstances which need to be corrected. Certain aspects of the Prices and Incomes Act are of this kind of legislation but it is doubtful whether there would be consensus about the need for it. The Factories Act, on the other hand, is unexceptionable in terms of a need.

(b) Legislation designed to produce services and resources which can be directly applied to the improvement of performance; the provision of state services to meet a perceived need. The establishment of the Central Training Council and the Training Advisory Service in 1958 following the recommendations of the Carr Committee in 1956 is an example. The provision of Government Retraining Centres is in the same category. There is a quite astonishing shortage of suggestions for this kind of government action in the various recommendations to the Royal Commission. The shortage suggests that the various parties were merely lifting their conflict relationships to a political level in demanding legislation in category a (above)—although, their own avowed respect for the voluntary principle should have suggested the inappropriateness of their recommendations. It also suggests, more dangerously, that the parties to industrial relations in Britain continue to be unaware of their own ineptitude, of the need for remedial action or of the sources from which it could be sought.

(c) Legislation designed, without coercing the parties, to alter the environment within which they operate so as to encourage them to respond in a predicted and desired direction. The structure and institutions of industrial relations are a complex response to the environment of employment; changes in the legal environment may therefore bring about a given response. The Industrial Training Act has added to the environment in this way, it does not force anyone to do anything, and is singularly imprecise about the duties of its creation, the Industrial Training Boards, but it provides the opportunity of financial incentives for firms investing in training and a financial disincentive for firms which choose not to.

What should be done to 'stimulate a higher standard of competence in industrial relations'? There is certainly no consensus either about the need for coercive legislation (category a) or the forms that it should take. There is a great deal of public concern about manifestations of industrial conflict but the concern is not general nor is it well-informed. The effect of strikes on the economy is not as damaging as the effects of sickness, accidents at work or redundancy, but strikes appear to be voluntary and wilful and, therefore, some people feel they should be stopped. The strike level in Britain is not high by comparison with other large and industrialised communities, and a measure of strike action is probably inseparable from a free society and from the kind of collective bargaining system of which we would all approve. The working out of industrial relations problems requires that interested parties should be heard and that they should be their own advocates; the regulation of serious conflicts is therefore not a process that can be short-circuited by the application of quick solutions which are deemed by some to be in the best interests of all.

Where the level of disputes is high in a particular industry it has often been shown to be the result of some institutional weakness, concerning the wage-payment systems or the disputes procedure, of the industry itself. This suggests, once more, the need to develop a higher standard of competence in industrial relations rather than generally to attack symptoms while causes are left undisturbed. 'Competence' is a nice word but it does not greatly assist anything, simply to tell managers and unionists to be more competent. What in the context of industrial relations, does competence mean? It would be impertinent to suggest that the parties to industrial relations need to be instructed at an elementary level, that they should be told to order their affairs with reasonable despatch, communicate clearly, apply costing techniques, engage in rational thought. If there are those who require improvement at this level there is no shortage of sources for their instruction and it is to be hoped that their survival will depend upon their seeking them. There are deeper needs for competence in industrial relations. The problems exist at three levels:

(a) The first concerns the need for those responsible for the conduct of industrial relations (and for the direction of industry) to achieve a better understanding of the motivation of and influences on human behaviour and human organisations. This is no mere injunction that people should behave better or with more sympathy for others. Social theorists are not often able to make predictive statements about behaviour in a given situation and managers should not be encouraged to look to them for instant solutions and easy techniques of manipulation and control. But social theorists have long been able to provide insights into the structure and interactions of organisations and groups. The work of Leonard Sayles in the United States and Joan Woodward in Britain is a clear demonstration of the importance of understanding the interaction of technical and social systems. No clearer statement of the relevance of this field could be found than the account given in Alan Fox's Research Paper for the Royal Commission, 'Industrial Sociology and Industrial Relations'. For industrial relations specialists to be ignorant of this area is roughly equivalent to turning out craft apprentices with no knowledge of hand tools.

(b) The second level is a practical extension of the first. It is not enough merely to administer the procedures of industrial relations effectively. The procedures must be relevant to the technical and economic circumstances of the industrial situation to which they are applied and they must keep pace with changes in that situation. Industrial relations structures must be an appropriate part of the total system. There are frequent examples of industries and firms in which the industrial relations and employment policies appear to be advanced and the specialist administrators competent but where technical and commercial innovations are introduced with the most careful planning but without apparent thought for the inevitable strains on existing employment policies. The assumption seems often to be that the inadequacies of employment policies can only be understood when they actually collapse and that they can then and only then be remedied. Changed production processes requiring completely new manning programmes are often superimposed on an existing wage structure (or on training programmes, or on selection methods) which cannot possibly stand the strain of the new requirements. Industrial relations and employment procedures are often efficiently maintained and operated, they are not often planned.

(c) The third level of competence is more elementary. Industrial relations procedures should be internally consistent and should not carry their own built-in risks of creating conflict. In some situations wages and salaries are paid on no recognisable basis of consistency or principle, the only payment 'structure' is one that has emerged from a complex of historical, accidental and expedient forces. In other situations a payment structure has apparently been 'planned' which affords no defensible internal relativities and no consistency of earnings. In some staff situations salary structures can only be maintained because their bases are concealed in secrecy. Payment by result systems can sometimes be criticised because, far from reducing tensions in industrial relations, they provide a battleground on which militant conflict is continuously invited.

It is at these three levels that competence in industrial relations must be improved. The improvement requires analysis, diagnosis and planning. The evidence seems to suggest that the attack must be directed at the place of work and at the actors in the system who are responsible for the design and maintenance of employee relationships at shop-floor level. National bargaining may survive and be effective, but only to the extent that it can incorporate and respond to variations in circumstances at the place of work. Discussing the problems of making incomes policy more effective, McCarthy wrote that 'a special responsibility needs to be accepted by the firm and those it bargains with. It may be doubted how far the institutional consequences of this situation have yet been realised by government, employers or trade unions, but there seems no reason to suppose that once it is appreciated, suitable institutions could not be developed.' The implications are wider than those concerning the effectiveness of incomes policy. Many of the institutions and the relationships they have formed in Britain may no longer be appropriate to the conduct of effective industrial relations. On the one side, it may be the firm and its managers rather than the employers' organisation which must be looked to as the responsible experts. On the other, it may be the workers, their immediate representatives and their co-ordinating committees rather than the 'official' union structures which will become more significant. The older institutions will not collapse because they will continue to have a variety of important functions to perform; perhaps the problems have largely resulted from requiring them to do too much. There is some evidence that changes in this direction are already beginning to take place.

But there are no panaceas. If we are to see responsibility pushed downwards and the authority and control of national institutions consequently begin to weaken, then we must also expect new stresses to appear. The national organisations, employers' and workers', exist largely to provide minimal protection for their members. If they are to become less involved in collective bargaining and analysis, then their protective cover is bound to be weakened. This, if it takes place, will result in more industrial conflict, not less. It is here, finally, that the case for more protective legislation may rest. If the national organisations have been criticised for being too defensive, and if the defensive control is to weaken, then defence must rest on the power that can be brought to bear in a particular firm, on a particular shop floor, in an industry or district. If responsibility is to be devolved then the only alternatives for minimal protection are that it will vary with the power of the participants (and with changes in the prevailing economic climate) or that a 'floor of rights' will need to be provided by legislation.[1] To some extent devolutionary changes are already taking place, but our attitudes to the change are unhelpful. The ineffective control exercised by unions and employers' organisations may be a symptom of such change, but we currently require them to correct rather than assist its process. Much of the analysis directed at the problems and many of the recommendations for correction are misconceived because they are directed at outmoded institutions and irrelevant relationships. If we cannot understand changes which are taking place it would be dangerous to apply improvements to a situation which we can understand only because it has disappeared. Perhaps we should wait and see.

[1] For employers as well as employees; firms can, after all, be driven out of business by militant trade unions, although this may happen more frequently in the United States than in Britain.

APPENDIX: The Report of the Royal Commission on Trade Unions and Employers' Associations, 1965–8

The Report of the Royal Commission was produced after this book had been completed. We suffered from writing under its shadow since its publication was likely to be a landmark in the study of British industrial relations. Because of its importance we have added this summary and comment on its recommendations. It may also give the reader the opportunity to check some of our own assertions although this inadequate summary should not prevent him from reading the Report itself. We do not think that the Report has required us to make any major readjustment in our own argument or conclusions.

SUMMARY

Collective Bargaining

'Britain has two systems of industrial relations. The one is the formal system embodied in the official institutions. The other is the informal system created by the actual behaviour of trade unions and employers' associations, of managers, shop stewards and workers.'[1] The two systems are in conflict and the result is disorder in factory relationships and pay structures. The remedy lies in the promotion of factory-wide agreements; national or industry-wide agreements

---

[1] *Report of the Royal Commission on Trade Unions and Employers' Associations* 1965–1968, H.M.S.O., June 1968, p. 12.

All other quotations in this section will be from the Report and the page number will be given in brackets after the quotation.

should be confined to matters which they can effectively regulate; there may be some additional advantages in guideline agreements.

The responsible agency in industrial relations and in the promotion of factory agreements should be the board of directors of the enterprise. Boards of directors should review industrial relations against *six* objectives:

1. To develop, together with trade unions representative of their employees, comprehensive and authoritative collective bargaining machinery to deal at company and/or factory level with the terms and conditions of employment which are settled at these levels.
2. To develop, together with unions representative of their employees, joint procedures for the rapid and equitable settlement of grievances in a manner consistent with the relevant collective agreements.
3. To conclude with unions representative of their employees, agreements regulating the position of shop stewards in matters such as: facilities for holding elections, numbers and constituencies, credentials, facilities for consulting and reporting to members, facilities for meeting other stewards, pay while functioning as a steward in working hours, paid day-release for training.
4. To conclude agreements covering the handling of redundancy.
5. To adopt effective rules and procedures governing disciplinary matters, including dismissal, with provision for appeals.
6. To ensure regular joint discussion of measures to promote safety at work.

In the pursuit of these objectives companies should:

a. welcome the exercise by employers of the right to join trade unions;
b. develop positive management policies on such matters as recruitment, promotion, training and re-training;
c. collect systematic information on which to base action and should make available such information as workers' representatives may reasonably require.

The Report recommends that a new Industrial Relations Act

should require companies with (initially) 5,000 employees or more, to register their collective agreements with the Department of Employment and Productivity or, if they have no agreements, to give the reasons why there are none. There are two purposes in this requirement: to emphasise the prime responsibility of the board of directors for the conduct of industrial relations and for the framework of collective bargaining, and to draw attention to aspects of industrial relations which the public interest requires should be covered by clear factory agreements wherever possible.

The Act should also establish an Industrial Relations Commission to investigate references from the D.E.P. on cases arising out of the registration of agreements. The D.E.P. should handle problems up to the point at which a reference is made to the I.R.C. The Report suggests no penalties for companies refusing to comply with recommendations of the I.R.C., but it proposes limited financial penalties for companies which neither register agreements nor explain their absence.

The Report suggests that the I.R.C. should be guided by the following principles:

1. That collective bargaining is the best method of conducting industrial relations and that there is wide scope for extending both the subject matter of collective bargaining and the number of workers covered by collective agreements.
2. That the test in dealing with disputes over recognition—other than a dispute between unions over recognition—should be whether the union or unions can reasonably be expected to develop and sustain adequate representation for collective bargaining purposes among workers, or a distinct section of workers, in the company or factory.
3. That a system of industrial relations must be judged principally by its effects in the company, the factory and the workshop. Industry-wide procedures and agreements should be confined to three issues which they can regulate.
4. Collective agreements should be written and precise.
5. Pay agreements should provide intelligible and coherent pay structures.
6. Agreements, wherever possible, should link improvements in

terms and conditions of employment with improvements in methods of operation.

7. Procedural agreements should be comprehensive in scope and should provide for rapid and equitable settlement of disputes over existing or new agreements.

8. It is desirable for each company or factory to be covered by a single set of comprehensive agreements applying to all the unions representing its employees. If this is unattainable, separate sets of agreements covering distinct groups of employees should be accepted by all the unions representing workers within each group.

The Report recommends that the extension of collective bargaining should be encouraged and goes on to other proposals:

1. Making void in law any stipulations in contracts of employment or in rules of friendly societies that an employee should not belong to a trade union.

2. Making the Industrial Relations Commission responsible for dealing with problems of trade union recognition.

3. Encouraging the replacement of wages councils by collective bargaining arrangements.

4. Section 8 of the Terms and Conditions of Employment Act should be amended. It should be made available to use in wages council industries and the consideration of claims under it should not be confined to the particular term or condition relating to the claim but should take account of the terms and conditions laid down by collective agreement as a whole.[1]

5. Compulsory and unilateral arbitration by the Industrial Court should be made available in industries or undertakings in which the D.E.P. has certified, on the advice of the Industrial Relations Commission following an inquiry, that arbitration could contribute to the growth or maintenance of sound collective bargaining machinery.

6. Arbitrators should be obliged by law to take incomes policy into account and should be encouraged to give reasons for their awards.

[1] This recommendation almost certainly relates to problems we discussed on p. 81.

Manpower and Training

The D.E.P. must 'rouse the country' to the gravity of the principles and practices of training and must be responsible for reform. Systems of training must accord with basic standards, including universal acceptability of qualifications which must meet objectively determined standards. Restrictive barriers to training based on age, sex or colour should be removed. Trade unions should revise their rules to ensure that no qualified worker is denied admission or the right to use his skills; workers claiming improper treatment should have the right of appeal to an independent body.

Strikes

'Unofficial strikes and other types of unofficial action in industry are above all a symptom of a failure to devise institutions in keeping with changing needs.' The D.E.P. should be enabled to set up statutory enquiries irrespective of whether a dispute exists or is threatened and the D.E.P.'s officers should carry the duty, in appropriate cases, of obtaining the full facts about unofficial and unconstitutional stoppages.

Dismissal

Employees should be protected against unfair dismissal by legislation stating that dismissal is justified only if there is a valid reason for it connected with the capacity or conduct of the worker or based on the operational requirements of the establishment. Invalid reasons for dismissal, including trade-union membership or activity, race, colour, sex, marital status, religious or political opinion, national extraction or social origin, should be specified.

Labour Tribunals

Existing industrial tribunals should be renamed labour tribunals and be extended to cover disputes between employers and employees arising from contracts of employment or from statutory claims against each other as employers and employees. Appeals against unfair dismissal should be made within five days of dismissal, seeking either compensation or, if both parties agree, reinstatement. Compensation should be limited to a ceiling equal to the wage or salary for two years, earnings of over £40 per week to be ignored.

Individual Rights in Relation to Trade Unions

Trade-union members should be given a statutory right to complain to the Registrar of Trade Unions and Employers' Associations about alleged election malpractices and the Registrar should be enabled to send an inspector to investigate. An independent review body of three members (a lawyer and two trade unionists) should be attached to the office of the Registrar. The review body would:

1. Receive complaints from unsuccessful applicants for admission to a trade union (or to its skilled section) alleging that their application had been refused on arbitrary grounds. If the complaint was upheld the review body could issue a declaration that the appellant should become and remain a member.
2. Receive complaints from workers dismissed as a result of declining to join a union.
3. Receive from members complaints of unjustifiable expulsion which caused them damage, or of penalties imposed on them which carried substantial injustice.
4. Adjudicate on disagreements between the Registrar and a union as to whether its rules complied with revised requirements.
5. The revised requirements for rules of registered unions should specify matters relating to admission, discipline (by the union), disputes (between members and the union), elections (including election of shop stewards), stewards' terms of office, authority and credentials.
6. A person in membership for, say, two years, should not have his admission questioned on any ground except found at the time of admission.
7. The review body would have jurisdiction, concurrently with the High Court, to try any case based on alleged breach of rules or violation of national justice. The review body would be able to award compensation.

The Law

The Law Commissions should undertake an urgent codification of labour law. An Industrial Law Committee should be attached to the Industrial Relations Commission in order to keep the law under review.

'Trade Union' should be a term reserved in law for an employee's organization and it should be defined as 'any combination of employees the principal activity of which is the regulation of relations between employees and employers, whether such combination is in restraint of trade or not, and which is registered upon the Register of Trade Unions and Employer's Associations' (p. 207).

Trade unions should be granted corporate personality and should register. New unions would be expected to register within a given period.

The Conspiracy and Protection of Property Act, 1875, and the Trade Disputes Act, 1906 (giving certain immunities to persons from criminal prosecution and civil action in respect of acts committed in contemplation or furtherance of a trade dispute), should be made expressly applicable to trade unions. The 1965 Trade Dispute Act should remain.

Section 3 of the Trade Disputes Act, 1906 (preventing an action being brought for an act done in contemplation or furtherance of a trade dispute on the ground only that it induces some other person to break a contract), and the Trade Disputes Act, 1965, should in future, apply only to registered unions and employers' associations.

COMMENT

The Report is as good as the research work that preceded it; its limitations result from the respect it showed to the researchers. It identified the principal features of British industrial relations and decided to encourage tendencies which were already present. The Report's implementation will introduce a necessary element of order and rationality into a situation of total disorder; in this sense the Report has gone back over the last 20 years and helps us to arrive at the point we should have reached. The Report will result in clarity and order but it has avoided issues which are irrelevant to the production of order, however important they are in their own right. Tomorrow's problems are left until tomorrow because the Commission's energies have been exhausted by producing a well-swept stable.

There is little reference to the most persistent and, so far, intractable problem, the new relationship that must be established with the state as a party to industrial relations. The Report argues, briefly, that the emergence of company and plant bargains will assist rather than threaten prices and incomes policy because the bargains will reflect the actual earnings and conditions they control and 'the registration of company and factory agreements would expose the whole process of pay settlement to the influence of policy' (p. 52). This assertion is optimistic because the logistical problem of controlling an infinitely greater number of agreements (and of testing their appropriateness to an even wider variety of circumstances) are likely to be considerable. The more disturbing problem is that the Commission was arguing the compatibility of its recommendations with Prices and Incomes policy at the time when the policy had finally become unacceptable to the British Labour Party and to the T.U.C.; in this sense it seems that a marriage has been arranged with a very sick partner. The Commission has no recommendations as to a replacement.

The distinction between the formal and the informal system is valuable and the criticisms made of the former are accurate and damaging. But the complete reinforcement of the informal at the total expense of the formal carries dangers. We argued in the text that national bargaining had been deliberately pursued because it was seen to have advantages over company autonomy and that the advantages were still real and might become more apparent with changed economic circumstances. The continued requirement for some element of control and state influence in earnings determination suggests, whatever the form of the particular policy, a continuing application of national criteria. It is likely to be more, not less, difficult to apply national criteria when the remaining vestiges of industry-wide influence and the institutions which applied it have been dismantled. The institutions were ineffective and their influence was weak, but a useful function should not be sacrificed because its performance needs improvement.

The Report sets out some 'principles' or 'objectives' which might help both the boards of directors and the proposed Industrial Relations Commission in their review of collective agreements. The guidance broadly recommends the entrenchment of trade unions, the extension of collective bargaining, the improved specification of agreements, the regulation of the position of shop stewards. It recommends, in short, an extension in the coverage of collective bargaining and an improvement in the quality of collective agreements. The intention is excellent and the explanation that their aims can only be achieved at plant level is acceptable, but there are doubts as to whether the instruments recommended by the Commission will achieve its ends. There are two levels at which this criticism can be made.

The board of directors is to be the responsible authority for industrial relations in the enterprise. The Commission is right to explain the necessary responsibility of the boards and to identify the plant, or company, as the arena in which this responsibility will be exercised. But the Commission's recommendations may not be sufficient to bring this responsibility home, there are no sanctions and no incentives. Secondly the subject matter for improvement is virtually confined to collective agreements. A major criticism of British industrial relations is that they are characterised by conservatism, smugness and self-satisfaction (there is strong evidence to support these charges in the Royal Commission's Research Papers). The production of tidier agreements does nothing to change this; more particularly it does nothing necessarily to incorporate industrial relations in the managerial planning process, to ensure intelligent forecasting of, and adjustment to, change.

The referral of company agreements to government agencies and the dual influence of the Department of Employment and Productivity and the Industrial Relations Commission, could conceivably have the opposite effect. An emerging tendency to measure the content of a company agreement against a Whitehall template might promote a degree of standardisation and inflexibility in agreements which could further remove industrial relations from a closer association with business and social planning in the firm or the plant. Reference to a central authority will require, or it will gradually produce, some sort of central norm (while at the same time dismantling the interest representing national institutions). But what is more necessary is a perceptive analysis of industrial relations in the plant in the context of its business environment. We would continue to argue the case for a consultancy service directed at the whole range of employment policies rather than a survey of collective agreements.

In terms of the Commission's recommendations concerning trade unions, it has been widely accused of protecting them from proper control. These accusations are probably wild in that more legalised control of the unions is likely to exacerbate problems of order rather than to assist in their solution. But there is another and less obvious sense in which the recommendations might have been designed to protect the unions. The argument runs through the Report that the unions are the only, and therefore the best, representatives of employee interests. This may be so, but unions become institutions and are subject to institutional rigidities and weaknesses. The weaknesses are corrected (if they are corrected at all) by pressure from below, but the effect of some of the Commission's recommendations may be to protect the unions from this pressure. The Commission describes unofficial strikes as 'symptoms of failure to devise institutions in keeping with changing needs', but they may also be symptoms of over-regulative procedures and of unions too conditioned to responsible behaviour. The Commission's recommendation could result in a considerable increase in official disputes (which would not please its already vociferous critics), or it could result in an attack on those elements in the trade unions most open to pressure from the membership. The amendment of Section 3 of the Trade Disputes Act, 1906, will provide protection from actions only against registered trade unions and may make a practical legal distinction between official and unofficial disputes. The movement towards plant bargaining and the whole trend of the Report is likely to enlarge and to formalise the role of the shop steward and, finally, to integrate him in well-regulated channels of conflict control. In this way the recommendations may serve to reduce pressure from below and so weaken the one force that prevented the further ossification of the unions.

The Commission's concern to protect the unions may have paradoxically rescued them from a threat from quite the opposite quarter. The recommendations that agreements should be registered, that stipulations in contracts of employment against union membership should be made void, and that compulsory arbitration may be unilaterally invoked where it can contribute to the growth of sound collective bargaining machinery, together mark a formidable defence of trade unions which might have unplanned consequences.

Such measures are likely to create a serious threat to the maverick employer who pursues anti-union but good employment policies. The threat will no doubt be applauded in its intention, but the existence of such employers has probably served as a spur to union activity which, in its absence, might have been more sluggish. The Commission, in other words, might have added to protection of the unions from the membership, protection from the independent employer. It is at least arguable that the last thing that the unions needed, in their own interest, was protection which might serve to increase an already considerable sense of self-satisfaction.

This whole line of criticism is strengthened by the almost complete absence of recommendations for the improvement of trade union government and administration (except in so far as they infringe the individual's natural rights). While the proposed examination of collective agreements by the I.R.C. suggests the existence of critical standards there are, apparently, no such standards conceivable against which trade union government and administration can be measured. Even in respect of the safeguards of members' rights it appears that the prime mover in defence of those rights must be the aggrieved member himself. It might be dangerous to assume that the public interest (or even the membership's interest) can rely safely upon the strong feelings of a union member. In this respect the unions, regarded throughout the whole Report as institutions of vital importance to the community, are to be treated virtually as closed and self-governing institutions.

A necessarily short comment such as this must condense the more critical reactions so that it runs the risk of appearing to damn where it might more frequently have praised. The Report is a clear and perceptive analysis of a complex environment, it has produced evidence where none existed before, and it will introduce order into a disordered situation while resisting the more choleric proposals for change. We have said that the Commission stopped short after clearing up the mess, but cleansing the stables was, after all, a task for Hercules.

Select Bibliography

Allen, V. L., *Militant Trade Unions*, Merlin Press, 1966
Baldamus, T. H., *Efficiency and Effort*, Tavistock, 1961
Bion, W. R., *Explorations in Groups*, Tavistock, 1961
Blau, P. M., and Scott, R. W., *Formal Organizations*, Routledge, 1963
Burns, T., and Stalker, G. F., *The Management of Innovation*, Tavistock, 1961
Clegg, H. A., *Industrial Democracy and Nationalization*, Blackwell, 1955
— *A New Approach to Industrial Democracy*, Blackwell, 1960
Coser, Lewis, *The Functions of Social Conflict*, Routledge, 1956
Dahrendorf, Ralf, *Class and Class Conflict in an Industrial Society*, Routledge, 1959
Dunlop, J. T., *Industrial Relations Systems*, Holt, 1958
Etzioni, A., *A Comparative Analysis of Complex Organizations*, Free Press of Glencoe, 1961
Flanders, A., and Clegg, H. A., *The System of Industrial Relations in Great Britain*, Blackwell, 1956
Flanders, A., *The Fawley Productivity Agreements*, Faber, 1964
— *Industrial Relations—What's Wrong with the System?*, Faber, 1965
— *Collective Bargaining: Prescription for Change*, Faber, 1967
Gouldner, A., *Patterns of Industrial Bureaucracy*, Free Press of Glencoe, 1954
— *Wildcat Strikes*, Antioch, 1954

Jaques, E., *The Changing Culture of a Factory*, Tavistock, 1951

Kahn, H., *Repercussions of Redundancy*, Allen & Unwin, 1964

Knowles, K. G. J. C., *Strikes: A Study in Industrial Conflict*, Blackwell, 1952

Labour, Ministry of, *Industrial Relations Handbook*, H.M.S.O., 1961

— *Written Evidence of the Ministry of Labour*, H.M.S.O., 1965

Lupton, T., *On The Shop Floor*, Pergamon, 1962

— *Industrial Behaviour and Personnel Management*, I.P.M., 1965

Milerson, G., *The Qualifying Associations*, Routledge, 1964

Mumford, Enid, *Living with a Computer*, I.P.M., 1964

National Board for Prices and Incomes, *Productivity Agreements*, Report No. 36, H.M.S.O., 1967

— *Pay and Conditions of Service for Engineering Workers*, Report No. 49, H.M.S.O., 1967

— *Payment by Results Systems*, Report No. 65, H.M.S.O., 1968

Niven, M. M., *Personnel Management: 1913–1963*, I.P.M., 1967

Odione, G. S., *Personnel Policy: Issues and Practice*, Merrill, 1963

Pribecevic, B., *The Shop Stewards' Movement and Workers' Control, 1910–22*, Blackwell, 1959

Reid, G. L., and Robertson, D. J., *Fringe Benefits, Labour Costs and Social Security*, Allen & Unwin, 1965

Roberts, B. C., *Trades Unions in a Free Society*, Institute of Economic Affairs, 1959

— *Industrial Relations: Contemporary Problems and Perspectives*, Methuen, 1962

Roethlisberger, F. J., and Dixon, W. D., *Management and the Workers*, Harvard, 1939

Royal Commission on Trade Unions and Employers' Associations (H.M.S.O.)

Research Papers:

No. 1 McCarthy, W. E. J., *The Role of Shop Stewards in British Industrial Relations*, 1966

No. 2 (Part 1) Marsh, A. I., *Disputes Procedures in British Industry*, 1966

No. 2 (Part 2) Marsh, A. I., and McCarthy, W. E. J., *Disputes Procedures in British Industry*, 1968

No. 3 Fox, Alan, *Industrial Sociology and Industrial Relations*, 1966

No. 4 *Productivity Bargaining and Restrictive Labour Practices*, 1967

No. 5 (Part 1) Hughes, John, *Trade Union Structure and Government*, 1967

No. 5 (Part 2) Hughes, John, *Trade Union Structure and Government*, 1968

No. 6 Bain, George Sayers, *Trade Union Growth and Recognition*, 1967

No. 7 Munns, V. G., and McCarthy, W. E. J., *Employers' Associations*, 1967

No. 8 Steiber, Jack, McCarthy, W. E. J., Marsh, A. I., and Staples, J. W., *Three Studies in Collective Bargaining*, 1968

No. 9 Whybrew, E. G., *Overtime Working in Great Britain*, 1968

No. 10 McCarthy, W. E. J., and Parker, S. R., *Shop Stewards and Workshop Relations*, 1968

Report of the Royal Commission on Trade Unions and Employers' Associations, 1965–1968, H.M.S.O., 1968

Runciman, W. G., *Relative Deprivation and Social Justice*, Routledge, 1966

Simon, H. A., *Administrative Behaviour*, Macmillan, 1945

Stevens, C. M., *Strategy and Collective Bargaining Negotiation*, McGraw-Hill, 1963

Sturmthal, A., *Workers' Councils: A Study of Workplace Organization on Both Sides of the Iron Curtain*, Harvard, 1964

T.U.C., *Trade Unionism*, 1966

Turner, H. A., Clack, G., and Roberts, G., *Industrial Relations in the Motor Industry*, Allen & Unwin, 1967

Walton, R. E., and McKersie, R. B., *A Behavioural Theory of Labour Negotiations*, McGraw-Hill, 1963

Webb, Sidney & Beatrice, *The History of Trade Unionism*, Longmans, 1920

Wedderburn, K. W., *The Worker and The Law*, Pelican, 1965

Woodward, Joan, *Industrial Organization: Theory and Practice*, Oxford, 1965

Index